Investment Trusts – A Complete Guide
by Andrew McHattie

•

The McHattie Group
St Brandon's House
29 Great George Street
Bristol BS1 5QT
www.tipsheets.co.uk

Authorised and regulated by the Financial Conduct Authority.

•

First published in Great Britain in 2021

ISBN 978-1-5272-8175-2

A CIP catalogue record for this book is available from The British Library.

•

Andrew McHattie MA (Cantab) runs the investment publishing company The McHattie Group, and has published the monthly Investment Trust Newsletter since November 1996. He is a qualified and authorised investment adviser.

Acknowledgements

This book is the culmination of many years of work on the fringes of the investment trust industry, interviewing managers, reviewing research, and providing advice to clients. I have benefited immeasurably from the help of so many people over the last twenty-five years, including the stockbrokers and research firms that allow me to access all of their work and attend their conferences; the management firms and their able marketing representatives who arrange manager meetings and the latest presentations and information; the AIC, with whom I have had a good relationship for a very long time; and numerous people in the industry, past and present, whom I would like to call my friends. There is not room here to acknowledge everyone, but I would like to thank those I troubled specifically to ask for permission to use their information in this book, so my thanks to Annabel Brodie-Smith, Christopher Brown, Richard Crawford, Piers Currie, Simon Elliott, Conor Finn, Alex Hayde, Michael Lindsell, Trevor Sayce, and Shivantha Thambirajah, all of whom responded quickly and with kind words of support.

My thanks to Morningstar for permission to reproduce two of their charts on page 53. © 2020 Morningstar, Inc. All Rights Reserved. The information contained herein: (1) is proprietary to Morningstar and/or its content providers; (2) may not be copied or distributed; (3) does not constitute investment advice offered by Morningstar; and (4) is not warranted to be accurate, complete or timely. Neither Morningstar nor its content providers are responsible for any damages or losses arising from any use of this information. Past performance is no guarantee of future results. Use of information from Morningstar does not necessarily constitute agreement by Morningstar, Inc. of any investment philosophy or strategy presented in this publication.

I must also give my special thanks to my wife, Sarah McHattie, both for her domestic patience while I wrote the book, and for her professional help with the editing. Of course, all remaining errors are entirely my own.

Table of Contents

Preface

I never set out to become an investment trust specialist. Frequently though, others shape your career path, and I have Lawrence Lever to thank for this turning. Lawrence, a former newspaper journalist with a sharp entrepreneurial mind that has brought him great success, came to me in 1996 with the idea of a publication giving regular advice on investment trusts. I had some knowledge of trusts through my work on warrants, and Lawrence had more, aided by excellent industry contacts and his great personal interest. We started the Investment Trust Newsletter together in November 1996 and found immediately there were always some great opportunities to be found. Lawrence moved on to greater things by forming the Citywire online media firm a few years later, so I took over the monthly task of writing the newsletter. It soon became a labour of love that I have kept up to this day.

For a while I ran a unit trust management company as well, and even managed a unit trust, but I kept the majority of my personal investments in investment trusts. Aware of the limitations of the open-ended structure, the advantages of investment trusts were always obvious to me. As an investor, an analyst and writer, and as an adviser, investment trusts have been central to much of my financial life for the best part of thirty years. I can see them continuing in that role for many more years to come.

Much as I favour investment trusts though, this is not simply an extended love letter to the sector. Investment trusts are far from perfect, and this book tries to present a fair picture of their risks and drawbacks as well as their merits. The sector has had its share of problems over the last thirty years, including a crisis with split capital trusts, new issues raising large sums of money and then heading south, and trusts suffering from too much gearing in a downturn. All are included in these pages.

It is difficult to claim truly comprehensive coverage of a large, diverse sector that has blurred edges and means different things to different people, but that is the intention here. To try and cover most important aspects I have split the contents into three different sections. I have tried to include real examples throughout, as I hope otherwise abstract concepts can be brought to life by reference to actual investment trusts. These will obviously date, so the plan is to refresh this content often, in new editions of the book, updating the examples and content as the industry changes, grows, and develops. Whilst thought by some to be a rather stagnant old backwater, investment trusts have proved themselves to be more than able to go with the flow in recent years, developing large new sub-sectors devoted to alternative assets, and refreshing some of the sector's oldest and largest trusts.

It's an interesting time to be publishing this first edition, but as I have found from my monthly publishing schedule with the newsletter, investment trusts are *always* interesting.

Andrew McHattie
January 2021

Introduction

This is an industry with a long and proud heritage, starting with The Foreign & Colonial Government Trust, founded in 1868 and still going strong as F&C Investment Trust (FCIT). The sector abounds with great stories, superior long-term profits, successful financing of new trends, and constant reinvention. Yet in spite of this longevity the sector is not very widely understood or appreciated, having long been overshadowed by the simpler form of unit trusts, or simply ignored by a British public without any great culture of stock market investment. That seems a great pity in view of the many advantages of investment trusts that have worked well to generate some excellent returns for more knowledgeable investors over long periods. It can take some effort to acquire that knowledge, but the good news is that the sector has rarely been in such great shape and ready to reward new investors who take the plunge.

The Basics

Very simply, an investment trust is a company with a public listing on the London Stock Exchange. It has a board of directors that oversee the company's operations, and a listing of shares that can be bought and sold for a price determined by supply and demand. So far that is just like Marks & Spencer or HSBC. Unlike other companies though, investment trusts do not manufacture goods or provide services to industry or consumers – their business is the business of investing. They exist to allocate their capital according to their stated objective, effectively pooling money from a large number of investors to spread the risk amongst a number of diverse assets.

Here's an example. Finsbury Growth & Income Trust (FGT) has a large number of shareholders who between them own £1.7bn of assets that are invested in 25 carefully selected companies including Unilever, Diageo, Hargreaves Lansdown, Burberry Group, and Heineken.[1] The trust receives dividends from these companies and seeks to benefit from their rising share prices. In this case, the trust's management is provided by an asset management company called Lindsell Train, and they are responsible for selecting its portfolio companies and making changes to those shareholdings. This is common, for the board of directors of an investment trust to assign responsibility for its investments to an outside firm of specialist managers. Sometimes a trust may have its own staff who perform this role, but whatever arrangements exist, the board is accountable to shareholders.

Buying a single shareholding in an investment trust gives you effective ownership of a much broader range of assets that would be difficult and much more expensive (and in some cases impossible) to buy directly. Investment trusts take advantage of the pooling

---

[1] Finsbury Growth & Income Trust monthly factsheet November 2020

of assets to pay a professional manager, deal more efficiently, gain more specialist knowledge, and generally allow you to benefit from investments you would probably never make yourself. At present the industry gives investors the chance to gain exposure to worldwide themes from the massive US technology stocks to Japanese smaller companies, UK micro caps, European shares, industrial property and warehousing, private equity, Vietnam, China, India, Russia, Brazil, hedge funds, gold mining, renewable energy, student housing, biotechnology companies, and much more besides.

Some of these choices are racier than others, but the point remains that by diversifying across a number of holdings with a portfolio of assets, investment trusts work effectively to spread the risk. Whilst there have of course been exceptions, the general rule is that investment trusts are less volatile and less risky than shares in single trading companies that can move in a much more extreme manner. Over recent years there have been numerous horror stories from so-called 'blue-chip' companies that investors thought were good solid holdings because of their size and importance, only to see them fall very sharply as problems arose. Shares in the telecoms giant BT Group, for example, slumped from a peak of 1520p in late 1999 to just 100p in September 2020. Shares in Barclays Bank peaked at 794p in 2007 and dropped to 93p by September 2020. Some investment trusts have also performed badly, but by spreading the risk they can often mitigate the worst impact of problems at individual companies.

The ability to moderate volatility can make investment trusts an attractive way to participate in the stock market in a sober and measured way, particularly for investors willing to invest with a long-term perspective.

There is also something wonderfully democratic about pooled investment schemes that treat all shareholders equally. The F&C Investment Trust (FCIT) says its original purpose was "to provide the investor of relatively moderate means access to the same opportunities and advantages as the very largest investors and diminish risk by investing across a wide area". For all investment trusts that is much the same now, and whether you are investing £500 or £500,000, you can achieve exactly the same pro rata benefits and costs.

The Closed-End Structure

One important point about the structure of investment trusts is that like normal trading companies, the number of shares in issue is fairly fixed, and will not normally change day-to-day. Those shares can change hands as different investors buy and sell them on the London Stock Exchange, but this does not affect the amount of money available to the manager to invest. Investment trusts are said to have 'permanent capital', unlike some other forms of pooled funds where the capital is withdrawn when an investor sells. Those types of funds have variable capital, a significant difference. For this reason, investment trusts are called 'closed-end funds' and are different from open-ended investment companies (OEICs), or what used to be called unit trusts. Those operate in a fundamentally different way, best illustrated by explaining what happens when an investor trades the shares or units, in this case a sale of £10m of stock in a £100m fund. In the case of the investment trust the outcome is completely different to that for the manager of an open-ended fund.

Example of Investors Selling £10m

Investment Trust	*OEIC*
£100m of shares	*£100m of units*
Manager has £100m to invest	*Manager has £100m to invest*
Investors sell £10m of shares	*Investors sell £10m of units*
Price adjusts and another investor buys those £10m of shares	*Manager cancels those £10m units*
Manager still has £100m to invest and does not need to change portfolio	*Manager has £90m to invest and must sell £10m of holdings*

This same process would work in reverse if a new buyer came in, and what this shows is that investment trusts are stable, with a 'closed' capital structure that means the capital stays put and does not flow in and out as investors come and go.

Pricing

As a consequence of the closed-end structure, the prices of investment trusts must be able to float and move freely to attract more buyers or sellers and achieve a balance in the market. What this means is that prices are set purely by the forces of supply and demand and may not reflect the value of the underlying holdings. If all of the holdings in an investment trust are aggregated and then adjusted for any cash or borrowings, a 'net asset value' can be calculated that reflects the true market worth of that collection of assets. This does not mean that the price of the investment trust will match that net asset value – it can deviate from it in either direction, lower (a discount) or higher (a premium), and because of the dynamic nature of stock market trading, the discount or premium can change to reflect current levels of supply and demand.

All investment trusts are listed on the London Stock Exchange. The exchange does have different tiers and you may sometimes see references to a 'premium listing' or a 'standard listing', but the differences mainly lie in the severity of reporting requirements and in reality there is little impact on investors. All investment trust shares will be identified using a ticker code, or EPIC (Exchange Price Information Code), or TIDM

(Tradable Instrument Display Mnemonic) that provides a quick method of unique identification. Thus, F&C Investment Trust is FCIT, and Finsbury Growth & Income Trust is FGT. These ticker codes are extremely useful as a shorthand way of referring to trusts and also as a way of ensuring correct identification – something that can be very important when there are trusts with similar names such as Henderson EuroTrust (HNE) and Henderson European Focus Trust (HEFT). The ticker codes generally relate quite directly to the abbreviated names of trusts, although some do have a more distinct personality, like 3i Group (III), Diverse Income Trust (DIVI), GCP Student Living (DIGS), the Hipgnosis Songs Fund (SONG), Urban Logistics REIT (SHED), and Gresham House Energy Storage (GRID). Wisely, Scottish American Investment Company decided to change its ticker code in 2019 from SCAM to SAIN. Separately, each share will also have a long numeric ISIN code – an International Securities Identification Number – that is another form of specific identification.

While dealing with abbreviations and acronyms, this might be a good moment to introduce the RNS, the Regulatory News Service system through which all major announcements are made. This quickly becomes a key source for all investors in stock market companies, and investment trusts are no exception. Whether they are releasing their latest net asset value calculation, or their annual results, or news of a change to their board of directors, all of this news will come through the RNS, which is readily available for all investors to peruse and examine.

The Scope of the Sector

Many simple questions have complicated answers. Simply asking the size of the investment trust sector and how many trusts are currently listed may not elicit a quick or straightforward response. One good reason for this is that the definition of investment trusts has changed over time, and the edges are not clearly defined. Even the trade body, the Association of Investment Companies (AIC) changed its name in 2006 from the old Association of Investment Trust Companies after a wave of issuance from offshore funds and AIM-listed investment companies. Whilst there is a specific tax definition of an investment trust,[2] in practice the industry includes a wider range of investment companies with a closed-end structure that operate in a broadly similar way. Still, at the mention of the FTSE 100 company 3i Group (III), a debate will quickly rage about its status and whether it counts as an investment trust alongside many other private equity investors. Similarly, there are a considerable number of property companies now classified as REITs (Real Estate Investment Trusts) which straddle the

[2] Technically, for HMRC, an investment trust must be a UK domiciled company that invests in shares, land, or other assets with the aim of spreading investment risk; it must be admitted to trading on a regulated market (which excludes the AIM) and cannot be a VCT or a REIT, both of which have different tax rules; it must distribute at least 85% of its income, and at least 35% of the voting shares must be public.

line between investment and trading. Whilst the majority of investment trusts are very clearly defined, there is this grey area to contend with.

For that reason, any calculation of industry size and scope should be considered an estimate, but there are some good approximations available. The AIC has some headline figures on the home page of its website, indicating 390 companies worth £209bn, as at the end of October 2020, those figures including 3i Group (III) and also VCTs, Venture Capital Trusts, another sub-sector on the fringes of the industry. The daily statistics provided by the stockbroker JPMorgan Cazenove contain data from 350 securities but exclude many smaller trusts. The scope of definition by the stockbroker Winterflood may be narrower, as they cited 327 investment companies in their Annual Review for 2020. Similarly, the annual 'Skin in the Game' review of investment company shareholdings by Investec Securities covered 303 investment companies. At the other end of the spectrum, the Morningstar investment trusts screener contains information on 470 securities, including multiple share classes and VCTs. A London Stock Exchange data search for closed-end investments found 492 securities, with multiple share classes for some trusts.

It is not easy to find definitive data, but of these organisations we think the AIC probably has the best grip on the sector, and the other sources cited do not appear to contradict its figures, so we'll accept those as a rough guide. For comparison, the monthly figures from The Investment Association for July 2020 state that the total funds under management in open-ended funds was just shy of £1300bn, so more than six times the size of the investment trust industry. Without needing to achieve precise measures, we can say confidently that the investment trust industry is considerably smaller in aggregate than that for open-ended funds.

So why is that? If investment trusts are cheaper, with better performance, and several other advantages, why are they so much less popular than open-ended funds? In part, the answer lies with a lack of education and participation. Apart from one greed-driven period when ordinary people were encouraged to chase quick returns from the privatisation spree of the late 1980s, there is very little culture of stock market investment in the UK, and few people have historically had sufficient knowledge or a stockbroking account. The easy appeal of being able to deal directly with a fund manager, buying 'units' that were simply priced on asset value, without any additional complications of discounts or gearing, meant that open-ended funds were the easier choice, backed by financial advisers who for many years were heavily incentivised to recommend open-ended funds in return for large commission cheques. The fund industry has also been promoted by some formidable marketing machines. Unlike closed-end funds, where the number of shares in issue is generally fixed, open-ended funds can expand and generate larger and larger management fees for companies that are able to advertise them successfully.

Performance

Just as single investment trusts measure their own performance against some sort of benchmark index, so it is handy to have some sort of measuring stick for the sector as a whole. The lack of a clear boundary means that no index will be comprehensive, but the FTSE All-Share Equity Investment Instruments Index (FTASX8980) or the FTSE 350 Equity Investment Instruments Index (NMX8980), which focuses on the larger sector constituents, may be as good as any other. In spite of their clunky names that mention neither investment trusts nor investment companies, these seem a decent proxy for the sector, although they do include VCTs and a small number of instruments not commonly associated with investment trusts.

Looking at its performance against the most well-known UK index first of all, the NMX8980 is well ahead of the FTSE 100 Index over all periods from one year to ten years.

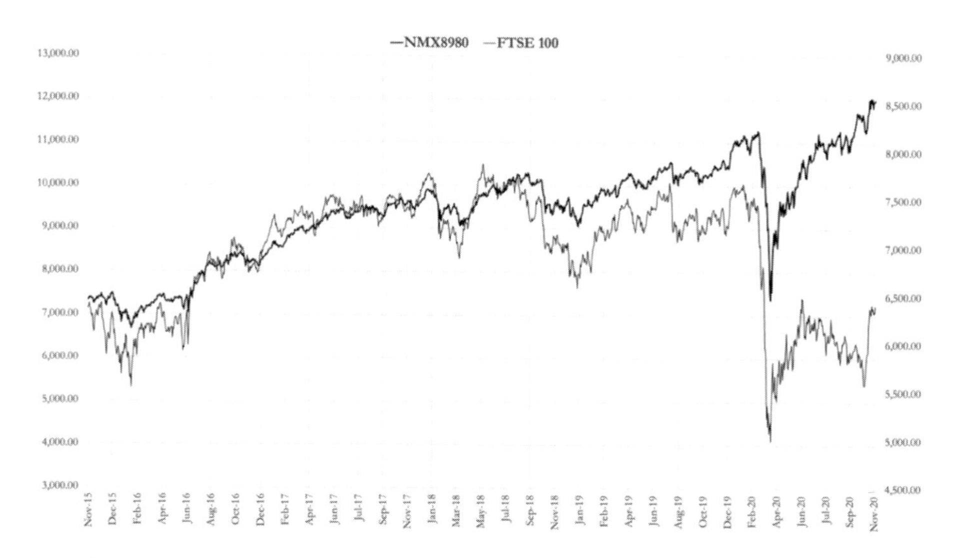

FTSE 350 Equity Investment Instruments Index (NMX8980) versus FTSE 100 Index, five years to 23rd November 2020

As the investment trust universe is international, this may not be a fair comparison, as UK shares have performed relatively poorly in recent years, certainly against more dynamic growth markets like the US. Against the much broader FTSE All-World Index, the investment trust sector has still outperformed, although the two lines are much closer.

FTSE 350 Equity Investment Instruments Index (NMX8980) versus FTSE All-World Index, five years to 23rd November 2020

These last few years have been good for investment trusts, and their considerable longevity obviously suggests they have delivered good results for investors for far longer. The industry is not resting on its laurels though, and has shown itself to be highly adaptable as new investment themes and trends emerge.

Recent Developments

Two major developments stand out as noteworthy over recent years as investment trusts have continued to develop and meet new challenges. The first has been a successful transition of ownership away from legacy institutions, and back to private investors, who have become a growing force. It is less easy to identify and quantify their holdings since the rise of platform stockbrokers and nominee holdings removed individual names from public share registers, but there is plenty of anecdotal evidence from the marketing departments of larger fund management firms who are increasingly keen to reach the retail market, and also from occasional references to the number of individual shareholders in trusts' reports and accounts.

This feels like a return to where investment trusts began, in some ways, as a way for smaller investors to participate easily and simply in big developing industries like the huge American technology companies or little-known companies in developing markets like Vietnam and Indonesia. Private investors can be wonderful long-term shareholders for trusts, something noted by Clare Dobie, a director of Alliance Trust (ATST). In a video on the AIC website about directors' responsibilities, Clare says that at her first Annual General Meeting (AGM) she met a shareholder who had inherited

additional inflation, so the low interest rates have remained in place for a far longer period than would have been envisaged at the time of the original cuts. The Bank of England's data for the base rate history since 1975 clearly shows that this period is highly unusual, and well outside of the previously established bounds.

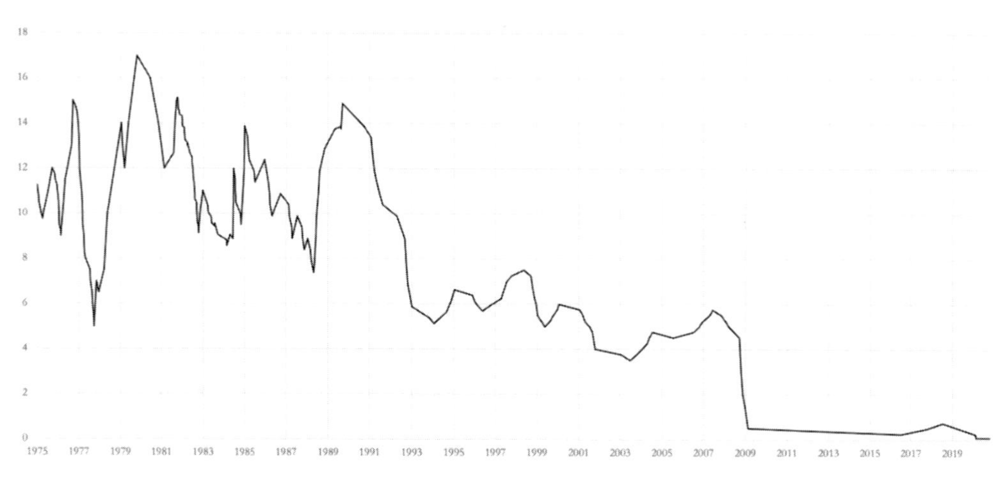

Base Rate History 1975-2020; source Bank of England

This extended period of low interest rates means it has been difficult for investors of all kinds to find yield. Bonds do not offer acceptable returns, interest-paying accounts are even worse, and whilst equities can offer decent dividends, these come with risk and volatility. The result is that these investors have gone hunting for higher yields from other types of less volatile assets, creating huge demand that the traditional financial instruments were no longer meeting adequately. After the thumping equity market falls of the financial crisis, the importance of real diversification rose up the agenda, and many larger investors began to focus on a multi-asset approach that also created an extra thirst for new types of assets.

As this demand has been unleashed by the lack of returns elsewhere, so the supply side has prospered at the same time. The second major contributing factor helping the rise of alternative asset investment trusts is that more stringent capital requirements and a generally tougher regulatory regime has meant that banks have withdrawn from many business lines, creating a void where they used to lend money and provide finance. Other financial operators have moved to fill that gap, including asset management firms. Some have used investment trusts as a vehicle to raise and provide capital to finance expensive assets, receiving cash flows in return, behaving much like banks have in the past. The closed-end structure is outstandingly appropriate for often illiquid assets that provide long-term returns, hence the growth of large new sectors at breakneck speed.

Just consider the renewables infrastructure sector, which did not exist in any way until 2013. If you are not already an investment trust aficionado, you may not have heard of Bluefield Solar Income Fund (BSIF), Foresight Solar Fund (FSFL), Greencoat UK Wind (UKW), NextEnergy Solar Fund (NESF), or The Renewables Infrastructure Group (TRIG). By October 2020, however, the thirteen trusts in this sector had combined total assets of no less than £10bn.[5] For comparison, the Japanese trust sector, which dates back to 1927 and contains well-known trusts like JPMorgan Japanese (JFJ) and Baillie Gifford Japan (BGFD) had aggregate total assets of just £3.3bn. Adding in Japanese smaller companies, another four trusts, took that total up to £4.6bn, still less than half of the size of the new renewables infrastructure sector.

Asset managers have chosen investment trusts over open-ended funds for these new types of investments because they are illiquid assets, not easy to sell quickly or to break up into small parts for sale. If you own shares, you can easily sell some if necessary to meet redemptions by holders of an open-ended fund wanting to sell, but if you own a wind farm, you cannot buy and sell individual turbines in response to the cash requirements of your investors. The 'permanent capital' structure of investment trusts makes obvious sense, as has become apparent during recent periods of market stress when open-ended property funds have been unable to realise their assets, even at distressed prices, when investors were clamouring to sell in a crisis. Many open-ended property funds were forced to suspend trading during the great financial crisis of 2007-08, and then – astonishingly, as if no lessons were learned at all – again during the Covid-19 pandemic in 2020.

That's not the only reason why open-ended funds should not be buying illiquid assets that they cannot sell in a hurry. Many of the best income-producing arrangements for certain types of property and for infrastructure and renewable energy assets in particular involve long-term contracts for 25 years or more that generate highly attractive and reliable cash flows, but of course these deals can only be struck by managers with permanent capital.

Whether or not you feel these alternative asset trusts are for you, it is becoming increasingly unwise and downright impossible to ignore them, even if you have always been a more traditional equity investor. They form a large component of the modern investment trust industry, meaning it is as well to be intelligently informed about them. Different types of assets can provide differing types of risk and return profiles for investors, and can provide uncorrelated returns that dampen volatility when combined, so it can be very useful to gain an understanding of each of the main classifications that will cover the majority of trusts. Equities still account for nearly half of all investment

[5] JPMorgan Cazenove Daily Statistics 2nd October 2020

trust assets, depending on how the industry is sliced up and measured, but the other side of the pie has been growing quickly.

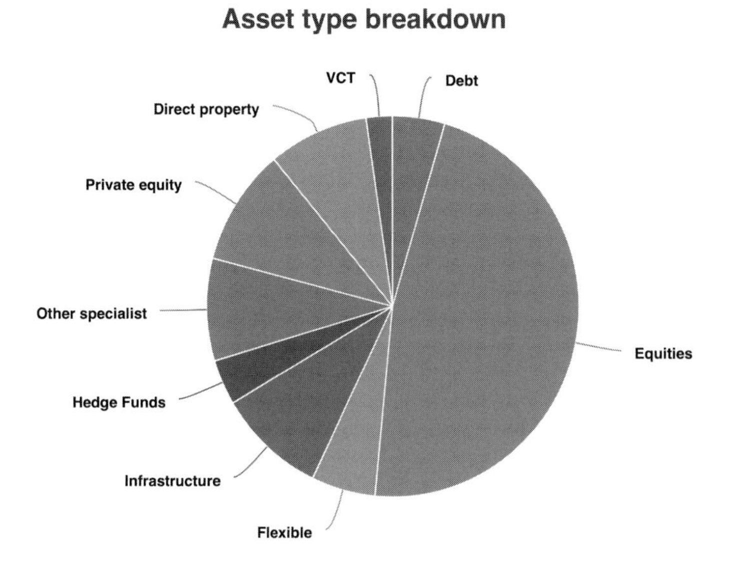

Asset type breakdown, AIC November 2020

Equities

Starting with the much-loved core of the industry, investing in equities is relatively simple to understand. The managers of the investment trust use the capital to pick a portfolio of shares from the quoted markets, which they can then trade freely to adjust the portfolio as market conditions change, and the value of that portfolio can be tracked and valued on a daily basis. It's normal for equity trusts to report their net asset value (NAV) each day, making them highly transparent.

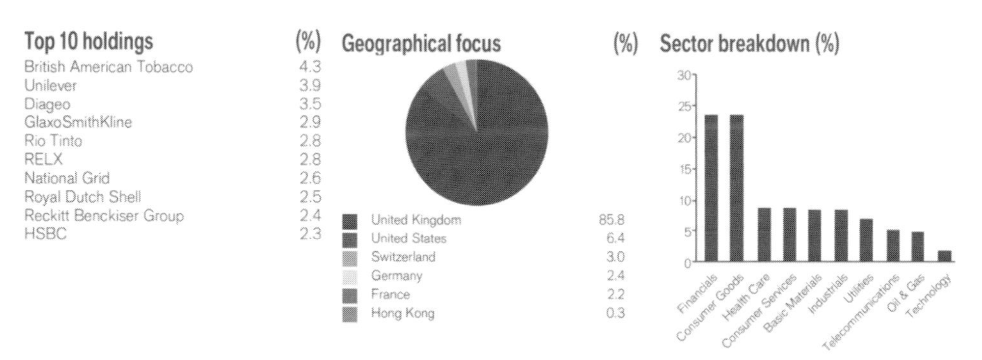

Extract from October 2020 Factsheet, City of London Investment Trust

In regular factsheets, equity managers will usually reveal their top ten holdings, and perhaps the geographical and sector breakdown, as well as some commentary on recent events and further information about the structure.

Often tucked away as well is the total number of holdings, which in the case of City of London Investment Trust (CTY) in October 2020 was 86. There is not a 'right' number here – the spread of holdings in an equity portfolio will vary quite a lot, depending on the management approach. It might be as low as 30 or so, indicating a concentrated portfolio that the managers may characterise as 'high conviction', or it may be much more broadly based, with upwards of 150 different shareholdings. A more concentrated portfolio generally indicates a higher risk, but with the potential for greater returns if the managers' selections are shrewd. For many years the concentrated portfolio run by the manager Alexander Darwall for European Opportunities Trust (JEO) delivered much better returns than its competitors, but it has hit some difficulties more recently with a large holding in a company called Wirecard that suffered from fraud, and some commentators are now suggesting its individual holdings are too large for a structure that is intended to spread the risk. At the end of October 2020 the trust's top two holdings, Experian and Novo Nordisk, each accounted for more than 10% of total assets, whereas for many trusts the largest individual positions might be around 4% or 5%.

Just as there is no definitive answer on how many holdings is the most appropriate, the same applies to how frequently the manager changes those holdings. This is called 'portfolio turnover' and can be measured by simply taking the total value of the shares bought or sold (whichever is greater) over a period, most frequently a year, and dividing it by the total net asset value. Investment trust managers are not traders – certainly not day traders – and their key task is to create long-term returns for their shareholders. That means that very often they will have a long-term mindset themselves, seeking returns over at least a three-year period, implying portfolio turnover of 0.33 as a maximum, and sometimes much longer. Alex Crooke, the manager of Bankers Investment Trust (BNKR) told the AIC in 2018 that he believed the trust had held HSBC continuously for 129 years and that it had owned a number of other shares for more than 30 years. Nick Train, the manager of Finsbury Growth & Income Trust (FGT) has famously said that his preferred holding period is forever, and he is well-known for his particularly low turnover. In their press advertisements running in late 2020, Baillie Gifford make a similar claim for Scottish Mortgage Investment Trust (SMT). They pose the question "how long do we invest in companies that we believe are delivering progress?" and answer it by saying "somewhere between five years and forever".

As with all portfolios of shares, investment trust equity portfolios will tend to move with the direction of global markets, but all of these investment trust managers are active managers, trying to use their skill, judgement, and resources to beat the market and achieve better-than-average returns, measured against a benchmark index. Not all active managers can win, of course, and there is a frequently repeated argument that passive index investment can be a better option much of the time, but that does not seem to be true for investment trusts, which have a good track record of performance. There have been some index-tracking trusts in the past, but there was very little demand for them, and they have disappeared.

In determining which shares the managers will buy, the scope of their investment universe will be set by the trust's objective, as laid down by the board of directors. This may specify a whole range of parameters, including geography, size of companies, the level of income, and the style of investment approach; and in addition to the publicly-stated objective, the manager will work within agreed limits for areas like concentration, turnover, and the level of borrowings.

On the whole, once managers have their boundaries, they can work within those to create an equity portfolio without difficulty. They can trade cheaply, at institutional rates of commission, and most of the time they can buy the shares they have identified, although the managers of larger trusts need to be aware of liquidity constraints that mean they might need to build positions over time, or invest in companies of a certain size. Commonly, this is one of the choices set out in the objectives anyway – certain trusts are 'large cap', investing in the well-known blue-chip companies that really represent certain markets; others are 'small cap', investing specifically in the smaller, up-and-coming growth companies, the blue-chips of tomorrow; and some are a mix, or 'all cap', meaning the manager is free to choose across the capitalisation spectrum.

That is certainly not the only way in which equity managers differ from one another – this is a pie that can be sliced in numerous ways. One very important consideration is whether there is a bias towards capital growth or income. Some trusts are aiming squarely for long-term capital growth, which can make them particularly suitable for younger investors with a long timeframe, no need to take any income from their investments, and a higher tolerance for risk. Other trusts seek a high income from their shares and pay out a welcome regular dividend to shareholders, giving up some scope for capital growth in return. Which type of trust you prefer will of course depend on your individual circumstances, and may change over time, but it has to be a good thing that the industry offers both types of trust. In reality, that's an enormous simplification, as there are many shades of grey between these black and white extremes, with yields ranging from zero all the way up to double-digits, with a great range of choice.

Before moving on from this particular way of segmenting the investment trust market, it is perhaps worth mentioning that the UK equity income sector has been a very popular sector for many years, as reflected in the number of trusts, their size, and their public profile. Trusts investing in UK shares for a mix of capital growth and income (and indeed, income growth) offer a sensible balance for many investors, plus a sense of familiarity that brings some comfort, and a level of simplicity as well. There is frequently no currency risk, if a trust is investing its pounds into UK shares listed in London (although the underlying companies will often have international scope and will trade in different countries), and judging the potential risks and rewards from a list of well-known UK company shares is arguably much easier than assessing a portfolio of loans or infrastructure projects.

In addition to trusts investing in UK equities or global equities, there are sector specialists that restrict themselves to specific areas that they believe have particular attractions and where they can add value with niche expertise. There are geographic specialists and sector specialists. The former include emerging markets, Europe, Asia, Japan, and North America, plus a few single-country trusts dedicated to China, India, and some smaller markets such as Thailand and Vietnam. The sector specialists include technology, healthcare, finance, natural resources, and environmental companies.

While you may accept that a specialist completely devoted to US biotechnology stocks might have much more knowledge and market information that would allow them to pick better shares than a lay person, you might feel that you can pick shares yourself, or perhaps replicate the top holdings of leading trusts by following their announcements. That is always a choice, but investment trust managers do have a number of advantages, and not just information advantages that spring from their greater resources. Professional managers with a certain presence in the market can secure preferential access to lucrative new issues or secondary financings at a discount, they can deal more cheaply, and of course investment trusts pay no capital gains tax on their dealings. The investment trust structure works well for equity investment, which is why it has thrived for so long and remains the largest single segment of the market today.

Natural Resources

One equity-related area that probably deserves its own section is natural resources – commodities like oil, natural gas, silver, gold, platinum, iron ore, copper, aluminium, and uranium – where these can be grouped together in a distinct asset class that behaves differently. Even though investment trusts like BlackRock World Mining Trust (BRWM), Baker Steel Resources Trust (BSRT) and Golden Prospect Precious Metals (GPM) principally take their positions by buying shares in mining companies, the impact of movements in underlying commodity prices can have a profound effect to drive these share prices independently of other macro factors. Against the main FTSE

350 Index, the FTSE 350 Mining Index (NMX1770) shows considerably more volatility and cyclical swings over almost any period.

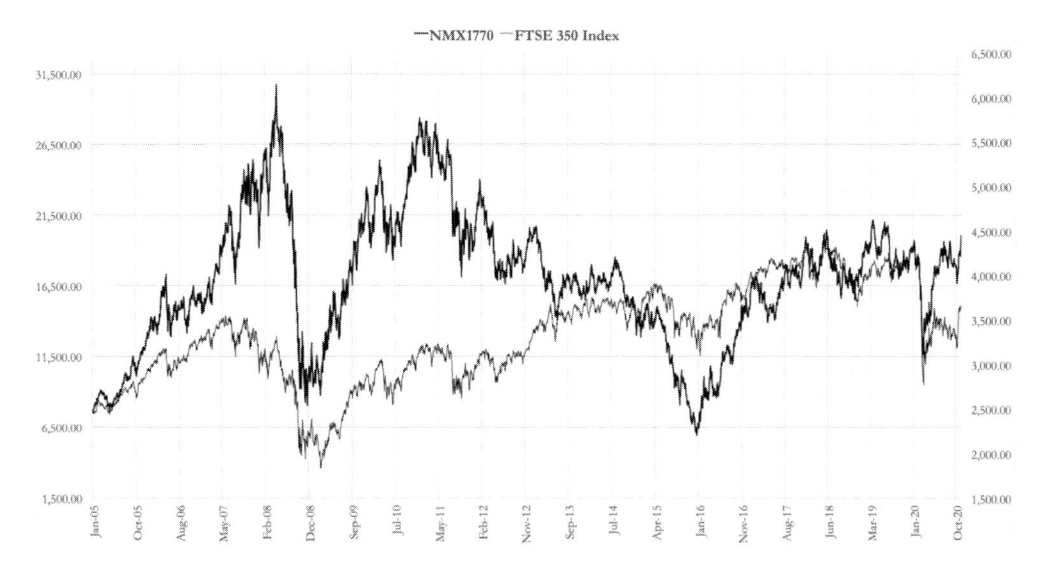

FTSE 350 Mining Index (NMX1770) versus FTSE 350 Index (NMX), 2005-2020

Commodities are commonly regarded as a highly cyclical asset class, particularly sensitive to economic growth in China, by far the biggest consumer of commodities, accounting for nearly half of the global demand for most major metals. Commodities can also be sensitive to a range of very specific indicators, including inflation, currency movements, and the weather, meaning that mining stocks are best analysed separately from other equities and have a host of idiosyncrasies of their own.

Gold, for example, can work well as a counterbalance to other commodities that react to cyclical demand swings. During times of economic stress, particularly if those involve political upheaval, a weaker US dollar, or calls for government stimulus packages that might have inflationary consequences, precious metals and associated mining shares can benefit from 'safe-haven' demand at the same time as the prices of other commodities are tanking. This was the case during the initial Covid-19 crisis, when the gold price rallied strongly.

Infrastructure and Renewables

Moving on to the first group of alternative assets, these are certainly not things you could buy for yourself, no matter your level of knowledge or dedication. Trusts investing in big infrastructure projects have brought this sector into the realm of the private investor. This was the first of the big new asset classes to emerge in the new wave, actually pre-dating the financial crisis, and it has arguably the highest profile. HICL Infrastructure (HICL), with net assets of almost £3bn on its own now and a constituent of the FTSE 250 Index, was the first of its kind in March 2006. The February 2006 Investment Trust Newsletter noted at the time that "it's a wonderful world out there, and the investment trust industry seems to be bringing more and more of it to your door. Being able to invest in exotic countries is old hat now – the latest trend seems to be asset diversification. In the hunt for value, investment trusts are moving into new areas of investment which were previously unavailable, we believe, to private investors".

The key attraction of the HICL launch (or the HSBC Infrastructure Company as it was called at that time) was an initial target yield of 5.75%. The managers explained they would buy infrastructure projects such as the Home Office headquarters in London, Bishop Auckland Hospital, Exeter Crown Court, and a Dutch high-speed rail link, typically acquired under Private Finance Initiative (PFI) or Public-Private Partnership (PPP) contracts. These were government-backed projects where the government had decided to contract out the work. In exchange for funding the building, project companies receive long-term operating contracts providing the right to operate those assets for a lengthy period of time – perhaps 20 or 30 years – and to receive inflation-proofed revenues for so doing. At the end of the contract the project is handed back to the government. The revenue is intended to be solid and predictable, and is not dependent on usage, with little (or no) impact from economic cycles or competition.

Fourteen years on, HICL had 117 infrastructure assets by March 2020 and has successfully delivered a total return of 9% per year to shareholders since its launch, outperforming the FTSE All-Share Index along the way. The basic premise, which has worked so well, is that the trust owns essential real assets that deliver resilient cash-flows from a protected market position. The dividend has grown by 35%, and the largest assets now include Affinity Water, the UK's largest water-only company; the high-speed rail line High Speed 1 that connects St Pancras with the Channel Tunnel; the A63 motorway in France; and Southmead Hospital in Bristol.

What investors are really buying into here, on the whole, are stable government-backed income streams, plus some scope for capital growth from the demand-based assets in the portfolio. The dividend yield is the big attraction, 4.9% for HICL in November 2020[6] and this would generally be regarded as a fairly low risk trust that should escape much of the regular volatility associated with equities. It is not risk-free, as shareholders in the trust discovered in 2018 when one of its construction partners, Carillion, went bust and eventually cost the trust £50m as cash flows were interrupted. Even so, infrastructure is not subject to the same day-to-day market movements as equity trusts,

---

[6] JPMorgan Cazenove Daily Statistics 24th November 2020

and it offers a different sort of return profile that many have described as more bond-like.

The renewables infrastructure sector is all about the build-out of a brand new power system to replace fossil fuels with environmentally-friendly sources of energy. Investment trusts have financed wind farms, solar farms, and more recently, battery storage facilities as these become ever more important for the UK's power generation. As with the social infrastructure of schools, hospitals, water and transport, the main focus here for investors is the generation of regular cash flows to fund high and growing dividends. These trusts arrived from 2013 onwards and are still being joined by newcomers. They have been largely successful to date, all delivering positive total returns over three and five years, and while investors have had to learn about the influence of subsidies, availability contracts, fluctuating power prices and climactic conditions, there has been high demand for their relatively stable dividends. All current signs point to a continuing need for greater investment and expansion in the sector, and of course its green credentials make this a popular choice for socially responsible investors perhaps allocating resources away from oil and gas.

Property

As a nation, Britain is in love with property investment. Generations have seen the value of their houses rise sharply in value, and people talk warmly of the solid attractions of 'bricks and mortar'. Buy-to-let schemes thrived to such a degree that the government needed to curb their attractions with changes to taxation. Commercial property is a little different though, and the classic trio of retail, office, and industrial is perhaps less familiar and somewhat less appealing to many investors, especially since the rise of internet shopping dented the prospects for retail property and the Covid-19 pandemic then raised question marks about future demand for offices too.

There has long been a niche property investment trust sector that does not really count as being an alternative asset class because these indirect property investors buy property shares. That is the case with TR Property (TRY), which gains its exposure through a portfolio of shares in the UK and Europe, such as Vonovia, LEG Immobilien, Arian, Gecina, Sergio, Deutsche Wohnen, and Safestore.[7] The trust does have a small collection of actual properties in the UK as well, but that is not its main focus. Another indirect investor, Schroder Global Real Estate Securities, was wound-up in 2016 after being considered sub-scale by its board.

The much larger sector that has emerged in recent years is in direct investment – trusts that buy buildings of various types and collect the rents as their income. These are

[7] TR Property factsheet August 2020

generally structured as Real Estate Investment Trusts (REITs) for tax purposes, but often considered part of the investment companies universe by analysts and investors. Some are generalist investors, sticking to those three primary sectors of retail, office, and industrial property, but a new breed has joined them over recent years, memorably named the 'meds, sheds, and beds'. These are healthcare facilities, warehousing, and student accommodation – three areas that have all attracted keen interest and performed well until the Covid-19 pandemic, which hit the demand for student rooms. A couple of particularly notable trusts here are Primary Health Properties (PHP), which has a portfolio of GP surgeries in the UK and Ireland and has developed a fine track record since 1996, expanding steadily to reach net assets of just under £2bn now;[8] and Tritax Big Box REIT (BBOX), which owns retail warehousing, distribution centres, and logistics hubs around the country and has also raised capital in several tranches to reach net assets of £2.7bn.

Property trusts do come in quite a few shapes and sizes, with different strategies and specialist realms. Dividend yields tend to be in the 4%-7% range, with some potential for capital growth as well. Property offers a 'halfway house' to some degree for investors who are less comfortable with newer, more exotic alternative assets, being relatively familiar but also able to work well to diversify portfolios that are largely based on equities. It remains worth bearing in mind, however, that a large proportion of British investors may have a large accidental overweight position in property on their personal balance sheets due to the appreciation in value of their principal residence. For that reason it is sensible to question how much diversification property investment trusts might be providing.

Private Equity

Private equity is not a new sector, but it has evolved and grown. Known many years ago under the title of venture capital, private equity is much as the name suggests – investing in private companies before their shares are quoted on public markets. There are some large private companies that have never needed to tap into public capital, either because they have grown gradually, or perhaps because of wealthy family owners, but most private companies are small and come with a higher level of risk. The unquoted nature of the shares also means they are harder to buy and sell, although there are active secondary markets that allow stakes to change hands. On the plus side, some of these companies are fast-growing and lowly-rated, meaning that huge returns can sometimes be achieved, many multiples of the investment value. Overall, the industry has a good track record of achieving investment returns a little higher on average than public markets, which is perhaps reasonable to expect to compensate for the higher risk.

---

[8] JPMorgan Cazenove Daily Statistics 1st October 2020

Outside of the world of investment trusts, the usual method of investing in private equity is through a general partnership, but this does require a certain scale, and more capital than many people would be able to commit, or would want to commit, without much flexibility. Using the investment trust structure – and again this is a universe that absolutely requires permanent capital – allows individual investors to participate with a small stake and also have daily dealing liquidity. It makes good sense, as does the diversification that investment trusts bring by pooling assets and making numerous investments.

The sector is actually split into two parts, the direct investors and the funds of funds. The direct investors really behave very much like equity investors. Using their own research and connections they identify companies they like, and then commit a certain proportion of their capital to buy a stake. HgCapital Trust (HGT), for example, has around £1.1bn of net assets invested in unquoted companies that are often buyouts in software and services businesses in northern Europe. Twenty investments make up the bulk of the assets,[9] led by Visma, a Norwegian cloud software provider, accounting for 21% of the net asset value. These direct investors tend to have more concentrated portfolios than their public equity counterparts, which seems intuitively rational, given the much higher levels of due diligence, paperwork, and ongoing focus required when buying an unquoted stake.

The second part of the sector – the funds of funds – avoid this concentration risk by committing their capital to funds instead of single companies, and as a result the 'look-through' portfolio is much more diversified across a large number of unquoted companies. HarbourVest Global Private Equity (HVPE) says that it has investments in over 9500 underlying companies,[10] a fraction of a very large and growing market. Helen Steers, the manager of Pantheon International (PIN), a private equity hybrid fund of funds, argues that private equity markets are growing while public markets are shrinking, increasing the opportunity set available.[11] It is worth noting though that many of these funds would not be available to you as an individual investor, not unless you were a well-established market participant with deep pockets. The best managers in the sector have restrictions on the amount of capital they can deploy, so contacts, reputation and longevity all count in this sector that is ultimately based on privately negotiated deals.

In practice, some investment trusts are pure direct investors and some are pure funds of funds, but the majority are hybrids that offer something in-between, perhaps with some direct co-investment alongside their fund partners. Whatever the approach, the

[9] HgCapital Trust monthly factsheet August 2020
[10] HarbourVest Global Private Equity Annual Report and Accounts 2020
[11] Webinar: Update on PIP and the private equity market, September 2020

managers generally have a tougher task on their hands to identify the potential winners and make the investments, which is why their fees tend to be higher as well. This can be a source of contention, particularly when success fees are typically built into the remuneration structure for managers, in the form of 'carried interest'. This can be a large figure that explains why some calculations of costs and charges seem to produce much higher figures for private equity trusts than for many others.

Historically, private equity trusts have also been lowly rated compared to the majority of the investment trust sector, frequently trading on a wide discount to net asset value. In part this is probably due to the reduced transparency of this sector compared to listed equity trusts, where the holdings are all known and can be tracked easily. Private equity trusts will not value their holdings on a daily basis, but typically do so every three or six months, leaving analysts and investors to estimate the net asset value in the meantime. This naturally introduces an element of caution and the need to introduce some margin for error, hence the lower share price ratings. Of course all trusts will say that they value their portfolio companies on a very conservative basis, and regular announcements of NAV uplifts when investments are exited (often through a trade sale, and less frequently by IPO) tend to support this assertion. The periodic changes in NAV that may occur when holdings are sold means that the maturity of portfolios is of relevance and will often be declared in shareholder communications.

The largest of all private equity firms in the UK is 3i Group (III), a FTSE 100 company with net assets of nearly £9bn[12] that is sometimes classified as an investment company, and sometimes not. 3i – investors in industry, in case you wondered - has private equity and infrastructure portfolios and announces its NAV in the same way as other investment companies, but the large premium to net asset value on which the shares trade[13] indicates it is not considered in quite the same way as its smaller competitors. This may be because of its overall size, dwarfing the rest of the sector, or because it acts as a manager of some private equity assets, or it may be because £3.5bn[14] of its assets are accounted for by one holding in the general merchandise discount retailer Action. 3i is not alone in having one particularly large portfolio holding, so this does not seem to disqualify 3i from its place at the head of the table. To settle the argument, the fact of the matter is that the company has been operated in the UK as an approved investment trust company since its listing on the London Stock Exchange in 1994.

A new sub-sector has been created in May 2019 under the title of 'growth capital', with three constituent trusts, Merian Chrysalis Investment Company (MERI), The Schiehallion Fund (MNTN), and Schroder UK Public Private Trust (SUPP). This

[12] JPMorgan Cazenove Daily Statistics 24th November 2020

[13] 18.2%, JPMorgan Cazenove Daily Statistics 24th November 2020

[14] 3i Annual Report and Accounts 2020

sector is for investors in unquoted shares that generally take non-controlling stakes in early to maturing companies, so something akin to private equity, but with some crossover to public markets. The Schroder trust is the former Woodford Patient Capital Trust, which transferred to the current managers in 2019.

Before leaving this sector it would be remiss not to point investors towards LPEC, a trade body with the task of representing, explaining, and promoting listed private equity capital. LPEC was founded in 2006 and is a very useful resource for material on the sector – visit www.listedprivatecapital.com.

Debt Funds

Direct lending, loans and bonds, structured finance, property debt, leasing, asset-backed debt, P2P lending ... the varieties of debt funds with a closed-end structure have proliferated over recent years as investment trusts have jumped into the vacuum created by the withdrawal of banking services in many sectors after the credit crisis of 2007-08. Some trusts have been spat out again, but others are here to stay.

Corporate structures for commercial firms vary widely, but quite commonly they are financed through some mix of debt and equity. Traditional equity investors will supply cash for the equity element at IPO and then trade these equities in the secondary market. Debt funds concentrate on the other part of the balance sheet, supplying cash for tranches of debt. Apart from a handful of trusts like CQS New City High Yield (NCYF) that trade in the secondary bond markets, the majority of these trusts are direct investors, issuing debt that is not traded subsequently on public markets. Add other debt instruments like mortgages and lease agreements into the mix, and the result is an array of income-oriented trusts that can be esoteric and difficult to understand. They have historically been of most interest to institutional investors, and certainly need careful examination, but the payment of very attractive dividend yields of 5%-8% without the risk of the equity market is a considerable draw in a low interest-rate environment.

When assessing debt funds, some of the main factors to consider are the health of the target markets, the intended returns, the risks of default, and as always, the quality of the managers. Throughout history, lenders have always had to contend with loans that have turned sour, so the managers of these trusts do need to have particular skills to perform due diligence, secure the loans against realisable assets, and assess the borrowers. Some debt funds have been able to generate reliable quarterly returns without any major problems or defaults, whereas others have found that their loan books have deteriorated quickly once economic conditions have changed. SQN Asset Finance, which became KKV Secured Loan Fund (KKVL), lost value very rapidly, as did Hadrian's Wall Secured Investments, which decided to wind-down and was eventually bought out. In the case of KKVL, the chairman said in September 2019 that its "underlying investment performance remains strong"[15] when the net asset value was 94.9p per share, only for the NAV to sink by 62% to an estimated 36.2p by November 2020.[16] The pace of this steep decline was never really explained clearly to shareholders who felt they were investing in a sector where risk was carefully assessed. There can be disasters in this sector, and it is not really a simple matter for shareholders or even experienced analysts to assess a debt portfolio in the same thorough way as an equity portfolio. Instead there has to be a higher level of faith in the manager and the valuers, if separate.

One sector that truly found itself in the wrong place at the wrong time when the Covid-19 pandemic hit and slammed the brakes on international travel was the aircraft leasing sector, a group of five trusts that buy aircraft and lease them to major international airlines like Norwegian Air, Thai Airways, and Emirates. Whether or not, with the aid of government support, the lease payments are eventually met in full, there have been interruptions to cash-flows and considerable fresh doubts about the residual value of the aircraft, resulting in heavy share price falls. The share price of DP Aircraft 1 (DPA) dropped from around US$0.77 in late February 2020 to just US$0.08 six months later.

That's a salutary tale of what can happen, but for some other specialist trusts in areas such as healthcare and infrastructure, this period was very much one of business as usual, indicating the importance of careful analysis as well as an understanding of the sector risk. Debt funds can offer steady returns that are much smoother than the regular daily fluctuations of equity trusts, but when something does go wrong, the impact can be swift and significant.

Hedge Funds

A relatively small sector in the investment trust world, hedge funds are something of a curiosity largely ignored by most participants. Whilst hedge funds are a massive global industry, with the benefit of highly flexible mandates and the useful ability to take short positions, some hedge funds have come under fire in the past for excessive leverage, lack of transparency, and for enriching their managers with excessive fees. This does not create an ideal match for the conservative and closely-scrutinised nature of the investment trust industry, hence the modest participations to date.

Of the hedge funds that are listed in London, BH Global (sterling share class BHGG) and BH Macro (sterling share class BHMG) both stood out with strong performances during the Covid-19 pandemic, but their solid returns were eclipsed by the remarkable

[15] SQN Asset Finance Income Fund Annual Report for the year ended 30th June 2019, released 30th September 2019
[16] KKV Secured Loan Fund valuation update 23rd November 2020

story of the dominant trust by size in this sector, with £6bn[17] of net assets, Pershing Square Holdings (PSH). It executed a trade so dramatically successful that it featured on the front page of The Financial Times, after manager Bill Ackman invested US$27m in some hedges in the form of credit protection on global investment grade and high yield credit indices that yielded an extraordinary US$2.6bn when he closed them out in March 2020. Even this stunning news failed to ignite interest in the sector, and Pershing Square itself remained on a wide discount to NAV that seems to reflect a lack of faith in the trust and perhaps in hedge funds more broadly.

Specialist Assets

There are of course many other investment trusts that are not covered by these broad sectoral summaries, in areas as diverse as reinsurance, the collection of ground rents, royalties from songs; and other trusts like Tetragon Financial Group (TFG, TFGS) that defy classification by having a spread of different interests. What this means is that some trusts don't receive very much attention and can 'fly under the radar' of most investors, allowing the eagle-eyed to pick up shares at bargain ratings on occasions. New angles are being found regularly as well, for investment into entirely new areas. In October 2020, for example, a new issue was announced for Home REIT (HOME), with plans to fund the acquisition and creation of new accommodation for homeless people in the UK. There are many sharp minds in the industry that will doubtless be on the lookout for many more specialised assets of the future.

Ancillary Businesses

Whilst the majority of investment trusts are pure investors, there are a small number with odd ancillary subsidiaries that can contribute to both income and capital growth. For many years, Alliance Trust (ATST) had a savings business that it sold to Interactive Investor in 2018, and Law Debenture (LWDB) has a separate independent professional services business that has been a part of its long history since 1889. This business is valued regularly and included in the net asset value, and of course its profits are a part of the trust's income.

It is more common to find that an investment trust may have a stake in its fund manager, and that can sometimes be highly significant. For Lindsell Train Investment Trust (LTI), the holding in the management firm, Lindsell Train Limited, is easily its largest holding at 47% of assets.[18] Similarly, Majedie Investments (MAJE) was a founding investor in the asset management boutique Majedie Asset Management, which was later appointed to manage substantially all of its assets. This holding

---

[17] JPMorgan Cazenove Daily Statistics 24th November 2020

[18] Lindsell Train Investment Trust monthly factsheet October 2020

accounts for just over 21% of the trust's assets.[19] This may seem incestuous, and it is reasonable to view it as a possible cause for concern. Arguably, this structure impinges on the independence of boards because it is in the portfolio's interest to maintain the same manager. Certainly it could act as an accelerant in any serious downturn when the assets of the trust fall, causing the assets under management for the management firm to decline, causing a lower valuation and a further self-reinforcing fall in the NAV of the investment trust. The investment trust industry worked hard in the early 2000s to root out the problem of cross-holdings between trusts that magnified the risks and led to an eventual collapse of a number of trusts, but as only a small number of trusts have significant stakes in their management companies, this is not currently viewed as a systemic issue.

[19] Majedie Investments monthly factsheet October 2020

Chapter 2: Types of Securities

Faced with such a dazzling array of different asset types, at least investors don't have to make tricky decisions about the type of share to buy, most of the time. The vast majority of trusts have a simple share structure with a single class of ordinary shares, and there has been a trend towards simplification that has reduced the number of complex share structures. That said, some variations do remain, and there are some quirks to watch out for.

Ordinary Shares

Most investors in investment trusts probably never own anything but plain vanilla ordinary shares, ubiquitous and standard, and the same for all shareholders. They are usually priced in pence, so a share price of 100 usually means 100p, but there are occasional exceptions such as Lindsell Train Investment Trust (LTI) which prices its shares in pounds. Some shares may be US dollar-denominated, and there are a few that are priced in euros. This may be off-putting for a newcomer, but in reality it is usually simple and seamless to deal through modern stockbroking platforms, where the currency conversion is all taken care of for you. There may be extra charges involved, so that is something to check before you deal.

From time to time, one of two events might happen that can be a shock to shareholders, although there is no actual direct impact. Ordinary shares can be sub-divided or consolidated. If a trust's board decides that its share price has become too high and unwieldy, perhaps making it difficult for smaller investors to reinvest dividends or to continue with modest monthly saving schemes, then it may decide to split the shares into smaller amounts. In October 2019, for example, BMO Global Smaller Companies (BGSC) decided to split its shares on a 10-for-1 basis, meaning that shareholders were given ten times as many shares, and the share price adjusted from 1360p to 136p. There was no net change in the value of the company or of individual shareholdings – this was simply a practical measure to allow small deals to be executed more efficiently. Even so, share splits can cause brief moments of panic when shareholders first see a much lower price. Conversely, trusts can also decide to consolidate their shares – the reverse of a share split – if the price has fallen to a very low level that may not look good optically and may incur a wider dealing spread.

'A' Shares

Here's an oddity. Hansa Investment Company (HAN, HANA) has two classes of listed shares, 40 million ordinary shares and 80 million 'A' shares. The two types of share are identical except for their voting rights – the 'A' shares are non-voting shares, meaning they do not carry any right to vote at the company's meetings. As you might expect, the prices of the two are similar, but not exactly the same. Historically, sometimes the ordinary shares have been slightly more expensive because they have voting rights, and sometimes the 'A' shares because they are more liquid. During the summer and autumn of 2020 the 'A' shares have largely had the upper hand, but the returns have been virtually identical from the two, so in practice the distinction does not seem very important. The choice probably rests more on their relative prices at the time, together with the importance you place on the voting rights and liquidity.

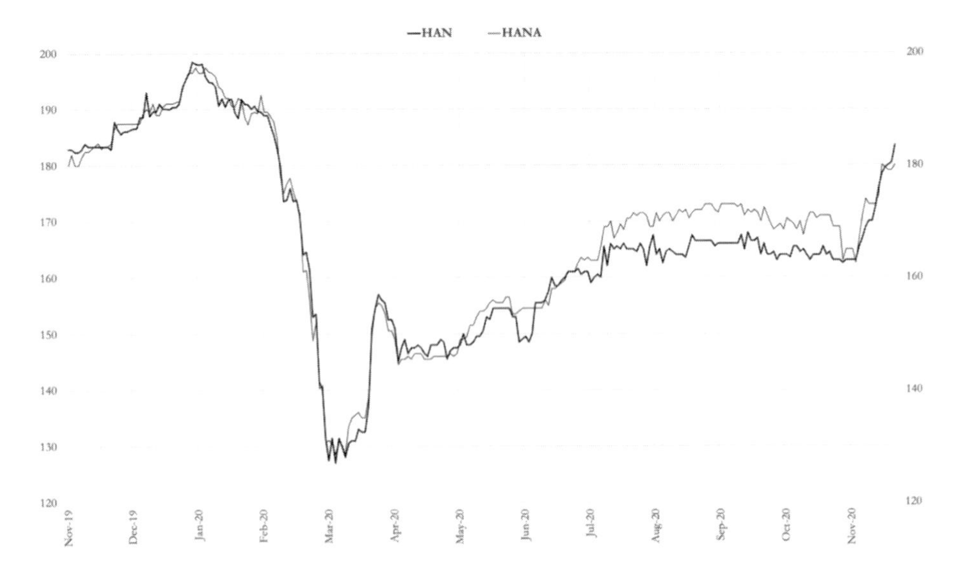

Hansa Investment Company ordinary shares and 'A' shares, one year to 24th November 2020

'B' Shares

And here's one more unique situation, this time for BMO UK High Income Trust, which has two classes of shares, ordinary shares (BHI) and 'B' shares (BHIB). This time the difference is nothing to do with voting – they are both voting shares, as usual – but to do with the tax treatment of distributions from the trust. The trust's Annual Report and Accounts contains a detailed explanation, but in a nutshell the ordinary shares pay dividends in the normal way, as income, while the 'B' shares distribute the same amount as a capital repayment. Which is more suitable for you depends on whether you have a preference for income tax or capital gains tax, with the latter offering more scope for tax planning. If this is not important – if you hold the shares in a tax-exempt wrapper like an ISA for example – then the ordinary shares are more liquid, or you can buy a 'unit' of the two shares combined in the ratio of three ordinary shares to one 'B' share. The two types of share generally trade at very similar prices.

From time to time, other investment trusts have considered a similar structure, but the relevance of tax preferences has been in decline over recent years as more investors use some form of tax-efficient account for their holdings. The current government is threatening some major changes to capital gains tax as well that may serve to move the two forms of distributions towards a much more equal tax rate, in which case there is again less reason to expect this particular formulation to proliferate.

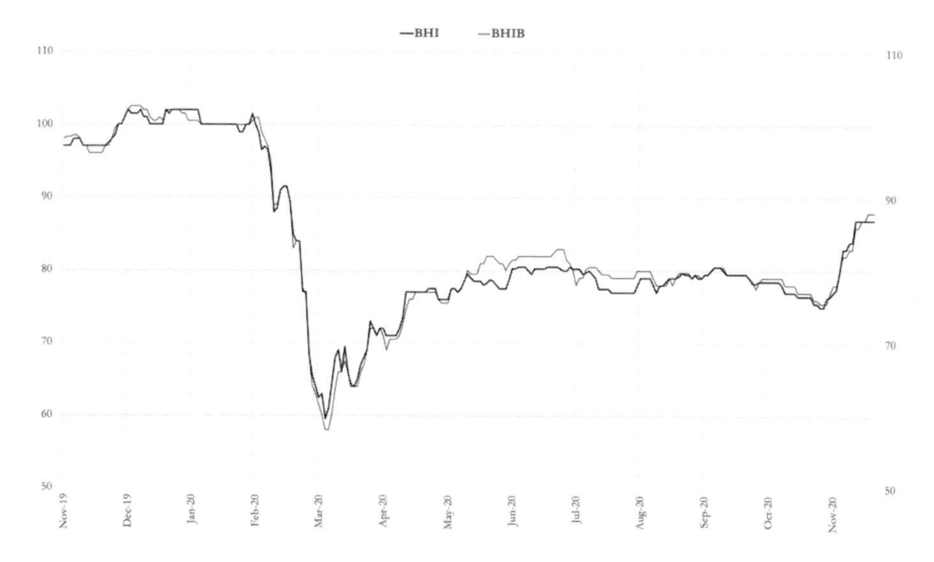

BMO UK High Income Trust ordinary shares and 'B' shares, one year to 24th November 2020

'C' Shares

From time to time you might notice something called a 'C' share on a certain trust, and then by the time you remember to look into it further, it seems to have disappeared. This is not your memory playing tricks – 'C' shares are temporary shares with a specific function for trusts raising additional capital.

When an existing trust wants to expand and raise more capital, it has a few options, and one method is to do so via a 'C' share issue to avoid any disadvantage for existing shareholders. One problem with expanding is that there is a period between the new capital arriving and therefore diluting the existing shares, and that money being invested and beginning to contribute to the returns. The effect of this 'cash drag' can be quite pronounced for alternative asset trusts in particular, which may take some time to fully invest the new cash into a pipeline of prospective illiquid assets. In principle, it could create an unfair situation where the prior shareholders returns are reduced, but the new shareholders benefit from a share of the pre-existing pool of assets, even if their capital remains uninvested.

The 'C' share structure works around this problem by classifying the new shares as 'C' shares with a separate pool of assets until, typically, at least 80% of the capital is invested (this percentage required can differ). At that point the 'C' shares convert to ordinary shares on an appropriate ratio of the respective net asset value of each pool. This may be some months later, and ensures a relatively fair outcome for all shareholders, old and new.

Here's a real example. In October 2019 the Hipgnosis Songs Fund (SONG) raised £231m from a 'C' share issue at 100p per share, to add to its 389.4m existing shares in issue, then trading at 107.5p, making the market pre-issue capitalisation £418.6m. This was a substantial addition of capital, but as the trust was deploying it into the acquisition of song catalogues, this would not necessarily be a quick process. Accordingly, the 'C' shares traded separately until 13th January 2020 when the trust announced that £214m of its £231m 'C' share pool had been invested, so the 'C' shares would convert to ordinary shares on the basis of the net assets attributable to the two share classes. The relevant NAV for the ordinary shares was 102.16p, and for the 'C' shares it was 100.08p, so on this basis each 'C' share was exchanged for 0.9796 of an ordinary share, with entitlements rounded down to the nearest whole share.

CULS

If you've never heard of CULS, don't be surprised. They are a rarity in the investment trust market, and quite easily ignored. For completeness though, these securities are Convertible Unsecured Loan Stock, a different class of listed security that has been issued by a small number of investment trusts to raise extra capital to provide gearing.

This has never been a large part of the market, but stepping back a few years it was an interesting sideshow that did throw up some anomalies and opportunities for the well-informed. Effectively it has nearly disappeared now, with just a couple of legacy CULS remaining, wiped out by a combination of the drive towards simplicity and the easy availability of cheap and flexible bank finance which has rendered them unnecessary.

In essence CULS are a hybrid between fixed interest and equity, allowing holders to obtain a higher yield than available on a trust's ordinary shares, but with exposure to a rising share price as well. The way they function means that holders trade off some of the potential upside of equity investment for the benefits of a higher yield and downside protection. The downside protection comes from repayment of the nominal value, the issue price, on expiry, but there is the potential to take up conversion rights as well that can yield more value if the underlying shares have been successful. For trusts, CULS have been a way in the past of raising a loan for structural gearing purposes at a lower interest rate than alternative sources of finance, but that period seems to have passed.

To explain further, let's take a look at one of the last remaining CULS in the market, the Aberdeen Standard Asia Focus 2025 CULS (AASC). Some £37m nominal of these were issued in 2018, partly as a roll-over option for some earlier 2019 CULS, and are listed on the standard debt segment of the Official List and traded on the London Stock Exchange's main market. They pay a bi-annual coupon of 2.25% per annum and investors have the opportunity to convert to ordinary shares twice yearly until the final redemption date on 31st May 2025. The ordinary share price (AAS) is 1042.5p[20] and the market price of the CULS is 98.5p.[21]

During May and November each year the conversion rights kick in, on the basis of 1465p nominal of CULS for one ordinary share. The nominal price is the issue price of 100p, so to reach the 1465p of nominal required to convert into one ordinary share worth 1042.5p, that requires 14.65 CULS, priced in the market at 98.5p (so worth 1443p, considerably more than the conversion right). Essentially, the conversion right only becomes interesting once the ordinary shares are over 1465p – below that level the CULS are really valued as bonds, so the 2.25% yield on the nominal of 100p translates to 2.28% at the market price of 98.5p. With the built-in capital gain on the planned redemption at 100p in 2025 the redemption yield rises to 2.61% (redemption yield calculators are freely available online to help with the arithmetic). That is better than the 1.4% yield on the ordinary shares, but not by a large enough margin to really attract attention, so there is not a great deal to draw investors to the CULS, which are not very actively traded. Whilst it is possible that in a period of higher interest rates or if bank finance dried up, CULS could see a renaissance, for the present time these look largely redundant.

Zero Dividend Preference Shares

Zeros, as these securities tend to be known, are quite similar to CULS in that they have been used by trusts to provide structural gearing, but in this case they are not paying a coupon or dividend and are pure capital instruments. They are issued with a certain 'redemption yield' with a fixed repayment price in the future, designed to be at the front of the queue in the priority for payouts and to be low-risk. For many years the industry proudly boasted that no zero had ever failed to be paid out in full. Sadly, that claim was ruined during the split capital crisis of 2001-02. Professor Andy Adams, who was quick to spot the danger at the time and has since edited a book on the subject,[22] says that to meet the demand for high yields when interest rates fell in the final years of the last century, a number of fund management groups created risky, unstable structures built on high levels of bank debt and cross investment holdings. In short order, when

[20] At close of business on 24th November 2020

[21] At close of business on 24th November 2020

[22] The Split Capital Investment Trust Crisis, Andrew Adams (Ed), 276pp, Wiley Finance 2004

markets fell and these highly geared trusts unravelled, 19 trusts were suspended from dealings. These ultimately tarnished the sector and halted the growth of what had been an interesting capital structure with different classes of share designed to meet the needs of different types of investor, and one that had served many investors well since the first launch in 1965.

That's why the number of zeros has dwindled to a total of 14 in November 2020.[23] Zeros are still used occasionally by trusts in preference to flexible bank debt, but as with CULS, the ready availability of cheap loans at low rates of interest makes it more difficult to justify the inclusion of fixed-term structured debt.

As some still exist, with many redemption yields in the 4%-7% range, these could be of interest, and a case study may help to understand how they work. Aberforth Split Level Income ZDP 2024 (ASIZ) is priced at 107.5p, and has a redemption price of 127.25p on 1st July 2024. Working out the redemption yield to that date, it works out at 4.76%.[24] The level of the ordinary shares is not relevant here, but the level of the assets is important, since there must be sufficient money to pay the ZDP holders. There are 47.56m zeros, so the trust needs £60.52m to pay them in full at redemption. At the end of October 2020 the trust had £149m of gross assets,[25] meaning the assets could fall by 59% before the zeros would not be paid out in full. Putting that another way, the cover is £149m/£60.52m, or 2.5 times. When assessing the risk, the cover is a key metric, and of course the volatility and quality of the underlying assets in the portfolio is another consideration.

Warrants and Subscription Shares

Just as CULS and zeros have been disappearing from the market, so the same is true of warrants and subscription shares, although for different reasons. Warrants are a type of security that carry an entitlement to buy a specific number of ordinary shares in a trust at a specific price, at a specific time in the future. Rather like options, they are pure capital instruments, with gearing, and they became very popular during the 1990s when the investment trust sector was expanding quickly. Warrants, which were also issued by some commercial companies, were used by investment trusts for one of two main reasons. The first was to perform the very specific function of closing the discount gap for new issues. At IPO, new investment trusts would frequently ask investors to pay 100p per share, but after the costs of the launch incurred by the trust, the opening net asset value would often be somewhere between 95p and 98p, meaning the initial investors were being asked to pay a premium, which would have been

---

[23] JPMorgan Cazenove Warrants, Subs and Convertibles statistics 24th November 2020
[24] JPMorgan Cazenove Warrants, Subs and Convertibles statistics 24th November 2020
[25] Aberforth Split Level Income factsheet, 31st October 2020

unpalatable at that time. By attaching free warrants to the issue shares on a 1-for-5 basis, trusts could bridge that discount gap because the warrants would have a market value of perhaps 25p-35p, or 5p-7p per share. They were a vital part of new issuance during this period, and having first appeared back in 1972, the number of investment trust warrants grew from under 50 in 1986 to 184 by 1995.[26] Some were also issued by trusts as a bonus for shareholders as trusts sought additional capital, as new shares would be created when the exercise rights of warrants were taken up – and the exercise price paid to the trust - at the end of their lives.

Subscription shares are much the same as warrants, an evolution of the same type of instrument with very little practical difference except for their eligibility for ISAs. During their years of popularity, warrants and subscription shares were very useful for the industry, helping to raise extra capital, and there were some tremendous returns on occasions for investors prepared to accept the higher risks of the gearing. At the start of 2013, VietNam Holding warrants multiplied 14-fold in three months.[27]

Active investors prepared to delve into the exercise terms and to use some basic mathematical analysis may mourn the near-death of the market in warrants and subscription shares, but it has virtually disappeared now. Vocal critics pointed towards the dilution that they caused by enabling holders to buy more shares at a lower price, but the main reason seemed to be increasing regulation and a growing dislike of complex leveraged instruments by institutional shareholders. As a result, in late 2020, only a handful of small issues remain, and those are set to mature by 2022. It did seem as though this part of the market, which had been so useful and so vibrant, might vanish altogether until CC Japan Income & Growth Trust (CCJI) announced in November 2020 that it was planning to issue new subscription shares as a bonus to shareholders in early 2021. Its ordinary shares rose on the day of the announcement, and if the issue is well received it could herald a re-think by boards and advisers keen to create new opportunities for shareholders to increase their investments. It is not easy to launch new equity investment trusts; nor is it easy for trusts on sizeable discounts to find a way to grow their capital base; nor is it easy for smaller trusts without any great reputation to find a way to differentiate themselves and attract new investors. Subscription shares are a potential answer, if the industry is prepared to listen.

---

[26] The Investor's Guide to Warrants (second edition), Andrew McHattie, 334pp, Pitman Publishing 1996

[27] Warrants Alert newsletter March 2013

Chapter 3: Size

From multi-billion pound investment trusts in the FTSE 100 Index down to those with just a few million pounds of assets, this is a universe in which the whales and the minnows swim together. Quite naturally though, less experienced investors may be drawn to the largest trusts. In a world of giant companies, dominated by US technology giants capitalised at more than a trillion dollars, there is a certain attraction in size. It comes with a certain swagger, suggesting success, resources, special expertise, and a marketing pull that smaller companies cannot match. Yet it can be a disadvantage too, as inefficiencies creep in, the value of exceptional individuals is diluted, and unexpected diseconomies of scale become apparent over time. In the investment trust sector, bigger is not necessarily better, but size is certainly a factor most investors will include in their selection process. It merits a closer look.

Choosing a Measure

It is easy enough to find figures for the size of individual investment trusts, but at the very start there is a decision to make as to which measure is most appropriate. We can choose from three – net assets, gross assets, or market capitalisation.

Net assets, first of all, measure the total value of the company's underlying investments, less any borrowings that are being used to provide gearing. The net asset value – NAV – is widely used as a performance measure, providing a level playing field and a true measure of the overall 'true' worth of a trust if it were to be liquidated immediately. It is not an easy figure to skew or manipulate, but neither is it an accurate indication of how much money a manager has to invest, nor the value that investors place upon those assets. It doesn't seem the right figure from either side of the fence.

Gross assets add that borrowing back in, to provide a measure of the total amount of money the trust can potentially invest, so for managers this may be a truer indication of size. If we compare the net assets of Merchants Trust (MRCH) and SDCL Energy Efficiency Income (SEIT) they are almost identical at £505m and £511m respectively.[28] Yet because Merchants borrows money to gear up, this increases its total assets being invested to £622m, whereas SEIT has no debt. Whilst it is certainly useful to know and understand what the figures are for the total amounts invested, using gross assets as a general measure seems somewhat arbitrary, particularly as borrowing conventions will vary from sector to sector as well as between trusts.

Market capitalisation is what investors 'see' as the value of a trust, but of course this is not the same as an asset value. The market capitalisation is simply the number of shares

[28] JPMorgan Cazenove Daily Statistics 24th November 2020

in issue multiplied by the share price, as determined by the supply and demand from investors. Discounts and premiums arise, so a trust can have £100m of net assets, yet be capitalised at £80m, £90m, £110m, or some other figure quite unrelated to the liquidation value or the amount of money at a manager's disposal. Market ratings can be heavily influenced by fashion, by recent performance, and by corporate policies to limit (or not) the size of any discount or premium. They can fluctuate quite widely, and it makes little intuitive sense to say that a trust shrinks in size when its discount widens.

Perhaps the real clincher for why market capitalisation is a flawed measure takes its cue from discount control mechanisms. Frequently these take the form of share buybacks, where a trust buys in its own shares for cancellation, thereby creating more demand and narrowing the discount, in theory at least. Potentially, then, a successful share buyback, reducing the number of shares in issue and shrinking the size of the trust, could improve the rating and boost the market capitalisation, creating the impression that the trust had actually grown.

These five paragraphs have essentially been a long-winded way of saying there is no perfect measure, and it does depend upon the context. For discussions about market liquidity for those needing to trade the shares, market capitalisation is clearly the most valid; when mentioning the clout that managers have in securing the best deals in the market, it is gross assets that matter. Overall, though, the best compromise may well be the figure for net assets, and that is the figure this chapter will generally use when talking about size, unless otherwise stated.

The Largest Trusts

Trust	Ticker	Sector	Net Asset Value[29]
Scottish Mortgage Inv Trust	SMT	Global	£15.8bn
3i Group	III	Private Equity	£9.0bn
Pershing Square Holdings	PSH	Hedge Funds	£6.0bn
F&C Investment Trust	FCIT	Global	£4.3bn
RIT Capital Partners	RCP	Flexible Investment	£3.2bn
Polar Capital Technology Trust	PCT	Technology	£3.1bn
HICL Infrastructure	HICL	Infrastructure	£3.0bn
Alliance Trust	ATST	Global	£2.9bn
Monks Investment Trust	MNKS	Global	£2.8bn
Templeton Emerging Markets	TEM	Emerging Markets	£2.4bn

[29] JPMorgan Cazenove Daily Statistics 24th November 2020

At the top of the net asset value pile by some distance is Scottish Mortgage Investment Trust (SMT), with £15.8bn of net assets. Originally founded in 1909, this highly successful global trust is managed by Baillie Gifford in Edinburgh and really reinvented itself under the stewardship of James Anderson, who became lead manager in 2000 and has since been joined by Tom Slater as co-manager. The managers are focused on identifying and investing in major long-term growth companies with the potential to deliver extraordinary returns. They take great pride in thinking differently from most other managers, deliberately questioning standard fund management beliefs about diversification, consistency, and shorter-term returns. The portfolio is very focused, with the largest 30 holdings accounting for 79.3% of assets,[30] and the managers describe themselves as owning companies rather than renting shares. Their thoughtful, philosophical approach seems highly distinctive, and best suited to long-term investors able to look past periods of volatility. The managers expect things to go wrong on the path to finding the kind of extreme payoffs they are seeking, pointing to research that finds the excess return of the US stock market since 1926 is entirely the result of the extraordinary lifetime performance of just 4% of the equities quoted during that period. That's why Scottish Mortgage is preoccupied with hunting for almost unlimited asymmetric upside, and why it has large holdings in the shares of some of the best-known growth companies of this modern period, including Tesla, Amazon, Alibaba, Tencent, Netflix, Spotify, Alphabet, and Zoom Video Communications.

Scottish Mortgage is in the company of three other global equity trusts in the top ten, joined by one each from private equity, hedge funds, flexible investment, technology, infrastructure, and emerging markets. Both Scottish Mortgage (SMT) and 3i Group (III) are constituents of the FTSE 100 Index, and Pershing Square Holdings (PSH) finally joined them in December 2020 after being denied a spot at the last moment during the previous reshuffle. F&C Investment Trust (FCIT) was in and out of the index three times between 1995 and 2009, and the former manager Jeremy Tigue used to joke about the trust being used as a contra-cyclical indicator, since it tended to enter the index when conditions were a little depressed for growth companies (and the trust was relatively resilient), and to leave again once activity picked up and investors became willing to pay up once more for future prospects. Further back in time, the other trusts to have made it into the FTSE 100 Index since 1984 are Edinburgh Investment Trust (EDIN), Globe Investment Trust, and Alliance Trust (ATST).

Large IPOs

Whilst the largest investment trusts are to an extent a self-selecting group of successful trusts, that is not necessarily the case with new issues, and those trusts that have raised

---

[30] Scottish Mortgage Investment Trust factsheet 31st October 2020

the largest sums at IPO. In fact their record is distinctly mixed and may serve as a warning against chasing over-hyped themes and managers.

The largest IPO in the industry until recently was the Woodford Patient Capital Trust, which raised £800m from enthusiastic investors in April 2015, when its shares started trading at an initial premium to their 100p issue price. They peaked at 119p in August 2015 and then fell back to a low of 73.2p in March 2018 as the trust encountered some difficulties with its fledgeling portfolio. In May 2018 the trust was relegated from the FTSE 250 Index, and that seemed bad enough until problems with unquoted holdings and with the manager's open-ended funds triggered a further sharp downturn that culminated in the collapse of the management company, the closure of the open-ended funds, a change of manager for the investment trust (now Schroder UK Public Private Trust, SUPP), and further declines in the share price down to 19p in early 2020.

To some extent this disaster mirrored the experience of many of the largest trust launches, which have raised capital on the back of mass optimism about a particular theme or strategy that has then struggled to meet high expectations. Launches such as Fidelity China Special Situations (FCSS), Amerindo Internet Fund, and further back, Mercury European Privatisation and Kleinwort European Privatisation, have proved disappointing. In the IPO market, it has become easy to squash the assertion that big is beautiful.

In 2018 another 'star' fund manager, Terry Smith, saw his Smithson Investment Trust (SSON) attract considerable demand. The trust's advisers increased the float size from an original £250m to £600m, and finally accepted a record £822.5m. The trust invests in a concentrated portfolio of global small and mid-cap companies, with almost half of the assets in the US and a heavy weighting towards information technology. To date it has performed very strongly and maintained a premium rating that has enabled it to issue more shares and reach an impressive market capitalisation of £2.0bn.[31]

The Advantages of Scale

Certain benefits accrue with greater scale, the most obvious being that a larger market capitalisation provides greater liquidity for larger investors to deal successfully. It is sometimes difficult for smaller private investors to appreciate that for wealth managers and institutions needing to deal in larger blocks of shares, it can be extremely frustrating if the normal dealing size is too small to accommodate those needs. In 2010 the minimum size required for an investment trust to be acceptable for wealth managers was thought to be £50m, but by popular consensus now, that figure is estimated at

[31] Smithson Investment Trust factsheet 30th October 2020

£200m or higher. Any trusts smaller than that risk being ignored, so it's a plus for larger trusts that they will most likely be on the radar of all sizeable investors.

One other aspect of liquidity is the dealing cost, in terms of the dealing spread on the shares. This will tend to be much keener for the largest, liquid trusts that attract a constant stream of deals throughout every trading day. Taking a one-day snapshot on 24th November 2020, for example, Scottish Mortgage Investment Trust (SMT), the largest of all investment trusts with a market capitalisation of £15.8bn, attracted 4242 trades during the day and the closing price showed a dealing spread of 1079p-1080p, so that is 0.09%. By contrast, Chelverton UK Dividend Trust (SDV), which has a market capitalisation of just £31m, attracted 15 trades during the day and closed with a dealing spread of 148p-150p, or 1.33%. When it comes to dealing on the stock market, the larger trusts have an undoubted advantage, both for ease and for cost.

Staying with the topic of costs, this is a much-quoted benefit of additional scale, cited whenever a trust is raising additional capital. This means that its fixed costs, such as the fees for listing on the stock exchange, paying auditors, directors and stockbrokers, and printing an annual report, will be spread over a wider base of shares, reducing the costs for all.

In recent years, as some trusts have grown very large, there has also been a growing trend for boards to negotiate tiered management fees with their managers, so the percentage fee drops once the assets pass certain thresholds. Picking out one of the larger trusts, Polar Capital Technology Trust (PCT) pays a base fee plus a performance fee, and the base fee is in four tiers. Tier 1 is 1% for net assets between zero and £800m; tier 2 is 0.85% for NAV between £800m and £1.6bn; tier 3 is 0.80% for NAV between £1.6bn and £2bn; and tier 4 is 0.70% for NAV over £2bn. What this shows is that shareholders have achieved some economies of scale as the trust has grown larger, reducing the overall cost incurred per share.

The majority of the largest investment trusts are reviewed fairly regularly in national newspapers, by the largest firms of stockbrokers and wealth managers, and so they are subject to a great deal of public scrutiny most of the time. This should help to maintain standards, and their relatively high profile should also be advantageous in attracting a continuous stream of new investors to buy the shares, replacing those who are selling or who drop off the shareholder register for other reasons. As a brief aside, the industry has been aware for a long time that it has an ageing demographic and has to raise its efforts to attract younger investors, no easy task.

Returning to the management fees, these can be very large in absolute terms. The managers of Polar Capital Technology Trust, for example, were paid a total of £18.3m for the year to 30th April 2020[32] - a hefty fee that is far in excess of the £542,000 paid to the managers of the much smaller Chelverton UK Dividend Trust.[33] This additional revenue enables the managers of larger trusts to devote greater resources to their task, perhaps in the form of extra professional managers and analysts, or a larger budget for third-party research, or the ability to conduct many more meetings. The additional 'clout' that comes from having more assets under management also means that trust managers may find they have improved access to talk directly to the senior management of major firms, as well as preferential access to placings or to restricted opportunities. This may be especially relevant for managers of alternative assets where agreements must be negotiated individually.

Managers themselves may also pay more attention to trusts that are larger and more important as fee-generators for their business. This is an unquantifiable advantage, but although all managers will point to their professional credentials and say they treat all clients with equal focus, they are both human and commercially-driven, so it is natural to spend more time and effort on the biggest clients. When most asset management firms will look after open-ended funds as well as investment trusts, plus private portfolios and pension funds, it has to be beneficial for the investment trust to be a sizeable chunk of their assets under management so that it does not need to fight for attention. A regular question posed by analysts is just how important an investment trust is to the managers.

One benefit of scale that may not be immediately apparent is additional flexibility with discount control. This is a technical point specific to investment trusts, which may adopt a range of measures to try to prevent their shares trading at a growing discount to the net asset value. One fairly common response is to use shareholder funds to buy back the trust's own shares, thereby supporting the market price (and if buying at a discount to net asset value, enhancing the NAV at the same time). For smaller trusts, this option is removed if they are concerned about buybacks making the trust materially smaller still, and they will often rule out this option as a result. For larger trusts, there is no great risk of share buybacks reducing the trust to an uneconomic size.

The Disadvantages of Scale

Very often, there is an advantage in greater size, but that is not always the case. For trusts that are seeking to invest in small niche areas where there is limited investment capacity, it can be a severe problem if they have too much money to invest. This is a real issue in areas such as UK micro-cap and in frontier markets. The River & Mercantile UK Micro Cap Investment Company (RMMC) invests into small UK

---

[32] Polar Capital Technology Trust Annual Report 2020

[33] Chelverton UK Dividend Trust Annual Report 2020

companies generally capitalised at less than £100m, where there are liquidity constraints, and the trust actually has a cap on its own size of £125m as a result. Once the trust's assets rise to more than £110m it returns capital to shareholders, as it has done three times since the trust's IPO (in June 2017, December 2017, and July 2018) to return the NAV back to around £100m, which is considered an optimal size. Some £42m has been repaid in total. The manager of BlackRock Frontiers Investment Trust (BRFI), which invests in some small out-of-the-way markets such as Kazakhstan and Kenya, has also spoken of a maximum size for efficient investment.

Potentially as well, with smaller trusts that have a lower profile, the manager may feel slightly more freedom to pursue what they regard as optimal investment policies without being hamstrung by the weight of expectation inherent in a larger mandate. Early-adopter investors looking for truly novel approaches or investment in new asset classes will usually be looking at smaller trusts, even though these may grow larger once the concept is proven. There are good reasons to be thankful for the existence of smaller trusts that bring extra colour, diversity, and choice to the sector.

One other type of investor will naturally find smaller trusts to be a happier hunting-ground as well, when looking for valuation anomalies and discount bargains. Although there are certainly exceptions, large trusts do on the whole tend to have higher public profiles, inviting lots of attention, and that means they will usually be priced more efficiently. Smaller trusts that few people may follow closely, less frequently dealt, can sometimes offer the greatest opportunities if you have the confidence to back your research and convictions. This has been the approach of Nick Greenwood and Charlotte Cuthbertson, who manage Miton Global Opportunities (MIGO), which has a portfolio largely comprising other investment companies. They deliberately target under-researched trusts, explaining "with many smaller trusts falling below the radar of wealth managers and, in particular, given the growth of alternative asset classes there is a lot of scope for mispricings".[34] Nick and Charlotte can provide plenty of examples, as can other investors who specifically seek out the second-rank trusts that are far from household names.

A Common Sense Approach to Size

In trying to answer the question of whether size matters, it is tempting to utter the simple common-sense answer "it depends". That's probably as good an answer as any, as it does depend on what type of investor you are, what sort of trust you are seeking, in what sector, and how long your holding period might be.

[34] Miton Global Opportunities Annual Report 2019

Various studies over the years,[35] and more ad hoc approaches, have tried to determine whether size is linked to subsequent market performance, and there appears to be very little evidence of any solid relationship. There are good and bad trusts of all sizes, although you might need a very good reason to invest in some trusts at the bottom end of the scale. There are some very small trusts in existence, including one called The Investment Company (INV) which is actually the second-oldest of all investment trusts but has been largely forgotten. A series of management changes over recent years is indicative of the struggle faced by the board, doubtless aware of the fact that they are the latest custodians of a historic trust, but one that is clearly sub-scale with just £15m of shareholders' funds at the end of June 2020. As a rule of thumb, you probably need a special reason to invest in trusts capitalised at less than £25m, and sometimes liquidity can be an issue for smaller investors. In tough market conditions, dealing spreads can widen dramatically on lesser-traded trusts as market-makers try to minimise their exposure, raising the risk of effectively being 'locked-in' to holdings you are unable to sell at a reasonable price – at the exact moment when you might need to. This happened during the Covid-19 crisis, when market turbulence caused some curious pricing. Canadian General Investments (CGI) saw its dealing spread widen out from 3.3% in January 2020 to 41.5% in April 2020; the spread on Premier Global Infrastructure Trust (now renamed Premier Miton Global Renewables, PMGR) shares widened from 3.9% in January 2020 to 20% in June 2020; JPMorgan Brazil (JPB) likewise saw its dealing spread gape from 4.9% in January 2020 to 12.2% in May 2020. In each case these were fairly illiquid trusts with a relatively small free float, so this was an example of small size being a disadvantage, but only in difficult circumstances. Once markets calmed themselves in the third quarter of 2020, the spreads returned to fairly normal levels. Once again, it depends.

[35] Including Mario Levis, University of Bath, Market size and seasonalities: the case of the UK investment trust industry, 1987

Chapter 4: Discounts and Premiums

If there is one investment trust topic that causes disagreements and furrowed brows, it's the question of discounts and premiums and how share prices deviate from their underlying net asset values. Remember, share prices are the result of the interplay of supply (selling) and demand (buying), and whilst there is usually a strong connection with the NAV, the elastic band can stretch quite far.

It may help to have a sense of 'normal' levels of valuations. At the time of writing the average discount for the investment trust sector (ex-3i) is 5.8%,[36] having ranged between close to zero and well into double-digits earlier in the year. That latest average is a little lower than has often been the case, but also much more volatile as was to be expected in a year of pandemic. A decade before, the average was more like a 9% discount, but in a much narrower 7%-11% range. As is always true of an average, it disguises a lot of variation amongst individual trusts, and we have seen discounts as wide as 60%-70% and premiums of 30%-50% from time to time. In November 2020 Tetragon Financial Group (TFG) was trading on a 61.0% discount to net asset value, while BBGI Global Infrastructure (BBGI) shares commanded a 27.1% premium.[37]

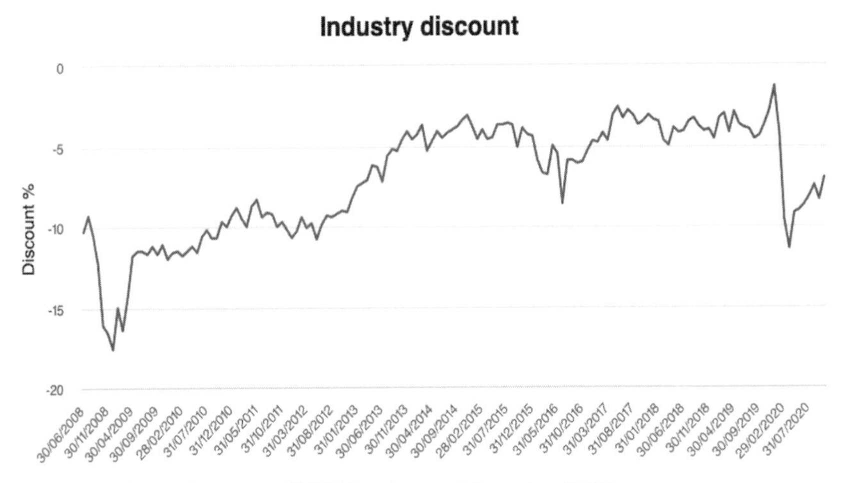

Average industry discount, AIC/Morningstar November 2020

Calculations

Starting with the basics, calculating a discount or premium is quite straightforward. Simply divide the share price by the net asset value, subtract one, then multiply by 100 to express it as a percentage. Here are a couple of simple examples:

---

[36] Winterflood Investment Trusts Daily Research Update 24th November 2020

[37] Both figures from JPMorgan Cazenove Daily Statistics 24th November 2020

Share price: 90p / Net asset value: 100p
Share price rating = ((90/100)-1)*100
Share price rating = -10% (discount)

Share price: 110p / Net asset value: 100p
Share price rating = ((110/100)-1)*100
Share price rating = +10% (premium)

If you prefer, there are free online calculators available that will do these simple sums for you, for example at www.tipsheets.co.uk/discountcalc.html. One small point that may be relevant if you are manually finding the share price and the NAV is that sometimes trusts may publish multiple NAVs under different assumptions. Generally, the NAV used is cum-income (so this includes any current year income) and fully diluted.

Alternatively, and even more simply, you can consult tabular information on public websites like Morningstar and Trustnet, or visit the AIC portal – they will all provide regularly updated figures. The simple figure for the premium or discount is a basic expression of how far the share price has strayed from the NAV. For context it is useful to compare figures across a peer group of similar trusts; to look at the high, low, and average figures over the last year; and to look for a graphical representation over time, if you can find one. At present, Morningstar (www.morningstar.co.uk) has good charts that show the progression of share prices against net asset values over time, for an easy visual representation of how the valuation might have changed.

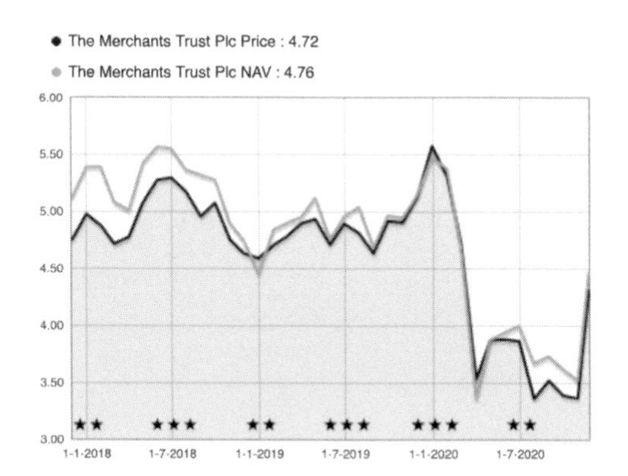

Merchants Trust (MRCH) share price and net asset value, three years to 25th November 2020. Source: ©2020 Morningstar Inc. All Rights Reserved. Reproduced with permission.

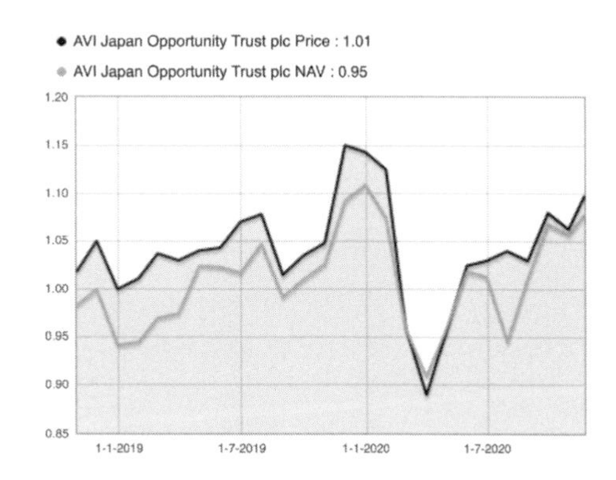

AVI Japan Opportunity Trust (AJOT) share price and net asset value, two years to 25th November 2020. Source: ©2020 Morningstar Inc. All Rights Reserved. Reproduced with permission.

If you are not too familiar with how pricing works and how it can vary over time, it might be a profitable use of an hour to flick through some charts like these, and in the majority of cases you will probably note there is a reasonably strong relationship between the NAV and the share price. There is an argument that long-term investors intending to hold shares over a period of many years should not pay the initial share price rating too much attention – and certainly not let it drive investment choices – since any subsequent change in the rating is likely to be fairly insignificant against the investment returns generated over a long period. That seems like sensible advice, but of course it is human nature to want to pay a fair price, and if you were buying goods in a supermarket then you might be attracted to goods available at a discounted price, and perhaps less inclined to buy those where a previous discount has disappeared. There's a great deal more to this subject for active traders, for investors who have a keen eye for the sharpest price, and also for those who worry that perfectly acceptable profits achieved by good management performance might be wiped out by a share price de-rating.

Z-Scores

For more sophisticated analysis of discount and premium movements, analysts use a measure called a 'z-score'. This calculates a single figure indicating whether the current rating is above or below the norm, but the arithmetic is more involved than just finding the divergence from the twelve-month average. Used by statisticians in other fields too, z-scores are standard scores indicating how many standard deviations a data point is above or below its mean level. A negative score indicates that a trust's rating is below its average and may therefore be cheap, and vice versa.

Working out the z-score obviously requires you to have the daily data for the discount or premium, but a couple of examples may again illustrate this sufficiently.

	Current Rating[38]	1 Year Average	Z-Score
Fidelity China Special Situations	-0.4%	-8.1%	2.2
Brunner Investment Trust	-12.7%	-9.9%	-0.6

In these examples, Fidelity China Special Situations (FCSS) shares on a modest 0.4% discount are considerably more expensive than they have been on average over the last year, so the z-score is positive; Brunner Investment Trust (BUT) shares are slightly cheaper than they have been on average, so the z-score is mildly negative.

[38] JPMorgan Cazenove Daily Statistics 24th November 2020

Discount Hunting

In most scenarios, discounts are a good thing. They mean a deduction from the usual cost of something, more for less, and it is no different for investment trusts. Buying the shares for less than the asset value means that you can get 'more bang for your buck' and have more assets working for you for each pound you spend. This can be a very attractive proposition, especially when a trust is generating income from its assets. If a trust has a net asset value of 200p, then that means the full 200p is working to generate income, and let's say for illustration it is invested in assets that earn 5% a year, and that the trust pays out all income as dividends. If you are buying at a discount, and perhaps pay 175p for your assets, then your prospective yield is not 5%, but 5.7%. The discount gives you a yield boost.

The fact that discounts can therefore be beneficial even if you have no reason to expect them to narrow means that many investors, not just traders and speculators, look for bargain discount ratings. Discount-hunting can also be worthwhile for investors if they believe there are good reasons for the discount to narrow, perhaps through improved performance, or a sector returning to fashion, or because it seems temporarily misaligned, or because of a new marketing and PR drive, or perhaps because there are some technical factors that appear to have depressed the price. For all sorts of reasons there is frequently a considerable focus on investment trust ratings, but experience shows that buying trusts purely for a wide discount is an unreliable path to profits. Asset performance is a much more important variable over any medium to long-term timeframe, and wide discounts can remain stubbornly wide for extended periods if a trust is out of favour. There is a behavioural bias around 'anchoring' on certain ratings for certain trusts. If a trust has been trading on a particular discount or premium level for some time, this can become a fairly concrete expectation for investors, that this is the normal and acceptable level for that trust.

Just as many investors like discounts and discount movement for the opportunities it throws up, for many professional advisers and investors in particular, there is a flip side. Discount volatility can be a rogue variable that throws a spanner in the works of the most carefully constructed client portfolios, and it must not be easy to explain to clients that although your analysis may have been correct and a trust performed well in asset terms, a widening discount means that it has fallen in value. This may not have anything at all to do with the trust itself. During bearish periods when sellers prevail, discounts naturally tend to widen across the board, which means that poor performance can be exacerbated and shareholders are hit by a 'double whammy' of falling asset values and worsening valuations. Discount volatility is an extra layer of risk.

Discount Control Mechanisms

Understanding that their shareholders don't want to see widely fluctuating valuations, a large number of trusts have instigated controls to try to manage the discount or premium, with varying levels of success. There are some trusts that deliberately stick to a rigid 'zero discount' policy that means they pull certain policy levers when the discount or premium blows out, and some achieve excellent results. Other trusts, by contrast, try very hard to reduce their discounts – this is much more of a problem than big premiums – but some fail and eventually give up the task, opting to wind up and return shareholders' money instead.

There are two types of discount control mechanisms, soft and hard. Soft DCMs are more like guidelines, and allow the board of a trust discretion and flexibility in how these might be implemented, whereas hard DCMs are intended as rigid rules that kick in once certain conditions, such as the level of the discount, have been met.

The most commonly used DCM, usually soft but occasionally hard, is share buybacks, used fairly extensively over the last twenty years. Investment trusts have the right to use their funds to buy back their own shares for cancellation, thereby injecting direct demand into the market and reducing the number of shares in issue. In theory that should help to tilt the demand/supply balance and encourage the price to rise against the asset value, reducing the discount. At the same time, it helps existing shareholders by slightly increasing the NAV as shares are purchased below their asset value. Often there we will be a soft trigger that the board can buy back shares at its discretion if the discount widens out beyond a pre-determined level such as 5% or 10%.

Whilst that might sound like unambiguously good news for all concerned, that is not the case and this policy attracts plenty of criticism. For smaller trusts in particular, reducing the number of shares in issue can reduce the liquidity and also increase the costs for remaining shareholders as the trust shrinks in size. For trusts that use borrowing, reducing the size of the equity base also increases their gearing, perhaps beyond the level initially intended.

Finally, there are also a lot of question marks over whether share buybacks actually work. Academic studies seem to suggest mixed results,[39] and market practitioners tend to reach the same conclusion, that share buybacks may work as a signalling mechanism to the market that the trust considers its rating to be unacceptable, but often their impact is short-term and the market reverts to its prior position as sentiment and the assessment of future returns regain prime importance.

---

[39] For example, The impact of hard discount control mechanism on the discount volatility of UK closed-end funds, Ahmed F Salhin, Investment Management and Financial Innovations, October 2013

It doesn't help when soft DCMs are implemented in a less than wholehearted fashion. The board of Phaunos Timber Fund undertook a strategic review in 2009 and considered its discount management options. It decided on a programme of additional communications together with "occasional share buybacks". It said that it would be monitoring the effectiveness of its programme. Almost two years later, in August 2011, the board said in its interim report, "share buybacks have been tried and had no impact". Fair enough, you might think, except that Phaunos had only spent US$2.8m on buybacks, less than 0.5% of its net asset value.[40]

Tougher measures are available, including tender offers that offer holders a partial exit at close to net asset value. Typically these might allow for 10%-25% of the assets to be tendered and cancelled, but like buybacks (this time without any enhancement to NAV), many of the same disadvantages of making the trust smaller make this a mixed bag for investors. Sometimes a tender that is fully taken up by shareholders can sound the death knell for sub-scale trusts. On occasions a struggling trust that might otherwise be under existential threat might offer a hard DCM to shareholders as a way of extending its life. India Capital Growth Fund (IGC) proposed a regular redemption facility to shareholders in May 2020, giving them the right to request the redemption of part or all of their shareholding on 31st December 2021 and every second year thereafter at an exit discount to NAV of a maximum of 6%. This effectively gave the manager a deadline to improve the performance of the trust and narrow the discount.

That particular corporate action was triggered by an upcoming continuation vote, which is another popular form of DCM that provides a focus and a deadline for both performance and the rating to be at acceptable levels. Many trusts have regular continuation votes, and some have contingent votes written into their articles of association. If the average discount to NAV at which Aberdeen Japan Investment Trust (AJIT) shares trade in the 90 days prior to its financial year end exceeds 10%, a continuation vote is required to be proposed to shareholders. The idea here is that if the discount is wider than the stated hurdle, prospective investors know that they are in with a chance of an exit close to NAV, so they have an extra incentive to buy in the knowledge that the risk of a significant widening of the discount from that level is less likely.

Fairly similar in practice is to establish a limited life for a trust at the outset. When the managers of a new trust are proposing a thesis that is specific to that moment rather than evergreen, a fixed life of a few years may be part of the initial structure, with some sort of vote or event thereafter. When AVI Japan Opportunity Trust (AJOT) came to the market in 2018 it followed the lead of Polar Capital Global Healthcare (PCGH) and Polar Capital Global Financials (PCFT) which were both launched to take

---

[40] Phaunos Timber Fund: playing with fire, Collins Stewart research report, 31st August 2011

advantage of time-sensitive opportunities identified by the managers. The AVI trust provides for a chance to exit all or part of holdings four years after the launch at close to NAV, and every two years thereafter. This should help to limit the discount, and if it follows the lead of the two Polar Capital trusts, then it can seek a longer life from shareholders once the initial term has passed.

Less mechanical approaches to narrowing discounts can include PR and marketing charm offensives; encouraging director buying; starting to pay, or increasing the level of, dividends; refining the investment policy to ensure it is well-aligned with investor preferences; or even changing the manager, as a last resort. Ultimately though, trying to fight the market is a difficult process that many boards have found fruitless. The name of discount control mechanisms implies much more agency than is the case in reality.

Arbitrageurs

If discounts are wide enough and trusts seem unable or unwilling to deal with them effectively, the door swings open for other market participants to join the fray. In the late 1990s and early 2000s, when many discounts on equity trusts were considerably wider, arbitrageurs, also called 'vulture' funds, bought sizeable stakes in certain trusts at a large discount, and then agitated for change to narrow the discount or for some sort of exit or reconstruction for them to sell out at a profit. Very often they were successful. Firms such as Sierra Trading, Millennium Offshore Partners, Carrousel Capital, and The Liverpool Partnership made waves and shook up boards with resolutions and proposals. Arbitrageurs called Laxey Partners and Elliott Advisors attacked Alliance Trust (ATST) and were eventually fought off after a bitter war of words, but the trust did change some board members, its manager, and eventually its whole investment strategy. Edward Bramson of Sherborne Investors Management battled with the board of Electra Private Equity (ELTA) and eventually seized control. These activist investors may not have been liked at the time, but their actions did serve to shake the sector out of some complacency and helped to shape the modern structure of the sector today where boards dare not ignore wide and sustained discounts for too long.

Premiums

Premium ratings used to be extremely rare and could usually be explained by something special relating to a particular trust, such as an additional business, or some scarcity value, or an asset that was likely to be revalued at a higher price. Since the expansion of alternative asset trusts that are more frequently valued on their yields, however, premium ratings are regularly to be found. In the infrastructure sector, or renewable energy infrastructure, premium ratings have become the norm, as big dividend payments that provide attractive yields have encouraged investors to pay more. Further, it is not possible to buy these assets more cheaply through open-ended funds priced at asset value, because they do not exist in that form. When equity trusts reach premium ratings, as they sometimes do, it is standard practice to search for an equivalent open-ended fund run by the same manager, which may then be cheaper.

If a trust is not high-yielding, why else might it trade at a premium? One reason is that the investment trust might be the only way for investors to gain access to an outstanding manager with a stellar track record. Even so, premium ratings can sometimes get out of hand, and the industry throws up an outstanding example in the case of Lindsell Train Investment Trust (LTI), managed by the high-profile and highly regarded fund manager Nick Train. This trust has traded at some extraordinary high premium ratings over recent years, as high as 100% (double the net asset value), causing the chairman of the trust to caution investors repeatedly about buying the shares on a large premium. In the trust's interim report for 2019, speaking about the share price fall from a peak above £2000 per share, at a 100% premium to NAV, to an end-September 2019 price of £1375, still on a premium to NAV, chairman Julian Cazalet said "if nothing else it was a ready reminder of the danger of buying shares in the company at an elevated premium to NAV, something that I continue to advise against with the premium around 35%". It is not very often that an investment trust chair will openly advise against buying his or her trust's shares.

Another potential reason for a premium is that a trust's latest asset valuation might be suffering from a time-lag. For equity trusts, daily valuations are no problem on the whole, and mean that the NAV is kept completely up to date. With alternative asset trusts though, and any unquoted investments, these will only be valued periodically, meaning that the quoted NAV could be based on some old data. If investors believe the 'true' NAV is higher, they might be prepared to pay a premium to the quoted NAV. The reverse can also be true, incidentally – that apparently large discounts can open up if outdated valuations exist in a falling market.

It is understandable why investors might be unhappy at their shares trading at a big discount, but less obvious why they might also be unhappy about a big premium. Whilst their shares might have benefited from some extra performance as a result, a premium rating reduces the yield and increases the risk of a 'double-whammy' decrease in rating during a sell-off. Trusts will generally keep a lid on premium ratings by issuing more shares – effectively the opposite of share buybacks. This helps to reset the supply and demand balance, enhances NAV, and expands the size of the trust to the benefit of all shareholders. Trusts can issue up to 20% more shares without going to the trouble and expense of issuing a new prospectus, and such issuance is known as 'tap' issuance that drips new shares into the market through the trust's stockbroker.

Quasi Open-Ending

If investment trusts can issue new shares and buy them back again, some argue they are no longer true closed-end vehicles, but have moved instead towards a quasi open-ended structure. This is normally directed at trusts as a criticism, but actually it may indicate that investment trusts have enough flex in the structure to allow them to adapt and serve investors well in changing circumstances. The really key difference is that the inflows and outflows of funds from issuance and buybacks are controlled and allowed by the boards and by shareholders, subject to limits, and only undertaken when the conditions are beneficial. Buybacks do not occur when shares are trading at a premium, as that would cut the NAV and disadvantage shareholders. Likewise, issuance at a discount will only take place on particular occasions when it has been sanctioned by shareholders. None of these flows are at the whim of jittery investors reacting to sudden changes in market conditions that can surprise a manager and require changing the portfolio at the worst possible moment. The divide between investment trusts and open-ended funds remains as sharp as ever.

Chapter 5: Gearing and Derivatives

In the investment trust world, gearing refers to the borrowing undertaken by some trusts, allowing the investment of extra capital to deliver additional returns to shareholders. Gearing can take different forms and is not always beneficial, so this is something for potential shareholders to assess. Another element, for some trusts, is how they use complex financial instruments to hedge or to enhance their returns. These too can increase the risk.

The Principle of Gearing

Often fêted as one of the advantages of investment trusts over open-ended funds, the ability to take on debt when appropriate can work well to boost long-term returns. Borrowing funds at 3% interest and then deploying them to earn a yield of 7%, for example, will provide a net benefit, and in this era of low interest rates, taking on cheap debt seems to make a lot of sense. For equity funds and those investing in economically-sensitive areas though, having gearing in a downturn can increase volatility and exacerbate losses. This is not a one-way street. For some boards, managers, and investors, remembering that investment trusts are intended to be conservative pooled vehicles, loading up with cheap money to pile into risk markets is not consistent with the need for prudent oversight and careful custody of investors' savings. For this reason, limits are imposed and gearing is generally used in modest proportions to add a little extra spice without making the risk level unpalatable.

Measurement

After quite a long period when different trusts expressed their gearing levels in different ways, the industry thankfully seems to have settled on a standard measurement. Simply, gearing is expressed as the amount of borrowing divided by the net asset value, expressed as a percentage. So if a trust with £200m of assets borrows £20m, the gearing level is 10%. Taking a real example, at the end of its financial year to 31st March 2020, The Biotech Growth Trust (BIOG) had £365,573,000 of net assets and £32,737,000 of loans, making its gearing level 9%.[41] The level of gearing will vary over time and will usually be disclosed in monthly factsheets as well as interim and annual reports.

Types of Gearing

There are two main types of gearing – variable and fixed. This first type, variable, is usually bank debt, organised as a facility that can be drawn down when desired, subject

[41] The Biotech Growth Trust Annual Report & Accounts 2019

to a maximum level. In the case of The Biotech Growth Trust (BIOG) it has a loan facility arranged with JPMorgan Securities, with interest charged at the US overnight banks funding rate plus 45 basis points. The loan is flexible in size, and it can be used at the discretion of the managers, subject to the limits set by the board. This is sometimes called tactical gearing, as the managers can use the debt facility strategically to buy more shares when they believe they are cheap. Over the last few years the end-of-year gearing level for BIOG has fluctuated between 3.2% (2017) and 11.1% (2016). Bank loans are the most usual way of financing variable gearing, but there are alternatives. Fidelity Japan Trust (FJV) uses long CFDs instead, which the trust says are cheaper than bank loans.

Fixed gearing, sometimes called structural gearing, is built into the capital structure of trusts with some sort of debt security like a zero dividend preference share, loan note, or debenture. As the name suggests, it lacks the flexibility of variable borrowing, but it does have the advantage of greater certainty and the chance to lock in a fixed interest rate. In 2015 Witan Investment Trust (WTAN) issued two long-dated loan notes, a £21m fixed-rate 20 year secured private placement note at a coupon of 3.29% and a £54m fixed-rate 30 year note at a coupon of 3.47%. Unlike variable borrowing these are not at risk of becoming more expensive if interest rates rise, but of course they won't become cheaper either if available interest rates fall. Many debentures and long-term structural debt instruments put into place before this current low interest rate era have proved to be a significant burden and drag on returns for some trusts. In recent years several trusts have been relieved to reach the final maturity for debt instruments paying coupons of 11% or more, and some like Brunner Investment Trust (BUT) have decided to swallow the high capital cost of early repayment. In mid-2018 the trust borrowed £25m at a coupon of 2.84% to partly fund an early repayment of £28m of debentures with interest rates of 9.3% (for £15m) and 6% (for £13m), due to mature in 2023. Wiping the slate clean came at a cost of £39.4m, including accrued interest, knocking 0.7% off the fair value NAV but obviously reducing costs from that point onwards.

One small extra point about long-term structural debt is that this will generally be 'marked to market' at fair value for the purpose of calculating the net asset value. This means that at times when gilt yields are falling, the value of the debt will rise and will, other things remaining equal, reduce the NAV – and vice versa. This tends not to be significant, but it can be confusing for investors looking at NAV announcements with up to four different figures, NAV ex-income for the period with debt at par value, NAV cum-income for the period with debt at par value, NAV ex-income for the period with debt at fair value, and NAV cum-income for the period with debt at fair value. The last one of these generally seems the best to use as the standard measure – it is, if you will, the NAV to have.

The choice between the two types of gearing, flexible or structural, will depend upon the circumstances of the time and the needs and preferences of the board and manager. It is not necessarily a straight choice between the two – some trusts have a blend of each type, and boards seem to generally assess the choices available when debt is taken on or due for renewal.

Limits and Limitations

Returning to our example of The Biotech Growth Trust (BIOG) and its 9% gearing, the managers of the trust have some freedom to draw on further borrowing if they wish, but this is subject to an absolute upper limit of 20%, the maximum permitted by the board. It is common practice for the managers to discuss any meaningful change in the gearing level with the board, so the board oversight is actually greater than it seems, but this is a published limit that is clear for all investors to see. Gearing is always capped, although the level is different for individual trusts. Fidelity China Special Situations (FCSS) had a gross gearing level (before netting off any short positions) of 25.2% at the end of its financial year to 31st March 2020,[42] within the limit of 30% set by the board. Pacific Horizon Investment Trust (PHI) had gearing of 4.1% at the end of its financial year to 31st July 2020,[43] well within the board's agreed range of gearing parameters, reviewed at each board meeting and between meetings if necessary. At that time the agreed range of equity gearing was -15% (i.e. holding net cash) to +15%, using a multi-currency revolving credit facility with The Royal Bank of Scotland.

Not all trusts use gearing, which is an option rather than a requirement. River & Mercantile UK Micro Cap Investment Company (RMMC), which invests in a concentrated portfolio of small UK companies, has no gearing because the managers say "we want to minimise risk, not take it on".[44] They believe in keeping things simple and avoiding any interference with the trust's principal aim of alpha generation through good stock picking. Gearing can be an unwelcome noise and distraction.

Whether or not they choose to, it is widely accepted that investment trusts can use gearing, and that the resultant magnification of returns, positive and negative, is a distinguishing feature of the sector. That is broadly true, but it is not quite universally true. There are in fact a small number of trusts that are unable to use gearing, due to a little-known technical quirk of regulation that arose in 2014. In response to the financial crisis of 2007-08 and a perceived gap in the regulation of certain alternative assets, mainly private equity and hedge funds, the European Commission introduced extra legislation to cover fund managers in these areas. This was the Alternative

[42] Fidelity China Special Situations Annual Report & Accounts to 31st March 2020
[43] Pacific Horizon Investment Trust Annual Report 2020
[44] Portfolio manager George Ensor, quoted in Investment Trust Newsletter September 2020

Investment Fund Managers Directive (AIFMD). Unfortunately for investment trusts, they fell within the classification as well, in spite of their independent boards, their reporting obligations under the rules of the London Stock Exchange, and their long history of generally strong corporate governance.

Even worse, and partly because the new rules were not really written with investment trusts in mind, the AIFMD had some unintended consequences. Managers of investment trusts had to register either as 'full scope' firms or as 'small registered UK Alternative Investment Fund Manager' firms, depending really on the scale of their operations, and slightly different regulations apply to each group. Regrettably, particularly during a period when there is so much talk about creating a 'level playing field' for all investment products, the regulations meant that some small or self-managed trusts had to choose between two of the traditional virtues of the sector – low costs and gearing. The problem is that for trusts such as Pacific Assets Trust (PAC), and Independent Investment Trust (IIT), the managers consider that full scope authorisation would be too costly and burdensome. They have chosen instead to opt for smaller company registration. Fair enough, but these sub-threshold managers are not authorised to use gearing, so effectively these new regulations have removed this benefit for certain trusts, effectively penalising them for not having a larger-scale manager. Certainly, it can be argued it has reduced their flexibility to fully exploit the structure and diminishes their attractions.

The Impact of Gearing

As gearing works in both directions, magnifying gains and losses, its effect depends on the direction of asset prices. It seems reasonable to argue that over the long-term the general trend of asset prices is up, so the overall effect of gearing is likely to be positive. This is what most studies seem to indicate. A study in 2000[45] by the stockbroker Cazenove assessed the impact of gearing on the twelve largest conventional investment trust sectors and found that gearing had added 5.3% to performance over the seven years to the end of December 1999. The 2018 study by Professor Andrew Clare and Dr Simon Hayley of the Cass Business School that sought to explain why closed-end funds outperformed their open-ended peers found that gearing was a minor factor, with some weak evidence that the timing of gearing added value.[46]

To measure the impact of gearing is quite tricky, to separate the effect of the borrowings from market performance, from stock selection, and from other allocation decisions made by the managers. Fortunately, more managers are now providing performance attribution analysis in their reports, allowing us to see the actual effect of

[45] Investment Week 26th February 2001

[46] Kepler Trust Intelligence Research Archive 27th June 2018

the gearing quite clearly. In most cases, it shows largely what we would expect – that gearing contributes to returns during positive periods and is a detractor during negative periods. The impact of gearing for Witan Investment Trust (WTAN) over the eleven years from 2010-2020 inclusive,[47] showed eight positive contributions and three negative, but all within the range of ±2%. Overall, for the majority of trusts it doesn't seem to be of prime importance, certainly not as important as which shares the manager picks or the sector allocation.

Gearing can certainly add risk though, and the time to be keenly aware of the level of gearing is when a bear market hits. On such occasions, highly geared trusts can quickly unravel as losses deepen. The property sector has traditionally used gearing, expressed as loan-to-value, which has become ubiquitous as REITs compete to provide competitive yields. During sharp downturns this can prove calamitous for trusts with high debt levels as they struggle to service the borrowing, which is called in by the banks because covenant levels are breached, and then the managers are forced to try to dump properties at a time when buyers are extremely scarce. In the great financial crisis of 2007-08, one example was Invista European Real Estate, which just managed to refinance in May 2014, by which stage its shares had fallen from their peak of 236p in March 2007 to a low of 1.06p in February 2014. The trust limped on for another year before shareholders agreed to put it into liquidation. Similarly, Tamar European Industrial Fund was another geared property fund that was caught out in the credit crisis when it found itself over-leveraged against a falling property portfolio and was forced to concentrate on asset disposals before it was acquired for 38.25p per share in 2014, well down from its peak of 124p in early 2007.

Negative Gearing (Positive Cash)

Sometimes trust managers may have negative views on markets, meaning they not only want to avoid gearing, but may want to move to a net cash position to protect value and to have funds ready and available to buy at the lower prices they anticipate. As key market participants with excellent sources of information and research resources, feedback from listed companies, and experience on the ground, managers can on occasions formulate strong market views. Even at these times though, it is unusual for a trust to move deliberately to a high cash position. Boards will usually have limits that govern this too, and the vast majority of managers will accept that shareholders are not buying their trusts as a way of accessing their market-timing skills. The prevailing view is that shareholders can express their own market views by buying and selling investment trust shares, and that for the majority of the time, portfolios should be substantially invested in pursuit of their published objective.

---

[47] Witan Investment Trust investor presentation October 2020

Cash positions tend to be built for other reasons instead. For equity trust managers, a high cash position might be the result of a receipt of funds from a takeover, or from a recent capital raise. For alternative asset managers with less liquid assets, a cash position might be the result of an interim period between a large asset being sold and another being purchased. In specific circumstances, if a trust is in wind-down mode, it may husband cash before returning it to shareholders. Outside of one particular sector, only rarely will a cash position be a strategic investment decision, and in these circumstances there is a risk that the 'cash drag' of uninvested capital will hinder both the absolute and relative performance. This happened with Fidelity Asian Values (FAS) for a period in 2017 when the manager, Nitin Bajaj adopted a cautious stance, but when markets fell back in 2018 this approach protected investor capital well.

There is one group of trusts that behave differently in this regard, and that is the small group of trusts classified in the 'Flexible Investment' sector that have a stated focus on absolute returns. Personal Assets Trust (PNL), for example, pays attention first and foremost to the risk of permanent loss of investment capital, and has cash amongst its asset allocation choices. At its last year end of 30th April 2020 it held 4.9% in cash.[48] For absolute return managers focused in part on loss avoidance, the choice not to deploy capital into risk assets is embedded in the investment proposition.

Use of Derivatives

Derivatives is a term that is often used pejoratively, to indicate high risk, recklessness, and complex financial engineering designed to confuse naïve investors. The reality is that many market practitioners use derivatives to reduce risk, to enhance income, to easily take short positions, and to back market judgements. Some investment trusts employ derivatives as part of their day-to-day work, even to use them as a distinguishing feature, while others may add them periodically for a special purpose.

Probably the most common use of derivatives is by a class of trust that most investors would consider conservative, namely equity income trusts. These trusts usually aim to provide a reasonable level of growing income, paid out as dividends to shareholders, and some have long and proud track records of maintaining those dividends. For the managers this brings a certain level of pressure to maintain the income in the trust, which can be challenging if company dividends are cut or if lower-yielding securities look more attractive. One solution to generating more income is to add a covered call writing strategy, which is used by trusts including Merchants Trust (MRCH), BlackRock North American Income (BRNA), and Schroder Income Growth (SCF) amongst others. In writing – or selling – an option over shares that it holds in its portfolio, the trust is giving the buyer of the option the right to buy those shares at a

---

[48] Personal Assets Trust Annual Report 2020

fixed 'strike' price within a specified period. In exchange for granting that right, the trust receives a 'premium' that provides income for the revenue account. If the share in question performs well and the option holder exercises their rights, the trust has to sell the shares at the strike price, which is likely to be below the market price, thereby forgoing some of the capital upside; if not, the trust pockets the premium and keeps its shares.

As Merchants explains,[49] its approach to option writing "is driven by the investment fundamentals on each stock we hold, rather than by a separate derivatives rationale. We write calls on portions of shareholdings that we are happy to sell at the strike price, provided that the premium income received is sufficiently attractive. The options written are typically short dated with most less than four months duration. The total exposure is closely monitored and is limited to 15% of the portfolio value with all option positions 'covered' by shares owned. From a holistic view, it can be argued that the overall strategy slightly reduces the trust's gearing to the equity market, neutralising a small part of the financial leverage. It tends to be more profitable in sideways or downwards markets but less profitable in rising markets". For income trust managers, option writing is certainly a handy addition to their arsenal and can be particularly useful for supporting income levels during tough periods. It is effectively trading some potential capital gain for certainty of income, and managers that use this technique do generally report that it has added to overall returns.

One other technique used less frequently to add modestly to income is to engage in stock lending in exchange for fees. Stock lending is a slightly controversial practice in the market that allows short sellers to pursue their strategies, but it can provide an extra income flow for trusts. Henderson Opportunities Trust (HOT) is one trust that lends its shares to others in the market. It started to do so in April 2018 and generated £49,000 of extra income in its first six months.[50]

BlackRock Throgmorton Trust (THRG) does something completely different, running a contracts for difference (CFD) portfolio that can provide gearing of up to 30%, but more commonly with a mix of long and short CFDs that results in a net market exposure of between 100% and 115%. In theory the trust could deploy the full 30% of permissible leverage into short CFDs to reduce the net market exposure to 70%. CFDs are agreements to exchange the difference in value of a particular security between the time the agreement is opened and closed, and operate on margin requirements, hence the gearing. The managers argue these additional instruments give them greater flexibility to adapt to changing market conditions and to try and profit from the full range of research outcomes, which does make sense. Sceptics have always

---

[49] Merchants Trust Annual Report for the year ended 31st January 2020

[50] Henderson Opportunities Trust Annual Financial Report for the year ended 31st October 2018

pointed to the very similar performance records of THRG and its sister trust with the same management firm, BlackRock Smaller Companies Trust (BRSC) until 2019, but recent periods have seen greater divergence in favour of THRG, which does break down the returns from its derivative contracts each year in its Annual Report. It shows a profit of £4.6m for the financial year 2018 and a profit of £11.9m for the financial year 2019. BlackRock Throgmorton is unique at present in following this strategy, which serves to differentiate this trust successfully from its peers, but the fact that other managers have not rushed to follow its lead suggests it may not be an obvious and reliable way to enhance performance.

For the majority of investment trust managers, derivatives are not a part of the structure of their regular portfolios, but they may still turn to them from time to time to take advantage of a particular market anomaly or a strong conviction that has arisen from their work and research. Often this is to hedge the main portfolio and protect returns, which is not a new idea. Jupiter Dividend & Growth purchased a FTSE put option for £13m back in 2003,[51] aimed at providing downside capital protection. More recently, Pershing Square Holdings (PSH) used credit protection derivatives to dramatically positive effect in the first quarter of 2020, Schroder Asian Total Return Investment Company (ATR) has bought put options, and Diverse Income Trust (DIVI) has used FTSE 100 Index put options on more than one occasion. Speaking at the Winterflood Investment Trusts Conference in London in early 2014,[52] DIVI's manager Gervais Williams said the risk-reward ratio looked attractive for the put options at the time of purchase because low volatility meant they were cheap. The cost of the strategy was modest at 1.6% of assets, providing downside protection for around one-third of the portfolio, but this meant the rest of the portfolio could stay fully invested. This put option turned out to be a small detractor to performance as markets kept on rising, and the same was true again for the next put option, kept as part of a strategy to place the trust in a strong position to purchase additional holdings at the time of a significant equity market setback. Finally, in the Annual Report for 2020 the trust's chairman was able to tell shareholders "for several years we have held a FTSE 100 Put option as insurance against a market fall, so when the UK stock market fell back in March 2020 this rose in value and was cashed in. This provided an additional £20m of new cash that was available to invest in additional portfolio holdings at a time when share prices were particularly low". This took patience, but did eventually pay off for the trust.

Derivatives positions can be idiosyncratic, as in the case of a 'total return swap' arranged by AVI Global Trust (AGT) and detailed in its 2019 Annual Report. In this case the trust had effective exposure to shares in another trust, Pershing Square

[51] Investment Trust Newsletter March 2003

[52] 23rd January 2014

Holdings (PSH) in exchange for a series of floating rate interest payments, and a simultaneous 'short' exposure to a number of PSH's US invested companies in return for receiving a series of floating rate interest payments. This sounds curious, but the point of these two deals was that the trust's net exposure was mainly limited to movements in PSH's discount to NAV and not to share price changes in its underlying investments. This was an example of financial engineering being used to fine-tune a holding to a very specific investment thesis.

A different kind of hedging is used by some trusts that have foreign currency exposure. In many cases this is left unhedged as an additional risk for sterling investors, or hedged with matching foreign currency borrowings, but derivatives may also be used to reduce the currency exposure that may otherwise have a major impact on the returns for sterling-based shareholders. The infrastructure trust BBGI Global Infrastructure (BBGI) has a partial hedging policy in place that aims to reduce the sensitivity of NAV to 3% for a 10% swing in foreign exchange.[53]

[53] BBGI Global Infrastructure investor presentation, Winterflood virtual investment trust conference 16th October 2020

Chapter 6: Fees and Costs

Investment management does not come cheap, and neither does a board of directors. Add in stock exchange listing fees, audit fees, transaction costs, borrowing fees, the cost of an AGM and an annual report, and the administration costs also mount up. These matter because charges eat into long-term investment returns – and because we all want value for money. It is worth considering how important investment trust costs are, who is responsible for them, how they vary, and of course how they compare with other forms of collective funds.

Measurement of Costs

Total cost ratio, total expense ratio, ongoing charges, reduction in yield, management expense ratio … there have been a number of different measures of costs that have been used over the years, gradually tweaked and refined to make them as useful as possible for comparing different trusts and different products. Two are current now, ongoing charges (OC) and reduction in yield (RIY), two quite different methods that give two quite different sets of results.

Ongoing charges, first of all, is the standard promoted by the AIC trade association and largely adopted by the industry. It is widely quoted by trusts in their communications with shareholders. It is defined as the annual percentage reduction in shareholder returns as a result of recurring operational expenses assuming markets remain static and the portfolio is not traded. The idea is that it provides shareholders with an indication of the likely level of costs that will be incurred in managing the trust in the future, although it is using past data.

Expressed as a percentage, annualised ongoing charges are divided by the average undiluted net asset value during the year to generate the final figure. Importantly, this does not include all expenses, as some are not considered to be operational and recurring. Performance fees are excluded, since those will vary from year to year, as are interest costs, transaction costs, restructuring costs, and some irregular legal and professional fees. The average ongoing charge for AIC member trusts, without VCTs or 3i Group (III), is 1.02%, or 1.15% if performance fees are included,[54] and varies markedly between sectors. In the global sector, which tends to have larger, well-established trusts that invest mainly in equities, the average OC is 0.50%, ranging from Scottish Mortgage Investment Trust (SMT) at 0.36% to EP Global Opportunities Trust (EPG) at 0.98%. For private equity, where the management fees are generally higher, the average OC is 1.27%, ranging from HarbourVest Global Private Equity (HVPE) at 0.55% to LMS Capital (LMS) at 5.69%.

---

[54] AIC statistics 24th November 2020

Reduction in yield (RIY) is the industry standard figure for the PRIIPS regime, prescribed by law. PRIIPS stands for Packaged Retail and Insurance-Based Investment Products, and the EU-based PRIIPS regulations that were enacted at the start of 2018 caused chaos in the markets for collective investments as providers scrambled to produce new documentation to conform to its requirements. RIYs are more comprehensive, including ongoing, one-off, and incidental costs and expressing them as a percentage impact on the potential return per year. The RIY will always be at least as high as the OC, and in nearly all cases, significantly higher. Portfolio transaction costs are included, as are performance fees, costs of borrowing, the cost of fund fees if the portfolio invests in other trusts or funds, and carried interest charges for private equity trusts. This last figure is especially important for the private equity sector, where these relatively high charges create some very high RIY figures, such as 6.08%[55] for ICG Enterprise Trust (ICGT), against its ongoing charges of 1.40%. For Scottish Mortgage Investment Trust (SMT) the RIY is 0.80%,[56] and for Majedie Investments (MAJE) it is 2.28%.[57]

It seems sensible to gather as much information as possible and to look at both the OC and RIY if you are concerned about the impact of costs on your investment. The OC is quite straightforward, but the RIY is clearly more complex because it includes more factors that may or may not recur over the future life of your investment. If a trust happened to use extra gearing or performed particularly well and paid a larger performance fee over the prior period, then it can appear expensive when in reality it may not be in future periods. It is not so easy to compare trusts on a like-for-like basis when some might have certain types of costs in their structure – such as financing costs - whilst others do not. Bear in mind as well that while the costs of borrowing are included, there is no way of including the benefits that might accrue from that borrowing.

Both the OC and the RIY relate to the costs of the trusts themselves, and do not include your own dealing costs of bid-offer spreads, stockbrokers' commission, stamp duty, and platform fees, or make any assumptions about your tax situation.

KIDS

Some kids can be troublesome at times, and that has certainly been true of the Key Information Documents (KIDs) for investment trusts, which are the documents required by the PRIIPS legislation containing the RIY figures as well as other information. The idea of these documents was to ensure that all investors were

[55] ICG Enterprise Trust Key Information Document produced 5th September 2019
[56] Scottish Mortgage Investment Trust Key Information Document produced 27th August 2020
[57] Majedie Investments Key Information Document produced 10th December 2019

reasonably well informed of the basic facts before committing to any deals, but their introduction at the start of 2018 proved difficult as market participants wrestled with the calculations and struggled to provide KIDs in the right format, to the right people. Some investors trying to deal through platform stockbrokers were left unable to trade in certain trusts for a period of weeks. Occasional problems still crop up, nearly three years later.

At their introduction, KIDs were criticised heavily by the AIC, which refused to host them on its website and called for them to be suspended, arguing that they were misleading investors about the potential returns.[58] This disapproval was mainly focused on the returns section, which postulates different scenarios based on recent performance, although the AIC did point out an issue with the KID methodology on transaction costs. They said "10% of investment companies with equity portfolios have KIDs showing transaction costs of nothing or which are negative (that is 'less than' zero costs). This implies that the process of making investments is either without any cost at all or, in some way, the opposite of a 'cost'. This is nonsense." Furthermore, the cost calculations seemed to make comparisons with open-ended funds unfair, and the cost disclosures apparently penalised trusts using the full array of possibilities within the investment trust structure, some of which carry costs, like the financing of borrowings. This sense of disquiet with the disclosures required by KIDs has rumbled on.

Management Fees

Paying the managers usually accounts for the biggest cost for an investment trust. The majority of trusts appoint external managers and pay them using an agreed fee that is usually a percentage of the net asset value. The fee may be tiered, and it may include a performance-related element, but the basic format is fairly standard across the industry. For equity trusts the fees tend to range from around 0.3% to 1% of net asset value per year, and for alternative asset trusts, where the management can be much more direct, involved, and hands-on, the annual fees are often 1%-1.5%, sometimes stretching up to 2% for private equity trusts, where fees are traditionally higher.

Until the start of 2019, the investment management agreement between Troy Income & Growth Trust (TIGT) and Troy Asset Management provided for an annual fee of 0.75% of the trust's net assets up to £175m and an annual fee of 0.65% of the assets over that amount. After 1st January 2019 the agreement was simplified to a straight annual fee of 0.65% of NAV, calculated monthly and paid quarterly. In the year to 30th

[58] Burn before reading, understanding and addressing the dangers of Key Information Documents, AIC, September 2018

September 2019 the trust paid a management fee of £1.5m,[59] by far the largest chunk of its overall ongoing charges of £2.04m. Based on average net assets of £223.2m for the year, the ongoing charges ratio worked out at 0.91%, with 0.67% of that accounted for by the investment management fee.

Moving on to an alternative assets trust, the fee structure is far more complex for The Renewables Infrastructure Group (TRIG). Here, the aggregate investment management fees are tiered, such that the fee payable is 1% of the first £1bn of the Adjusted Portfolio Value, 0.8% of the APV between £1bn and £2bn, 0.75% of the APV between £2bn and £3bn, and 0.7% of the APV in excess of £3bn. The APV means fair market value, taking into account any project financing, less any other debt held other than the acquisition facility. Once the aggregate investment management fee is calculated, it is then split 65% to the investment managers InfraRed Capital Partners and 35% to the operations managers Renewable Energy Systems. Further, the agreements stipulate that 20% of the fees up to an APV of £1bn are to be settled in ordinary shares, so the whole arrangements are far more complicated than for many other trusts and take some sifting through. Overall, in its financial year to 31st December 2019,[60] TRIG paid £14.26m in management fees, out of total expenses of £15.83m, based on an average NAV of £1.61bn for the year. The ongoing charges percentage was 0.98%, down from 1.12% the previous year as the trust had grown.

One additional layer of complication that has often been included in fee structures is a performance fee, an extra payment typically earned if the growth in the NAV for a trust exceeds that of an agreed benchmark. The idea is that performance fees can allow managers to participate in the success of a trust, thereby aligning their interests with shareholders and ensuring the managers are well incentivised. A performance fee can also be balanced by trading it off against a lower base fee, which can work for all parties. Performance fees have been falling in popularity though as the industry strives for simplification, and as shareholders push back against some examples of large fees that have not seemed fair or warranted. In May 2012 a survey[61] of conventional AIC-member trusts found that 48% had a performance fee arrangement, whereas that figure has dropped and Winterflood estimated at the start of 2020 that 30% of the investment companies sector retain an incentive element to their fee arrangements.[62]

There are concerns that performance fees can encourage excessive risk-taking as managers chase outsized returns, and this was one reason why they have been prohibited for US mutual funds since 1971 unless they are symmetric, meaning the manager loses compensation for underperformance. Those don't exist in the

---

[59] Troy Income & Growth Trust Annual Report and Financial Statements 2019

[60] The Renewables Infrastructure Group Annual Report & Financial Statements 2019

[61] JPMorgan Cazenove, Performance fees: a hurdle for investors ahead of the RDR, 22nd May 2012

[62] Winterflood Annual Review 2020

investment trust sector (although it was tried in 2002 by a trust called Britannic Smaller Companies), and it hasn't helped that the upward-only performance fees have occasionally got out of hand. One of the most famous, or rather infamous, examples of performance fees in action occurred during the technology boom, when Henderson Investors earned a huge performance bonus from Henderson Technology Trust (later to become Polar Capital Technology Trust, PCT). At that time the management fees were based on whether the trust outperformed the FTSE World Index rather than a specific technology benchmark, and in the year to March 2000 the managers earned an overall fee of £48.6m, of which £43m was a massive performance bonus.

In 2020, BMO Real Estate Investments (BREI) found itself in an awkward position at the time of its annual results that included the start of the Covid-19 pandemic. It reported a negative NAV return, and a -24.9% share price total return over the period. The property portfolio did outperform its MSCI index though, as it had over three years, and as a result the manager was eligible for the maximum performance fee. The board said it was "conscious of the sensitivity of paying performance fees in a market of negative returns" and negotiated a 50% reduction with the manager before scrapping the performance fee altogether.

Performance fee arrangements are usually carefully written now to avoid this scenario of paying larger fees at a time when shareholders have lost value. One key clause usually added too is a 'high water mark' that means managers are not paid extra if the assets fall by 10% one year and then rise by 10% the next. The high water mark means that previous losses must be recovered first. For Real Estate Credit Investments (RECI), for example, the manager receives a fee of 1.25% of net asset value, plus a performance fee equal to 20% of returns in excess of 7% per year. If the trust was not that successful in any given year and no performance fee was paid, then the 7% hurdle rate starts from the beginning of the period (the next day after the last performance fee was payable), and is cumulative, so any lost performance must be made up. No performance fee was paid in the year ending 31st March 2020, just the base fee of £4.14m as the company ended the year with £337.2m of net assets.[63]

Management costs have been falling across the industry in recent years, with boards regularly announcing they have agreed slightly lower fee arrangements. This is excellent news for shareholders, but some of the absolute numbers for management fees in the multi-millions still seem very high for the work being done. The problem for boards, who might prefer to cap fees or even move to a fixed fee system, is that they could alienate highly successful and highly-rated managers, and if they decide to move away then that could signal very real problems for the trust. In the spring of 2018 Invesco Perpetual Enhanced Income (IPE) could not agree revised fee terms with the managers

[63] Real Estate Credit Investments Annual Report and Accounts 2020

and Invesco Perpetual resigned, ushering in a period of uncertainty that was resolved a couple of months later when the parties reached a settlement.

Directors' Fees

Often the second largest cost after the management fees, board fees are a necessary part of running an investment trust with an independent set of non-executive directors. A survey published in October 2020[64] by Trust Associates, a consultancy providing advice and support in relation to the governance and management of investment companies, provided details of fees paid to directors in the year to 31st March 2020. The average fee for a chairman was £47,308 with a median fee of £40,000; for the audit chairman the average was £35,985 and the median £32,000; and for other directors the average was £31,141 and the median was £27,500. These figures are all for non-executive directors, so the executive directors of self-managed trusts have been excluded. These fees have risen steadily every year over the past decade, and are also higher for larger trusts over £500m compared to their smaller counterparts, and for Channel-Islands registered companies compared to UK-registered companies.

The balance here is between cost and the need for investment trusts to have high-calibre boards, made up of professional and experienced individuals with the skills to oversee the business of the trust, examine the fund manager's approach and returns, sign off the accounts, and on occasions make really key, even existential decisions about changing manager, policy, or style. It's an important role, so perhaps those board fees, which rarely seem to be questioned or challenged, count as money well spent.

Investment Trusts versus Open-Ended Funds

For many years it was easy for advocates of investment trusts to make fairly glib claims about how much cheaper investment trusts were compared to open-ended funds. Around the turn of the century this was a fairly clear-cut win for investment trusts, and a study by an independent firm called Fitzrovia International in 2000[65] found that unit trusts were on average 60% more expensive than comparable investment trusts, with annual total expenses of 1.38% against 0.83%.

To some extent the Retail Distribution Review (RDR) ended that era at the end of 2012, when open-ended funds could no longer pay hefty commissions to introducing agents. That signalled a closing of the gap and an erosion of the historical advantage held by investment trusts. Since that time, a number of studies have shown the competition is much closer.

---

[64] Investment Companies Non-Executive Directors' Fees Review 2020, Trust Associates, October 2020

[65] Reported in Citywire Investment Trust Insider, 23rd February 2000

In 2016[66] the investment research firm Tilney Bestinvest identified 47 pairs of open-ended funds and investment trusts with similar mandates run by the same teams. They found that in 53% of cases the open-ended funds had lower ongoing charges. Around the same time, the stockbroker Canaccord Genuity published very similar results by investigating 51 pairs of trusts and funds, finding that 23 investment trusts (45%) had a lower ongoing charge, 27 (53%) were more expensive, and one was in line. Once their proud boast was called into question, some investment trusts did react quickly with fee cuts, and within three years the previous status quo might have been restored. A study by the platform stockbroker AJ Bell in 2019[67] found that 60% of investment trusts were cheaper than their comparable open-ended vehicles, with ongoing charges of 0.91% against 0.97% respectively.

Whatever the exact outcome of any particular analysis, the general picture now is that there seems little difference between these two types of collective vehicles in cost terms. There are far greater differences in flexibility, style, governance, performance, liquidity, and the structural suitability for certain types of assets. Cost is not the big factor it once was.

Trusts with the Lowest Costs

Searching for the cheapest investment trusts may not be the best way to pick future winners in performance terms, but it is interesting to see which trusts can make a particular virtue of their low cost base. The two tables below rank the ten cheapest trusts by ongoing charges (OC) and by the more detailed reduction in yield (RIY), with liquidity funds excluded.

	OC[68]
JPMorgan American (JAM)	0.18%
Fair Oaks Income (FAIR)	0.22%
Independent Investment Trust (IIT)	0.24%
The Schiehallion Fund (MNTN)	0.27%
Law Debenture (LWDB)	0.30%
Hansa Investment Company (HAN)	0.31%
Highbridge Tactical Credit Fund (HTCF)	0.34%
Blackstone/GSO Loan Financing (BGLF)	0.36%
City of London Investment Trust (CTY)	0.36%
JPMorgan Global Core Real Assets (JARA)	0.36%
Scottish Mortgage Investment Trust (SMT)	0.36%

[66] Reported in ThisisMoney.co.uk, 6th September 2016
[67] Reported in FTAdviser, 15th July 2019
[68] AIC statistics 24th November 2020

	RIY[69]
Independent Investment Trust (IIT)	0.24%
JPMorgan American (JAM)	0.62%
Baillie Gifford UK Growth (BGUK)	0.68%
Aurora Investment Trust (ARR)	0.75%
Baillie Gifford European Growth (BGEU)	0.76%
Invesco Income Growth (IVI)	0.76%
Finsbury Growth & Income Trust (FGT)	0.80%
Scottish Mortgage Investment Trust (SMT)	0.81%
BlackRock Smaller Companies Trust (BRSC)	0.83%
Personal Assets Trust (PNL)	0.83%

The Importance of Low Costs

Especially now that the costs of investment trusts seem to be broadly in line with open-ended funds, you might think it is not really necessary to focus too much on the fees and charges. There is a risk these could distract attention from other factors more likely to play a part in future investment returns, and they are seldom at the top of any analysis or discussion of investment trusts. As long as they are within the normal threshold levels and do not stand out, most investors seem prepared to gloss over them and focus on other aspects of the investment management process. Not everyone agrees though. The stockbroker Canaccord Genuity argued in 2016[70] that in a low growth, low inflation, low interest rate environment, ongoing charges could have a much greater dilutive impact on returns, particularly when compounded over the long term. For that reason they argued that costs merited greater scrutiny, and the maths does suggest that costs are important for long-term investors. A 7% return achieved over ten years implies £1000 would grow to £1967 without any charges, but a 1% annual charge knocks this down to £1779 and a 2% charge reduces it to £1607. If you have spotted a valuation anomaly that you expect to be corrected within a few months, and that is your investing timeframe, then costs should be well down your list of concerns. If you are looking for a long-term savings vehicle, they become much more relevant.

[69] JPMorgan Cazenove Daily Statistics 24th November 2020

[70] Canaccord Genuity, Adjusting to a world of lower numbers, 13th October 2016

Chapter 7: Benchmarks and NAV Performance

Once, literally, a surveyors' mark cut into a rock or wall to help determine altitude, a benchmark has become known as a point of reference, a criterion, a touchstone. For investment trusts, needing to measure their individual performance against a reasonable comparator, some sort of benchmark index is highly useful. Understanding how they are used and what they mean can help to place past performance into context, as can comparative tables comparing peer group trusts or other types of collective funds. As frequently as we hear that past performance is not necessarily a guide to the future, we still seek guidance from how investment trusts have delivered for shareholders over past periods. It's one measure of quality we can use to help make informed judgements when selecting single trusts from large groups of competitors.

Choosing a Benchmark

The majority of trusts have benchmarks that are used as a measuring stick for their own performance, good or bad. For equity investment managers in particular, they generally ask to be judged over multi-year periods, but also against a relative measure instead of an absolute measure. They cannot control the direction of markets, but as active investors they control their stock picks and how the trust's portfolio performs in relation to others. This is why they are paid – to do better than a simple low-cost passive tracker investment – and investors need to know whether they are delivering on that promise. If they fail for any lengthy period, not only will managers miss out on any associated performance fees, but they will be at risk of losing their mandate as well.

Relevance is most important for a benchmark index, as is the ability to replicate the index, its independence, and its risk level. Cynics may also suggest that managers are incentivised to pick an index they think they can beat, but of course in a fast-changing world any bias of that nature may not last very long, no matter how much back-testing managers may have done to check that their particular methodology has worked in the past.

Picking an index that makes sense to all concerned can be a straightforward matter. If you are a Japanese smaller companies trust manager, you will pick an index that tracks the performance of Japanese smaller companies, but even then there is an array of indices from which to choose. Atlantis Japan Growth Fund (AJG) measures its performance against the Topix Index (total return); AVI Japan Opportunity Trust (AJOT) and Baillie Gifford Shin Nippon (BGS) both use the MSCI Japan Small Cap Total Return Index, in sterling terms; and JPMorgan Japan Smaller Companies (JPS) uses the S&P Japan Small Cap NR Index. For trusts with broader investment remits, the range of potential indices is enormous – one estimate puts the number of indices on the US market alone at 5000.[71] Few investors will extend their due diligence to checking the constituents of benchmark indices, so there is an element of trust that managers and boards have agreed on suitable choices.

Benchmarks will sometimes change. This is sometimes related to a significant change in the constituents of a benchmark index, perhaps related to new issues or takeovers; or more often a shift in the emphasis of a trust's investment strategy. Thus, Polar Capital Global Financials Trust (PCFT) changed its benchmark in early 2020 at the time of its continuation proceedings, moving from the MSCI World Financials + Real Estate Net Total Return Index to the MSCI ACWI Financials Net Total Return Index (both in sterling with dividends reinvested). The trust had underperformed its old benchmark in the prior period, and slightly underperformed it in the near-seven year period since inception, but explained the new index was more appropriate in view of the trust's level of portfolio exposure to emerging market financials equities and its limited portfolio exposure to real estate equities. In September 2019 Witan Investment Trust (WTAN), which has a multi-manager portfolio that has been gradually shifting away from the UK, changed its benchmark composition from a mix of 30% FTSE All-Share Index and 70% of four international indices, to 15% FTSE All-Share Index and 85% FTSE All World Index. Again, this makes sense as it more accurately reflects the true composition of the overall portfolio, allowing a truer measurement of the stock picking skill rather than whether the UK happens to underperform or outperform. This type of 'blended' benchmark composed of more than one index is not uncommon for trusts with objectives that overlap more than one standard area.

Whilst equity-based trusts will normally pick an equity benchmark, for absolute return trusts that are seeking to protect investors capital as well, their more conservative positioning would likely mean constant underperformance during bullish periods and vice-versa. For this group of trusts, an absolute return target matches their objectives more closely. This is why Personal Assets Trust (PNL) does not have a benchmark, demonstrating that they are not necessarily required, and Ruffer Investment Company (RICA) has the objective of achieving a positive total annual return, after all expenses, of at least twice the Bank of England Bank Rate.

For alternative asset managers, benchmarks are also harder to find, and will not usually form a part of the trust's reporting. Civitas Social Housing (CSH), which invests in care-based community housing and healthcare facilities in the UK, does not have a formal benchmark. For the purposes of displaying its total shareholder return in some sort of context it does compare its share price to the FTSE All-Share Index and FTSE 350 REIT Index, but with a caveat that these are not very direct comparisons.

---

[71] Investopedia, An Introduction to US Stock Market Indexes, 13th April 2020

Similarity to Benchmark

Where a benchmark does exist, there is no requirement for a trust's portfolio to mimic it or to bear much relation to it at all. Very often, concentrated portfolios in particular will bear very little resemblance to the benchmark. Smithson Investment Trust (SSON), where the managers run a very concentrated portfolio, say exactly this, noting "the investment manager's investment style is such that performance is likely to deviate from that of the benchmark index". The MSCI World SMID Cap Index is the trust's benchmark, capturing mid and small cap representation across 23 developed market countries. It has 5121 constituents,[72] whereas the trust has a total of 31 holdings.[73] The managers could hardly be more blunt about how they view the benchmark, saying in their trust's 'owners manual' that "although we will provide an appropriate equity index for you to measure us against, and you may of course have comparators of your own, we can assure you that we pay no attention to how similar or different our portfolio is to that index. In other words, we regard the benchmark as of some benefit for performance measurement, but of no benefit to portfolio construction".

Some other managers do take a different view and describe themselves as 'benchmark aware', meaning that they are definitely trying to beat that specific collection of stocks and will know whether they are underweight or overweight in each position. They will be mindful though of avoiding the charge of being 'index-huggers' or 'closet index trackers' that have been widely criticised for charging relatively high fees without any meaningful chance of delivering exceptional returns for investors.

Active Share

The extent to which managers are truly active can be measured, to make this an objective matter rather than one of opinion and rhetoric. By 'active' we are not talking about how much they trade, but rather, how the portfolio is actively different from the benchmark index. This method of measurement was developed by a pair of US professors at the Yale School of Management, Martijn Cremers and Antti Pestajisto in 2006,[74] and has been fairly widely adopted since. The key principle is that an active equity fund manager can only outperform a benchmark by taking positions that are different. The calculation for 'active share' compares the portfolio holdings of a trust to that of the benchmark to work out the percentage of the portfolio that is different from the benchmark index. Thus, active share will always be between 0% and 100%, and a high figure indicates a higher active share, of greater deviation or differentiation. A higher active share indicates greater potential for beating the benchmark (and equally

---

[72] MSCI World SMD Cap Index 30th September 2020

[73] Smithson Investment Trust monthly factsheet October 2020

[74] How Active Is Your Fund Manager? A New Measure That Predicts Performance, KJ Martijn Cremers and Antti Petajisto, 31st March 2006

a higher risk of failing), as well as helping to measure the 'alpha' or added value from stock selection when combined with a measurement of tracking error.

Active share is something increasingly mentioned by managers, particularly those that have a narrow focus. Mobius Investment Trust (MMIT), which only invests in a small number of companies, acknowledges this explicitly, saying "we recognise that our high active share (+99%) will result in short term disparities with the wider market, but will act as a source of alpha as the benefits of our engagement with each portfolio holding are borne out".[75] Baillie Gifford Shin Nippon (BGS) lists the active share in its monthly factsheet.[76]

Additional Uses of the Benchmark

In addition to its primary use as a yardstick for measuring investment returns, benchmark indices are also used to compare other metrics. In management presentations, figures such as P/E ratios and return on equity (RoE) are often compared to the benchmark to illustrate the portfolio characteristics.

NAV Performance Tables

Following a list of investment trusts where you have a linked RNS newsfeed means being consistently bombarded by net asset value announcements, released to the stock exchange on a daily, weekly, or quarterly basis. The market is quite transparent on how net assets are performing, and thanks to the internet, live information is now more freely available to private investors than ever before. Individual trusts will offer news links to their regular releases, and will have summary and often graphical information in their monthly factsheets. For broader comparative data, a number of websites offer access to tabular information that is updated daily, including Morningstar, Citywire, Trustnet, Money Marketing, and QuotedData. If you prefer traditional communication and want to browse performance tables in paper form, it's more difficult as more sources have migrated online. The AIC stopped its printed monthly information service quite a number of years ago. When the Investment Trust Newsletter published a Statistical Supplement in paper form in 2015 it was intended as a one-off but has actually become an annual fixture after being received with some enthusiasm by subscribers.

All of these sources generally group investment trusts by sector and list NAV returns over different time periods, often stretching from one month or three months to six months, one year, three years, five years, and sometimes beyond. Trusts may be ranked

---

[75] Mobius Investment Trust Annual Report for the period ended 30th November 2019

[76] 94% as at 31st October 2020

in their sectors, and undoubtedly this statistical information is extremely useful for checking track records and seeing how investment trusts stand up to the competition. Whilst managers usually judge their performance against their benchmark, many investors judge them much more against their peer group trusts.

It's a general rule when looking at statistics that you still need to engage your brain and look at them enquiringly. Performance figures are by nature backward-looking, and if an individual manager has changed, or a trust has moved management firms, or changed its mandate, altered its gearing policy, or shed expensive past borrowings, then those historic numbers really may not be much of a guide to the future. Sometimes they are though, and if you can see that an impressive trust has beaten the opposition regularly in the past, then this may lead you to examine that particular trust more closely. The numbers only tell part of the story, and uncovering further information on the risks taken to achieve past performance, the consistency, and the evolution of the portfolio and management technique will likely prove useful.

Bear in mind the dividend policy as well. If a trust is paying out large dividends to shareholders, this may hinder NAV growth, but the total returns are generally what matters, over the long-term in particular. If you are looking for a long-term savings vehicle and can be patient, then it is probably the three-year, five-year and ten-year historical returns that are most relevant to consider. Any trust can have a great quarter, or a disastrous one, so short-term NAV performance is bound to be more variable.

Chapter 8: Dividends

Many shareholders want an income from their investments in the form of regular dividends. Investment trusts can offer a high income, and there is one peculiar advantage that means the dividend stream can be more reliable. That's why you will probably have read about the sector's 'dividend heroes' that have raised their dividends continuously for many years, through thick and thin. At a time of low interest rates, widespread uncertainty, and dividend cuts by many well-known stalwarts of the UK economy, this special quality has become a major attraction.

Dividend Policies

If you recall the formal tax definition of a UK investment trust, it must pay out a minimum of 85% of its income received each year, so you might think that all trusts pay dividends to their shareholders. That's not the case. Some are actually structured as offshore investment companies, where different tax rules apply, and others invest in pure capital instruments that do not produce revenue, so there is nothing to pay out to shareholders. To discover whether a particular trust is likely to pay dividends it can be useful to check whether it has done so in the past, but also to look at the annual report and other communications from the trust to find the board's dividend policy. It is the board's decision to recommend dividends (and shareholders must approve them at the AGM), not the manager, and their policy will usually be stated very clearly as part of the trust's objective or in a separate section devoted to dividends.

In some cases the aim to achieve a high and growing income is front and centre; sometimes trusts are seeking a mix of capital and income growth; and sometimes income is not part of the objectives at all. Where dividends are of prime importance this is sometimes embedded in the trust's name, like Bluefield Solar Income Fund (BSIF), which has the objective "to provide shareholders with an attractive return, principally in the form of regular sterling income distributions, by investing in the UK into, primarily, a portfolio of solar energy infrastructure assets". The Diverse Income Trust (DIVI) has the objective "to pay shareholders a good and growing dividend income – principally derived from those paid by a portfolio of listed UK companies".

Dividend Basics

In simple terms, dividends on shares are a little like receiving interest on a savings account. They represent a payment on your invested capital, and whilst not guaranteed, it is possible to select trusts that are likely to continue paying a growing amount to shareholders every year. Often, though not always, the dividends that trusts pay out reflect the income they have themselves earned from their invested assets, so as a shareholder the dividends are your share of the bounty. If you own a share worth

100p, the trust might pay you a dividend for the year of perhaps 4p, translating to a dividend yield (dividend/share price) of 4%. So an investment worth £50,000 would receive a dividend of £2,000 in this example, and it is easy to understand how dividend flows from a sizeable portfolio can become a very useful source of cash, even if few investors ever quite reach the position of John D Rockefeller, regarded as the richest man in modern history, who is often quoted as saying "do you know the only thing that gives me pleasure? It's to see my dividends coming in."

Timing and Frequency

Trusts can choose to pay dividends annually, like Lindsell Train Investment Trust (LTI), which declares a single dividend payment for the year every June; or six-monthly, like JPMorgan Russian Securities (JRS), which declares two dividend payments in January and September; or quarterly like Merchants Trust (MRCH), which declares four payments in January, April, June, and September; or even monthly, like the aptly-named TwentyFour Select Monthly Income Fund (SMIF). There has been a trend over recent years for investment trusts to move increasingly towards quarterly payouts, perhaps because of improving technology or the growth of platform stockbrokers which has made the administration easier and cheaper. The AIC said in 2019[77] that over half (54%) of its income-paying members pay quarterly dividends, up from 46% in 2017. Only 16% now pay an annual dividend, down from 23% in 2017.

It is really a matter of personal preference, whether the timing of payments matters to you. It might if you have a seasonal pattern to your income requirements, with large bills or other outlays at a particular time, or if you want to 'smooth' your income throughout the year. The AIC has introduced a useful suite of tools on its website called 'Income Finder', including a graphic display of when dividends are paid in the year, and you can even search for trusts that are likely to pay income in the months that you need it.

The Mechanics

Shareholders about to be paid a dividend do not need to claim it in any way – it is paid directly to the holder, usually these days into a stockbroking account. When a trust declares its dividend along with other financial results, it will at the same time specify three more dates, the ex-dividend date, the qualification date, and the payment date. European Opportunities Trust (JEO) is not an income trust, but it does still pay a small dividend to shareholders, most recently declared with the annual results for the year ended 31st May 2020, announced through the RNS on 23rd September 2020. The trust

[77] More than half of income-paying investment companies now paying quarterly dividends, AIC press release 20th May 2019

stated "a resolution to declare a final dividend of 3.5p per share will be proposed at the Annual General Meeting on 16th November 2020, payable on 27th November 2020 to shareholders on the Register of Members on 23rd October 2020. The ex-dividend date is 22nd October 2020."

There is quite often some confusion around these dates. Starting with the ex-dividend date, this is the date from which the shares will trade 'XD', without the dividend entitlement. In theory this means the share price ought to fall by the amount of the dividend, although this is not necessarily the case. The date of record is the next day, so this is the date on which the share register is checked for the details of the shareholders that will receive the dividend. This often causes confusion, but it makes sense once you remember that the London Stock Exchange uses a T+2 settlement system, so trades are settled and reflected on the shareholder register two days later. In order to receive the dividend, you must have bought the shares the day before the ex-dividend date – not on the ex-dividend date – and so the record date is two days after that, to be consistent. This is not too important for the majority of investors, but if you wanted to finesse your timing at some point to tweak the balance of your capital and income returns, then these dates become more relevant.

The payment date is some time later, and there can be a long wait on occasions. Often the payment date is about a month after the ex-dividend date, so several weeks after the original declaration date, but the timing will vary depending on the structure of the company and the date of the AGM. Some real examples are shown below.[78]

	Declaration Date	**Ex-Dividend Date**	**Payment Date**
European Opportunities Trust	23-Sep-20	22-Oct-20	27-Nov-20
Bankers Investment Trust	30-Sep-20	22-Oct-20	30-Nov-20
Henderson EuroTrust	02-Oct-20	22-Oct-20	25-Nov-20
TR European Growth Trust	08-Oct-20	22-Oct-20	27-Nov-20
CQS Natural Resources Gr & Inc	08-Oct-20	22-Oct-20	30-Nov-20

Although there may be small variations in the dates from year to year, most companies stick to the same rhythm of regular payments, and because these are based around the trust's financial periods you can usually expect the dividends to arrive on a regular recurring schedule. If you hold your shares in nominee form through a stockbroker, as is most common, the dividend will simply be added to your account on the due date. The same generally applies to regular saving schemes administered by investment trust managers, if you have asked for the dividends to be reinvested. If not, or if you own a certificated holding, then the dividends will be paid directly to you by cheque, or directly into your nominated bank account.

---

[78] Dividend data.co.uk, 16th October 2020

Dividend Heroes

Many investors who were expecting regular dividend payments from commercial companies in 2020 found themselves disappointed when the Covid-19 pandemic caused many companies to cut, postpone, or stop their dividend payments entirely. Link Asset Services, a leading third-party administrator, reported that in the second quarter of 2020[79] UK dividends had fallen by 50% and that it expected full-year dividends to be around 40% lower. In the second quarter, 176 companies cancelled their dividends altogether, and another 30 cut them. Even Royal Dutch Shell slashed its payout by two-thirds, its first reduction since the Second World War.

Dividends are not always reliable, but the investment trust sector has built a tremendous record of continuous dividend growth, and the AIC collates the names of those that have consistently raised their dividends for 20 or more years in a row. Collectively, these 21 trusts are known as its 'dividend heroes'.

AIC Dividend Heroes[80]	Consecutive Years of Increase	Yield 13/03/20
City of London Investment Trust (CTY)	53	6.0%
Bankers Investment Trust (BNKR)	53	2.6%
Alliance Trust (ATST)	53	2.2%
Caledonia Investments (CLDN)	52	2.3%
BMO Global Smaller Companies (BGSC)	49	1.6%
F&C Investment Trust (FCIT)	49	2.0%
Brunner Investment Trust (BUT)	48	2.9%
JPMorgan Claverhouse (JCH)	46	5.2%
Murray Income Trust (MUT)	46	5.0%
Witan Investment Trust (WTAN)	45	3.2%
Scottish American Investment Company (SAIN)	40	3.4%
Merchants Trust (MRCH)	37	7.2%
Scottish Mortgage Investment Trust (SMT)	37	0.6%
Scottish Investment Trust (SCIN)	36	4.8%
Temple Bar Investment Trust (TMPL)	36	6.1%
Value & Income Trust (VIN)	32	6.1%
BMO Capital & Income (BCI)	26	4.7%
British & American (BAF)	24	27.6%
Schroder Income Growth (SCF)	24	5.9%
Invesco Income Growth (IVI)	22	5.2%
Perpetual Income & Growth (PLI)	20	6.8%

[79] Link Asset Services UK Dividend Monitor Q2 2020
[80] AIC, 16th March 2020

That's an impressive list, headed by trusts that have raised their dividends for shareholders every year for more than half a century. These include some of the grand old trusts of the sector, solid names that savers rely on for a growing annual income. They are in traditional sectors such as UK equity income, global equities, flexible investment, global smaller companies, and global equity income.

It would be misleading though to suggest that only the oldest trusts can offer this sort of reliability: the AIC also compiles a useful list of 'the next generation of dividend heroes' – trusts that have raised their dividends for at least ten consecutive years, but fewer than twenty.

AIC Next Generation Dividend Heroes[81]

	Consecutive Years of Increase	**Yield 20/03/20**
Aberdeen Standard Equity Income (ASEI)	19	9.8%
TR European Growth (TRG)	17	3.9%
Athelney Trust (ATY)	16	4.8%
BlackRock Smaller Companies Trust (BRSC)	16	3.2%
BlackRock Throgmorton Trust (THRG)	16	2.7%
Henderson EuroTrust (HNE)	16	3.4%
Henderson Smaller Companies (HSL)	16	4.4%
Artemis Alpha Trust (ATS)	15	2.2%
Murray International (MYI)	15	6.5%
Witan Pacific	14	2.5%
BlackRock Greater Europe (BRGE)	14	1.6%
Edinburgh Investment Trust (EDIN)	14	7.6%
Henderson European Focus Trust (HEFT)	12	3.3%
HICL Infrastructure (HICL)	12	5.8%
Schroder Oriental Income (SOI)	12	5.3%
Standard Life UK Smaller Companies (SLS)	12	2.2%
Aberdeen Asian Income Fund (AAIF)	11	6.0%
Henderson Far East Income (HFEL)	11	8.4%
International Public Partnerships (INPP)	11	5.4%
CQS New City High Yield (NCYF)	10	11.7%
Fidelity Special Values (FSV)	10	4.5%
Law Debenture (LWDB)	10	6.0%
Lowland Investment Company (LWI)	10	7.4%
Schroder UK Mid Cap (SCP)	10	5.4%
Tetragon Financial Group (TFG)	10	10.4%

[81] AIC, 23rd March 2020

This list of a further 25 trusts includes some newer trusts and is populated by a more diverse range of sectors, including European smaller companies, Asia Pacific, and infrastructure. Some of these have only come into being as investable concepts in the last couple of decades.

For many investors this consistency of dividend growth is extremely valuable. If you want to be a 'buy and forget' saver with only a passing interest in the stock market, these trusts may be ones to consider for a commitment that does not require constant analysis and switching. When making any selection though it is important to look beyond the basic yield figure, which won't tell the whole story. For these trusts with long unbroken records of dividend growth there is one other very important factor – the 'special sauce' that gives investment trusts a major long-term advantage over commercial companies and other forms of collective investment funds.

Revenue Reserves

Whilst investment trusts are required to pay out 85% of their revenue as dividends, that leaves an all-important 15% that boards can decide, at their discretion, to retain as 'revenue reserves' that can later be used to top-up dividend payments during lean times. This allows investment trusts to smooth their dividend payments, which is how those dividend heroes have been able to sustain such lengthy records of consistent annual improvement. Some revenue is squirrelled away during good times to use in the inevitable bad times that result from the cyclical nature of the economy and stock markets.

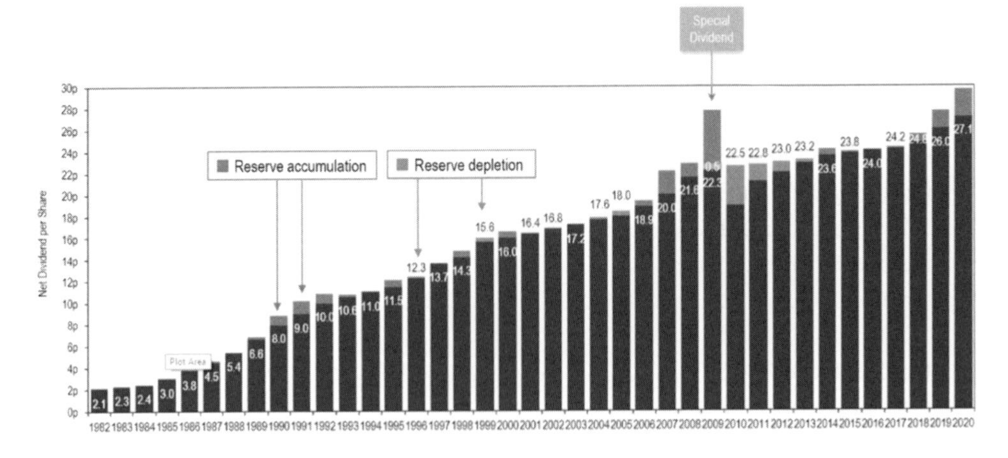

Merchants Trust Dividend Record 1982-2020; source AllianzGI/Merchants Trust
Past performance is not a reliable indicator of future results

Merchants Trust (MRCH) provides a good example, and this chart shows how the trust builds revenue reserves during strong periods of good underlying revenue growth, like 1989-1993, 2006-2009, and 2018-2020; and then uses some of those reserves to maintain dividends during downturns such as 2004-05 and the aftermath of the credit crisis in 2010-2013.

Trusts decide individually how much revenue to keep in their revenue reserves, and this will depend on a number of factors including longevity. Younger, newer trusts have to start from zero and build reserves from scratch, so they do not have the advantage of historic reserves that have been created by more established trusts. Many trusts will express their reserves as a multiple of the most recent year's dividend, so Merchants' revenue reserves of 28.2p are sufficient to cover the annual 27.2p dividend 1.04 times. There is no 'right' level of revenue reserves, but many trusts will aim to retain cover for between one and two years' dividends. Some are more extreme, such as Caledonia Investments (CLDN), which says "the board's objective is to ensure that the annual dividend is fully covered by investment income for the financial year, although the company has available distributable reserves of £1,775m, broadly equivalent to 53 years' payment of the current annual dividend, which could be used to smooth any investment income shortfall".[82]

It is worth remembering that although two infrastructure trusts do appear on the AIC's list of next generation dividend heroes, the majority of alternative asset trusts are relatively young and have not built high levels of revenue reserves, or retained earnings. Some trusts go further and make a virtue of their 'full payout' dividend models that aim to pay out substantially all of the current year income to shareholders. The prime beneficiaries of revenue reserves are equity trusts that are arguably most at risk of volatility in their underlying revenues from company dividends. It was notable when the Covid-19 pandemic struck, equity investment trusts seemed to have an edge in terms of the strength of dividends, as many alternative asset trusts cut their dividends, including SQN Asset Finance (now KKVL), Marble Point Loan Financing (MPLF), Volta Finance (VTA), DP Aircraft 1 (DPA), Picton Property Income (PCTN), BMO Commercial Property Trust (BCPT), Tritax Big Box REIT (BBOX), CVC Credit Opportunities (CCPG), and Fair Oaks Income (FAIR).[83]

Job Curtis, the seasoned manager of the 'dividend hero' City of London Investment Trust (CTY), made the point at an AIC media webinar[84] after a very tough year for dividends in 2020 that if the trust's revenue reserves were to be fully depleted at any point, then the board could decide to top up the dividend with capital reserves. These

---

[82] Caledonia Investments Annual Report 2020
[83] Investment Trust Newsletter May 2020
[84] AIC end of year media webinar, 8th December 2020

are gains realised from investments and therefore available for distribution to shareholders, amounting to £271.8m at 30th June 2020. The main point here is that these long-established investment trusts have plenty of different levers to pull to maintain their superb dividend records, which would not be relinquished lightly.

Special Dividends

In 2009 Merchants Trust paid a special dividend of 0.5p per share on top of its regular dividends of 22.3p per share. This reflected a one-off event in the form of a £2m recovery of VAT for the period from 1990-1996, so the trust decided to pay out this non-recurring income in a form that did not add to its obligations for the following years. Special dividends are not very common in the investment trust industry, where most operations are very routine, but they do arise a little more frequently from alternative asset trusts more likely to benefit from one-off receipts. These can sometimes be a matter of policy as well. GCP Asset Backed Income (GABI) has a stated annual dividend target and will pay special dividends when portfolio returns have exceeded expectations, hence an extra 0.25p per share for shareholders in addition to the targeted 6.2p in 2019.[85]

Some special dividends are larger in scale. Symphony International (SIHL), a hybrid public-private equity Asian trust, has the policy to reward shareholders from the gains made on partial exits and distributions on investments. This has led to some chunky periodic payouts of special dividends, but as the name implies, these are not regular and not to be relied upon.

Other dividend policies are unorthodox, such as for Chelverton UK Dividend Trust (SDV), which says that once its retained revenue reserves are equal to double the historic core dividend, the trust will distribute all additional current period revenue as a special dividend. At its year-end of 30th April 2019 it had retained revenue reserves of £4m, or 19.19p per share, representing 199% of the expected core annual dividend of 9.6p per share. In the financial year 2020 it kept the same core dividend and did not pay a special dividend because the reserves had declined to 16.5p per share.

Dividend Cover and Capital Distributions

Just as there is an elastic relationship between the net asset value and the share price for investment trusts, so it is with the revenue a trust receives from its investments and the money that flows out again in the form of dividends. The relationship between revenue and dividends is called the dividend cover, and if the two match, then the dividend cover is 1.0 times. If dividend cover is 1.2 times, sometimes expressed as 1.2x

[85] GCP Asset Backed Income Fund, RNS, special dividend declaration 23rd October 2019

or 120%, then that means the dividend is more than covered by current year revenue, which means it should be more secure. If a trust is using revenue reserves to top up the dividend during a difficult period, then the dividend may be uncovered, meaning the cover is less than 1.0 times. On occasions, alternative asset trusts may start to pay a high dividend from launch, initially uncovered but with the plan that as the funds are fully invested and the portfolio takes shape, so revenue will start to cover the dividend.

This raises the question of how a new trust can pay uncovered dividends when it has had no time to build revenue reserves. The answer arrived in 2012, when the tax rules changed to allow investment trusts to pay dividends out of capital profits. This change was not met with much enthusiasm initially, but as the period of low interest rates has lengthened and the thirst for income has grown, so more trusts have decided it is an attractive proposition to pay a dividend out of capital, even if they do not have sufficient revenue.

It's worth stepping back for a moment to 2001, when the European Assets Trust (EAT) adopted a high distribution strategy, which it could do because it was a Dutch-domiciled company. It decided to pay shareholders a dividend equal to 6% of the year-end NAV each year, even though its investment realm of European smaller companies does not tend to produce high dividends. It argues this enables investors with high income requirements to diversify into an area that is not typically income-producing, but EAT was a curiosity until recently. Over the last couple of years, perhaps after observing the popularity of high-yielding alternative asset trusts, a number of equity trusts have adopted a new policy of paying dividends from capital, often at a fixed percentage rate. For some trusts this has been seen as a way of attracting new investors who would otherwise ignore a non-dividend paying trust, and a way of narrowing the discount to net asset value. Some wealth managers have extensive mandates that require some level of dividend, and by adopting a capital distribution policy, even trusts in traditionally capital-focused areas such as biotechnology can qualify as dividend-payers. International Biotechnology Trust (IBT) is paying a dividend equal to 4% of the year-end NAV in two equal tranches in the following year, and JPMorgan Chinese went one step further when instituting a similar policy at the end of 2019 by changing its name as well to JPMorgan China Growth & Income (JCGI).

Other investment trusts which pay dividends out of capital include Aberdeen Emerging Markets Company (AEMC), BB Healthcare Trust (BBH), BlackRock Latin American (BRLA), JPMorgan Global Growth & Income (JPGI), Martin Currie Asia Unconstrained (MCP), Montanaro UK Smaller Companies (MTU), Princess Private Equity (PEY), and Securities Trust of Scotland (STS).

The resulting increase in demand is real, and trusts using this technique have often succeeded in trading on better ratings. There is a counter-argument though that this is effectively sleight-of-hand, financial engineering designed to create an entirely artificial dividend that is unrelated to the trust's revenue. Dividends paid from capital are simply slicing off a piece of investors' capital and returning it to them on an annual basis. When investment trusts have tried clever techniques in the past to increase demand it has sometimes ended in tears, as was true at the time of the split capital crisis. Such artfulness, while signed off by shareholders and in no way dishonest, also seems somewhat at odds with traditional investment trust virtues of simplicity and rectitude. From questionnaires completed by delegates at its 2019 investment trusts conference, the stockbroker Winterflood reported that 52% of respondents were negative on enhanced dividends. The problem is that these 'fake' dividends eat into the capital returns for long-term investors, the real constituency for investment trusts. Capital that is paid back is either no longer deployed, or investors have the cost, irritation, and possible tax consequences of needing to reinvest the dividends. This may eventually prove to be a temporary fad of a low interest rate world.

REITs

Real estate investment trusts operate under different tax rules, and that affects their distributions to shareholders as well. REITs are required to distribute 90% of the tax-exempt profit from their property investments and businesses to shareholders in the form of a Property Income Distribution (PID). They may also distribute income from other activities in non-PID form. The dividends paid by REITs may therefore be made up of PID or non-PID income, and this is relevant for UK taxpayers because of the way in which this income is treated. If you hold the shares in a tax wrapper like an ISA or a SIPP, this is not of great concern. Picton Property Income (PCTN) paid quarterly dividends amounting to 3.5p per share in the year to 31st March 2020, all of which were PIDs.[86] Likewise, the four dividends amounting to a total of 8.25p per share paid by Regional REIT (RGL) in 2019 were entirely PIDs.[87]

Dividend Growth

Receiving a high dividend can be very welcome to help with regular expenses or as a supplement to income, but in a generally inflationary world, a high and growing dividend is even better. Remember, those dividend heroes have raised their dividends each year, not simply maintained them. Checking on the growth rate of dividends can be useful, as trusts that can sustain a high growth rate in the dividend may accelerate your payback meaningfully. Take the example of a stock yielding a static 3%, meaning an investor will recoup the original cost of the share in 33 years, from dividends alone. If that dividend stream grows by 5% per year, the time to recoup the original

[86] Picton Property Income Annual Report 2020

[87] Regional REIT Annual Report and Accounts for the year ended 31st December 2019

investment is slashed to just 20 years,[88] so the potential dividend growth is as important as the starting dividend yield.

Choosing Capital Growth or Dividends

Even though dividend returns are widely recognised as an important component of long-term growth, there is a trade-off between capital growth and dividends. Investment trusts that are very focused on growing your capital, in areas such as technology, private equity, or smaller companies, are much less likely to pay substantial dividends, whereas many debt trusts, or those focused on certain alternative assets such as specialist real estate, infrastructure, and renewable energy will expect most of their returns to be in the form of income. Which suits you better is very much a personal question and will depend on your circumstances and preferences. If it is possible to generalise a little though, there is a life cycle argument that younger investors earning an income from work will often express a preference for long-term capital growth, and then switch gradually into more income-producing assets as they reduce risk and seek non-employment income later in life.

There is a small group of curious hybrid investment trusts that cater exactly for this need by combining a traditional structure with different share classes with segregated pools of assets. One is BMO Managed Portfolio Trust (BMPI, BMPG), with two classes of share with two separate investment portfolios: the income shares, where the investment focus is to provide an attractive level of income, together with some capital growth; and the growth shares, where the investment focus is to achieve capital growth. The ability to switch between the two share classes annually, in a tax efficient manner (without triggering a capital gains tax event), offers flexibility to those investors whose requirements may change over time. Invesco Perpetual Select Trust (IVPU, IVPG, IVPB, IVPM) has four separate classes, namely the UK Equity Share Portfolio, the Global Equity Income Share Portfolio, the Balanced Risk Allocation Share Portfolio, and the Managed Liquidity Share Portfolio. The capital structure permits quarterly conversions between the four share classes without triggering a disposal for capital gains tax purposes. JPMorgan Elect (JPE, JPEI, JPEC) offers three share classes, Managed Growth, Managed Income, and Managed Cash, again saying "the aim is to provide the choice and flexibility for investors to manage their investment strategy throughout their lives".[89] JPMorgan European (JETI, JETG) also offers a choice of Income Shares or Growth Shares.

In principle, these trusts seem like a good idea, serving a common need while minimising administration, tax implications, and the need to make difficult decisions

---

[88] The Little Book of Big Dividends, Charles B. Carlson, 2012; adapted for use on fidelity.com

[89] am.JPMorgan.com, 19th October 2020

when choosing between a myriad of different investment trusts. The reality, sadly, does not always match the concept. The BMO trust was launched in 2008 but did not complete any share conversions until 2018, hindered by the requirement for a high minimum aggregate number of shares laid down by the board to justify the cost, later halved. The greater issue is that if you are driven by tax considerations you may be compromising on your choice of fund manager or portfolio, when with careful management any tax liability can probably be minimised.

Dividend Reinvestment

Many investors end up choosing a middle path between capital growth and income, blending the two in a portfolio that is more focused on total return, including at least some dividend payments. That money can be withdrawn and used for other purposes, or it can be used to bolster future capital and income prospects by reinvesting the dividends and buying more shares. Reinvesting dividends makes a huge difference over time to long-term returns, such is the power of compounding. Schroders have calculated that a notional US$1000 invested in the MSCI World Index at the start of 1993 would have grown to US$3231 by March 2018, an annual growth rate of 5.9%. Adding in reinvested dividends boosts that notional return to US$6416, nearly double the amount and implying an annual growth rate of 8.3%.[90] Many similar studies show the same sort of result – that reinvesting dividends can provide a considerable turbo boost to long-term capital returns.

There are different ways to reinvest dividends, depending on the size of your portfolio. Some stockbrokers will allow you to opt for automatic reinvestment at a small charge. Hargreaves Lansdown will reinvest income automatically, if chosen, when the income reaches £10 per holding, with a 1% charge, minimum £1, maximum £10. Interactive Investor offers a similar service for dividend reinvestment for a minimum of £10, with a charge of £0.99. This can be cost effective for smaller investors, and means you can gradually build up the number of shares held in each income-paying investment, thereby raising the dividend payments every year if the rate of the dividend is maintained or increased.

An alternative for larger investors who might be seeing greater dividend flows that are available for reinvestment is to wait for these to build up in the cash account to a reasonable minimum, say £500, and then choose to reinvest that as a lump sum in whatever holding is considered best value at the time. This can be a very satisfying form of portfolio maintenance that allows you to rebalance or to focus on particular opportunities that may arise, without having to add extra cash to your portfolio. If Mr

[90] How investing dividends has affected returns over 25 years, David Brett, Schroders.com

Rockefeller had the chance to reinvest his dividends in a modern stockbroking account, it's a fair bet he would take great pleasure in that too.

Chapter 9: IPOs and Winding Up

Novelty is a great salesman. Most of us like shiny, new items, fresh out of the box with no blemishes and the promise of improvement and a better life ahead. It's the same with investment trusts. The lure of a new issue at the initial public offering (IPO) is strong, that chance to get in on the ground floor, to buy on day one and pick up shares in a trust with no legacy issues or hangovers, no shadows over its reputation, no archaic clauses or structures, no old debts, and with some sort of unique investment proposition. With lots of press coverage, maybe a video pitch by the manager, and a colourful marketing document too, IPOs are tempting, but it is always worth assessing each new trust on its individual merits. Some make more sense than others.

There are decisions to be made when a trust will on occasions reach the end of its life too and face a winding up, as the assets are sold off and the proceeds returned to shareholders. This need not be a negative outcome – it can sometimes be the result of an opportunity exhausted or some extraneous corporate influence – but just as some trusts make a noisy entrance, some make a quiet exit.

Recent IPO Activity

If we work backwards through time from the present day, 2020 was obviously an atypical year because business was interrupted by the Covid-19 virus lockdown. Only one IPO got away prior to the lockdown, that being the Nippon Active Value Fund (NAVF), which sneaked under the finishing tape just in time and raised £103m. There was then a flurry of activity in the autumn, following the traditional quiet period over the summer months, where there were some mixed results for a group of attempted launches that hit almost simultaneously. Home REIT (HOME) raised £240.6m, just shy of its £250m target, Round Hill Music Royalty Fund (RHM) raised US$282m, Triple Point Energy Infrastructure Company (TEEC) raised its minimum of £100m, and Schroder British Opportunities Trust (SBO) struggled to its minimum of £75m. A proposed UK trust launch from a specialist boutique called Tellworth was abandoned, as was the Buffettology Smaller Companies Investment Trust. The Ecofin US Renewables Infrastructure Trust asked for a short extension of the timetable to see if it could reach its minimum of US$150m.

2019 was a fairly quiet year for IPOs as well, with eight new trusts – The Schiehallion Fund (MNTN), Octopus Renewables Infrastructure Trust (ORIT), US Solar Fund (USF), JPMorgan Core Real Assets (JARA), Aquila European Renewables Income (AERS), RTW Venture Fund (RTW), Riverstone Credit Opportunities (RCOI) and Cameron Investors Trust (CIT) raising a combined total of £1.36bn.[91] With three

---

[91] Winterflood Investment Companies 2020 Annual Review

renewable energy infrastructure and another four alternative asset trusts, only the small-scale and short-lived securitisation of a family trust called Cameron Investors Trust[92] stopped alternative assets from claiming a clean sweep.

In 2018, 17 new trusts raised £2.6bn in total at an average size of £153m.[93] The list was headed by Smithson Investment Trust (SSON), which raised a record £822.5m at launch, joined by Tritax EuroBox (BOXE), Hipgnosis Songs Fund (SONG), Baillie Gifford US Growth (USA), Ceiba Investments (CBA), Mobius Investment Trust (MMIT), M&G Credit Income (MGCI), Merian Chrysalis Investment Company (MERI), Gresham House Energy Storage Fund (GRID), SDCL Energy Efficiency Income (SEIT), Augmentum Fintech (AUGM), JPMorgan Multi-Asset Trust (MATE), Odyssean Investment Trust (OIT), AVI Japan Opportunity Trust (AJOT), Ashoka India Equity (AIE), Marble Point Loan Financing (MBLF), and Gore Street Energy Storage Fund (GSF).

2017 was a busy year, with 19 new investment trusts raising £2.9bn at an average size of £153m.[94] The main theme was the quest for yield, and Winterflood noted "the average yield target of an IPO in 2017 was 5.7%, with the majority of funds offering yields of between 4% and 7% once fully invested". Only two of the 19 did not have a specific yield target, and there were a number of REITs seeking to invest in specialist types of property. BioPharma Credit (BPCR) led the field by raising £611m at launch, followed by PRS REIT (PRSR), Greencoat Renewables (GRP), Triple Point Social Housing REIT (SOHO), Aberforth Split Level Income (ASIT), Aberdeen Standard European Logistics Income (ASLI), Residential Secure Income REIT (RESI), Impact Healthcare REIT (IHR), Warehouse REIT (WHR), LXi REIT (LXI), Supermarket Income REIT (SUPR), Jupiter Emerging and Frontier Income (JEFI), AEW Long Lease REIT (AEWL), Gabelli Merger Plus+ (GMP), EJF Investments (EJFI), Tufton Oceanic Assets (SHIP), Downing Strategic Micro-Cap (DSM), ScotGems (SGEM), and TOC Property Backed Lending (PBLT).

If 2017 provided a good illustration of the momentum that can build behind a sector when it is in favour, 2016 served to show what happens when momentum is halted by an unexpected macro event, in this case the Brexit vote that greatly unsettled markets and slammed on the brakes for new capital being invested. There were only four new issues in 2016, raising just £630m and providing the evidence that the IPO market is highly sensitive to prevailing market conditions and to the importance of timing. Some trust launches are fortunate to get it just right; others can find themselves scuppered through no fault of their own when the market tide turns.

---

[92] Cameron Investors Trust raised £10m and was de-listed before the end of the year following a reconstruction
[93] Winterflood Investment Companies 2019 Annual Review
[94] Winterflood Investment Companies 2018 Annual Review

much stock the market-makers can find at that moment. New issues are also free of stockbroking charges and stamp duty, and there is no dealing spread, so there is a saving for all investors buying at launch. In most cases, because launches are well managed by sponsoring stockbrokers, the price in the market on the first day of dealings will be at a slight premium, making it more expensive to buy immediately afterwards.

On occasions too, the initial premium may be large if the manager has a particularly strong reputation, or if the sector has been in great demand from investors and peer group trusts are trading on high ratings. This was the case with Octopus Renewables Infrastructure Trust (ORIT), which had a strong case at launch and was well received, raising £350m against its £100m-£250m target to invest in solar and wind assets. The shares were offered at IPO for 100p each and started trading in December 2019. They started trading at a premium to both the NAV and the issue price, opening at 103.4p, closing in the market on the first day at 106.8p, and moving over 110p the following month.

Drawbacks of IPOs

Some IPOs are obviously unique, but on other occasions trusts are seeking to join existing developed sectors with a subtly different investment model. Very often that means that comparable assets are available through existing trusts at a better price. Since the disappearance of warrants and subscription shares, investors at IPO have nearly always been asked to pay a premium for the assets at launch (once costs are deducted), often 100p for initial assets of around 98p. Trusts do not know their initial NAV at launch, since this depends on the amount of capital raised. M&G Credit Income Investment Trust (MGCI) estimated its initial NAV at 98.8p in its prospectus, based on an assumption of initial gross proceeds of £250m. When it actually raised just £100m from the IPO in November 2018 the initial NAV would have been lower, and its first announced NAV was 97.94p.

Paying a premium for a new trust means that when compared to established trusts on a discount, the new one may be more expensive at a time when it also has the extra costs of investment to come. For income-producers, there has of course been no opportunity for a new trust to build revenue reserves to protect the dividend, nor is there a public track record to examine, nor is there much if any independent research. New issues are backed by clever marketing and by paid-for reports, so it often pays to look at them with a sceptical eye.

There is a broader question surrounding the timing of new issues and whether these are by necessity marketing-led. It is a lengthy, expensive and time-consuming task to launch a new investment trust, and managers, sponsors, brokers, and all the other stakeholders have a definite vested interest in ensuring that the offer gets away successfully and raises the minimum capital required. This means that IPOs often target 'hot' fashionable sectors that are in demand, perhaps at the wrong moment in the cycle, closer to a peak in valuations rather than a trough. IPOs are also timed for periods of market strength and are notoriously difficult to launch during bearish periods when prices are low. Contrarian investors are unlikely to be attracted to IPOs, and for the rest of us the prudent approach is to assess the market opportunity critically.

Except in cases where a significant premium seems likely to be maintained, there is often limited cost in waiting a year to see how new trusts bed in, and whether the managers actually found it as easy to invest their cash balance as they believed. If a concept is genuinely new, or if a new approach really is being adopted, then all of the back-testing and conceptual arguments in the world may be no substitute for waiting to see the portfolio in action, in real market conditions. A patient assessment once more market information is available can be sensible, particularly as analysts have to go through a learning process as well to understand the real risks and nuances of new sectors.

It can take some time in certain cases for managers investing in illiquid markets to get their money into the market and actually put it to work. Riverstone Energy (RSE), an oil and gas investor that came to the market in October 2013 had only 37% of its assets invested by May 2015, and that is not a unique case. One further drawback is that if a new trust is paying a dividend this is likely to be at a reduced level initially, while the trust gets invested. If a higher dividend can be obtained from an existing trust, that additional income may cover any premium or dealing costs incurred to switch into a new trust one year down the line. US Solar Fund (USF) said at launch in March 2019 that it was aiming for a target annual dividend of 5.5% of net assets once all solar power assets were operational, but an initial target dividend yield of 2%-3% prior to that. It has subsequently said that it expects to start its full dividend payments in 2021.

The Good, the Bad, and the Ugly

There are good and bad trusts in most sectors, and over recent years there have certainly been good and bad IPOs. As all journalists know, the disasters make for much better stories than investment trusts that have performed as expected and hit their targets, but plenty of new trusts have done well for investors. Alternative asset trusts have been a particular success in recent years, delivering a high income for investors at a time when yield has been very scarce. HICL Infrastructure (HICL) broke new ground when it was launched in March 2006 and has since delivered a high yield that has also grown by 35% over 13 years, alongside a share price that is up from 100p to around 170p and a portfolio that has grown to £3bn.[95] The same has been true for renewable

[95] HICL Infrastructure factsheet Summer 2020

energy trusts and for those in emerging sectors such as healthcare. BB Healthcare (BBH), an investor in global healthcare equities, launched in late 2016 and by 30th September 2020 had grown its net assets by 83.8%,[96] placing it in the top ten performers over the last three years.[97] Another trust that has done very well, thankfully breaking a run of calamities for record-breaking IPOs, is Smithson Investment Trust (SSON), which raised a record £822.5m from its flotation in 2018. From an issue price of 1000p the shares have risen to over 1500p by October 2020.[98]

Turning now to those that did not work out so well, a great example – probably the greatest example - of the mistiming of new issues is from 1994. That was the year that Bill Clinton and Boris Yeltsin signed a nuclear accord, the film Schindler's List swept the Oscars, and the Channel Tunnel opened. The privatisation of state-owned assets was also all the rage. Two large management houses – Kleinwort Benson and Mercury Asset Management – went head-to-head in competition, both launching huge investment trusts dedicated to European privatisation stocks. The Kleinwort European Privatisation Investment Trust (known as KEPIT) raised £480m, and the public offer of shares was three times oversubscribed. Its fund-raising success, which set a new record, was then eclipsed shortly afterwards by the Mercury European Privatisation Investment Trust (known as MEPIT). This trust was aiming for £575m and raised £540m, another record.

The public was enthused by the idea of privatisation, which had already proved for many a way to make a fast buck. In the 1980s, the privatisation of businesses such as British Gas, British Telecommunications, Jaguar, British Airways, Rolls Royce, British Steel, and the water and power utilities had proven successful. Investors had made good money from the launches and were hungry for more. By 1994 the trend was sweeping across Europe, hence the rationale and demand for these trusts. Within the first couple of months of its life, KEPIT had already participated in six European privatisations in France, Italy, Turkey, Sweden, the Netherlands, and Denmark.

Unfortunately this promise soon turned sour, and neither trust was ultimately successful. The Kleinwort trust only ran until November 1996, when it was unitised and the majority of investors exited with cash. The Mercury trust soldiered on for longer, becoming the Merrill Lynch European Investment Trust, but finally winding-up in September 2004, worth less than when it began.

At the height of the technology boom in early 2000, Amerindo Internet Fund raised £400m, well in excess of its original target, as investors clamoured for exposure to the

[96] BB Healthcare Trust Monthly News September 2020
[97] JPMorgan Cazenove Daily Statistics 16th October 2020
[98] Share price on 21st October 2020 was 1574p

new digital economy. Five years later the founders of the management company were arrested in New York on alleged fraud charges and the trust was liquidated. Framlington NetNet.Inc Fund, another launch from the frenzied period in 2000, quickly turned into another debacle that cost over-excited investors dearly. A year after launching with net assets of £100m it was left with just £7.8m.

Trusts can sometimes turn around. Fidelity China Special Situations (FCSS) was perhaps an example of hubris when the highly-successful UK equity manager Anthony Bolton tried to replicate his strategy in China. Straight from the IPO in 2010 it proved to be a more difficult task than expected, with the trust encountering fraud and all sorts of difficulties as the learning curve steepened. After the first flush of enthusiasm that took the shares up to a premium-rating and a peak share price of 129p in November 2010, the shares were down at 70p within eleven months. Following a change of manager in 2014 the trust eventually found its feet and has since been a strong performer, up to 374.5p by October 2020.[99]

The story of another high-profile fund manager is very well known. The name of Neil Woodford has been dragged through the media in bloody fashion over the last couple of years after his nascent fund management company collapsed ignominiously. A star UK equity income manager at Invesco Perpetual, Neil Woodford was the darling of a big sector in the open-ended fund world and had control of billions of pounds worth of assets when he decided to cash in and set up his own asset management firm in 2014. He kept the mandates for his huge open-ended funds and in the spring of 2015 the IPO for Woodford Patient Capital Trust was announced to considerable fanfare and demand based on his high reputation. From an initial target of £200m the trust's offering was oversubscribed and was scaled up to a then record-breaking £800m. The shares surged to an initial premium and peaked at 120p, but they struggled thereafter as performance was poor. Like Anthony Bolton, Neil Woodford was investing a substantial portion of the funds into a different market segment than the one where he had built his track record, in this case very small and unquoted companies. In 2017 the trust sought permission to increase the percentage invested in unquoted stocks, raising the risk profile higher, in spite of the trust's new Key Information Document at the start of 2018 classifying the risk as 3/7 on its risk spectrum, which always looked dubious. The trust was relegated from the FTSE 250 Index in May 2018, and as confidence ebbed away, the manager's open-ended funds that shared many of the same holdings were hit by massive redemption requests and were suspended, ultimately being wound-up and bringing down the management company.

Unlike the open-ended funds, which were unable to meet investor demands to sell and were suspended, causing considerable hardship to some investors unable to retrieve

---

[99] Share price 374.5p on 21st October 2020

any of their remaining money for many months, the investment trust structure proved far superior and allowed investors to trade in and out freely without any need to halt dealings. The price wasn't great though, down to below 30p by the time the trust's board moved the management mandate to Schroders and renamed the trust as Schroder UK Public Private Trust (SUPP).

Some intended IPOs never get off the ground at all, having found that the demand from the initial marketing never materialises, or that markets dip at an inopportune moment during the process. Tellworth British Recovery & Growth Trust had been seeking £100m for an IPO but found insufficient demand to meet the minimum target in October 2020. Most often, when trust launches are 'delayed' or 'postponed' those are euphemisms for 'abandoned', but occasionally a trust IPO does succeed second time around, sometimes with a tweak to the terms. This was the case for ICG-Longbow Senior Secured UK Property Debt (LBOW) in 2013 and for Hipgnosis Songs Fund (SONG) in 2018.

Types of IPO

IPOs are not a 'one size fits all' proposition. Depending on the size of the issue, the intended market, the complexity of the underlying assets, the type of listing, and the preferences of the participants, there are a number of possible routes available to raise funds. The simplest and probably the cheapest is to stick to a placing of shares to professional investors, something that may be the result of regulatory restrictions on providing access to retail investors. Stockbrokers and banks that promote new issues have to be careful to ensure that they are marketing to suitable investors who can reasonably be expected to understand the risks, and there are a host of rules. For trusts that are listing on the specialist fund segment of the London Stock Exchange, which specifies that it is for institutional, professional, professionally advised and knowledgeable investors, an offer open to the public is not appropriate.

Access to the public is patchy, depending on the specifics of each trust launch. If IPOs are targeted at retail investors then it is usually quite straightforward to subscribe for shares through a platform stockbroker, through an adviser, or directly. On other occasions it is very difficult for private investors to gain access, although an initiative from a company called PrimaryBid is trying to level the playing field with its goal to allow "everyday investors fair access to public companies raising capital. PrimaryBid always ensures that retail investors transact at the same time and at the same price as institutional investors".[100] There are issues with links to accounts such as ISAs and SIPPs, but PrimaryBid is taking its first steps towards a fairer market.

---

[100] PrimaryBid.com, 21st October 2020

Secondary Fund-Raising

Much as they might grab the spotlight, IPOs are really the supporting actors in the capital markets for investment trusts. Surprising as it may seem for the closed-end structure, there is considerable scope for trusts to raise additional money after IPO, and this is a route that has been very successfully followed by premium-rated trusts that have expanded gradually over time with several tranches of extra capital.

In 2019, IPOs represented £1.4bn of the total of the £8.9bn raised by the sector, and as the chart from the stockbroker Winterflood[101] shows, secondary fund-raising by trusts that are already listed on the London Stock Exchange is consistently more substantial.

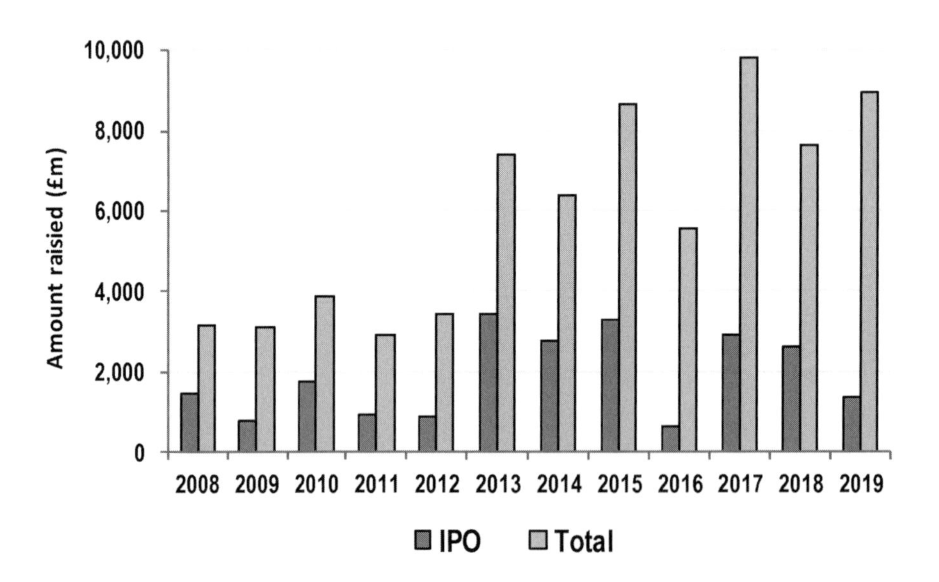

Amount of fundraising 2008-2019; source Winterflood Annual Review 2020

Trusts usually raise additional money when the managers have identified a particular opportunity or a pipeline of assets that they wish to acquire, and it may be part of a defined strategy to grow to an optimal size. This model has worked particularly well for alternative asset trusts in new areas, where they have proved the concept and then gone on to expand through several fundraisings. It makes sense for these managers, when acquiring physical assets such as infrastructure, property, or renewable energy projects, to have capital available in tranches rather than all at once, when it is difficult to invest in a single swoop. The Renewables Infrastructure Group (TRIG) has

[101] Winterflood Annual Review 2020

underperformers or trusts that have lost their rationale in a way that open-ended funds do not.

A less dramatic example was Aberdeen Private Equity Fund, which had long struggled to attract investors and narrow its wide discount to net asset value. In 2017 a value investor in the guise of another investment trust, British Empire Trust, took a large stake, and at the end of the year the trust agreed to sell its entire investment portfolio at a modest premium to its 31st October 2017 valuation, net of associated sale costs. The capital was then returned to shareholders. As with UKML, the trigger for the corporate activity here was the wide discount to NAV that created the surplus value ripe for picking. The other item of note here was the signpost of a rising stake in the trust prior to the corporate action – something that was also true before the bid for the property trust Kennedy Wilson Europe, also in 2017.

Around the same time, the Berlin property investor Taliesin Property Fund reported a recommended all-cash offer from Blackstone Group at a 16% premium to the trust's NAV and roughly a 10% premium to the share price before the bid. In this case the motivation was different, and the bid was more about the high investment demand for scarce high-quality Berlin residential property. The same was probably true for Hansteen's 2017 purchase of Industrial Multi-Property Trust.

Perhaps the most dramatic takeover over recent years though was John Laing Infrastructure, a £1.4bn infrastructure trust that was taken out in July 2018 at a substantial premium to net asset value. A consortium of two fund managers bid for the trust at a 19.8% premium to NAV, saying that the mature cash flow profile from the portfolio matched the long-term nature of their institutional and pension fund mandates. That was a good example of portfolios of alternative assets being worth what a buyer is prepared to pay. All valuers say they are conservative and use accepted methods to calculate a fair market value for the assets, but until they are sold these valuations are always estimates.

Rather like takeovers for cash, mergers are occasional events in the sector. At the start of 2019, Primary Health Properties (PHP) expanded by merging with MedicX Fund, providing considerable scale and presence in the market for GP surgeries. More recently, in July 2020, the board of Perpetual Income & Growth Investment Trust, who had been conducting a search for a new manager, concluded the best outcome was to merge with Murray Income Trust (MUT), with an opportunity for a partial cash exit thrown into the deal. For sub-scale trusts in particular, or those where the boards feel the original investment rationale has run out of momentum, mergers can make sense to refresh the approach and gain scale, thereby saving costs and improving liquidity at the same time.

There is an argument that with such a focus on liquidity by many investment trust buyers, plus the aftermath of the Woodford scandal and the MIFID II regulations, there could be more pressure on boards to consider scaling up by combining with other trusts. The stockbroker Numis Securities said in a report issued in July 2020 that a process of "creative destruction" took place after the financial crisis and that with plenty of sub-£200m trusts and others with "undifferentiated strategies" there is plenty of scope for action again. It highlighted a number of trusts with a high level of overlap in their strategies or portfolios, and in some crowded sectors there do seem to be trusts that could usefully join forces to create new signature trusts with greater market clout. Some of these are even within the same management company, such as BlackRock Smaller Companies Trust (BRSC) and BlackRock Throgmorton (THRG); and JPMorgan Mid Cap (JMF) and The Mercantile Investment Trust (MRC). It may take a period of turbulence to shake the sector first, but more mergers may well be a feature of the sector again at some stage.

This does not necessarily mean it is a viable investment strategy to try to pick trusts that might be taken over or be the smaller party in a merger. The problem with buying such trusts is that they can be serial underperformers and in the absence of any corporate action their discounts look well justified by the lack of liquidity. It is one thing to recognise that the investment trust sector as a whole might benefit from some rationalisation, but quite another as a small investor to try to roll the dice and pick the trusts that might benefit.

The game is different for larger investors, of course, who can take meaningful stakes and engage with boards directly to persuade them to accept change. At various times in the past, particularly in the late 1990s and early 2000s, the sector has seen activist investors coming in to extract value from wide discounts and sleepy non-executive boards. The public nature of investment trust performance, which is under constant scrutiny in this information age, also means that underperformers cannot remain under the radar for long, so there are reasons to believe that future waves of corporate action are likely to sweep through in the wake of a big market upset.

Ticking Clocks

As one of the tools used to battle persistent discounts, continuation votes, or discontinuation votes, are in place for quite a large number of trusts. These require shareholders to assess the continuing viability of trusts on a regular basis, and because these dates are specified and known in advance, some scheduled votes will act like ticking clocks for managers and boards under pressure. Boards sometimes enact change before continuation votes that they suspect they might otherwise lose, and they can also be used as deadlines for improvement. Some trusts may impose their own separate timetables for improvement, as was the case for Witan Pacific Investment

Benefits of IPOs

The lists of recent issues support one of the central arguments for IPOs, that in a continuously changing world we need new trusts to provide access to new ideas, new asset classes, and new highly-skilled managers. Some of those will endure, and others may pass quickly, but without a dynamic sector creating new waves, investors might never get to dip their toes into the water.

IPOs have always served this function, from emerging markets in the late 1980s and early 1990s to frontier markets later on, from the demutualisation of building societies to new fintech companies, from infrastructure to renewable energy, from post-financial crisis credit opportunities to peer-to-peer lending, from student housing to song catalogues. It is this constant renewal and regeneration that keeps the sector in existence and keeps investment trusts relevant to this day. The ability of the industry and the structure to adapt and to embrace new opportunities as they arise is not just good for the industry, but for investors who need access to the latest themes and the most innovative fund management techniques to ensure they are maintaining the best performance they can.

For all IPOs, whether they are focused on a new area or not, the marketing period before flotation provides a great deal of information to all interested parties, through initial flyers to the final prospectus, backed by manager meetings and roadshows, or virtual roadshows in 2020, and usually with some keen press coverage. In terms of transparency, manager access, and having the investment thesis clearly articulated, this is a great period for investors to gather all the information they need to make a decision from a position of knowledge. The prospectus in particular is a highly detailed document that includes a full run-down of the risks that have been identified as well as the investment case and a granular breakdown of how the company will be structured and run. The prospectus for the Round Hill Music Royalty Fund (RHM) issued in October 2020 ran to 151 pages.

It is reasonable to make the point that IPOs tend to have a clean modern structure, without the problems that older trusts can sometimes have with expensive debt or restrictive management contracts, or assets reaching the end of their lives. Most importantly, the mandate and objective has also been constructed to suit the prevailing opportunity and circumstances, so the manager can create the portfolio as they wish, rather than wrestling with yield targets or limitations that no longer make sense. Managers of older trusts are sometimes asked what they might change if they were starting with a clean slate.

For larger investors, IPOs can be an attractive entry point because they can often buy exactly the number of shares they wish to buy, without worrying about liquidity or how

Trust, which said in February 2019 that the trust must justify its active management investment approach. The board determined that if the trust did not beat its benchmark over the three years to 31st January 2021 it would advance proposals that would include a full cash exit close to NAV for shareholders. At various times thereafter it was possible to buy the shares on a double-digit discount, and then before the final deadline arrived, in July 2020, the board announced a change of management firm and strategy. The move to become Baillie Gifford China Growth Trust (BGCG) led to a sharp re-rating.

Changing Managers

It is the prerogative of the board of directors to ensure they are employing the best managers to achieve their objective, and changing the manager is one of the biggest internal corporate actions they can take, though not a decision taken lightly. This may take the form of discussions with the asset management firm to strengthen the team or to change the personnel, but it could also signal a more radical shift by awarding the mandate to another firm. In that case one consideration is the notice period required by the existing managers, and sometimes in the case of impending change the board will give 'protective notice' to managers to ensure that a timely changeover can be made without the expense of compensation once a new manager is selected. If a mandate is up for grabs, a 'beauty parade' of potential managers is often the result – a selection process that will involve the managers pitching their case to the board, who will have taken soundings from shareholders about exactly what style and methodology they might prefer.

Having your name on the trust is no guarantee whatsoever of longevity or continuance. Many trusts are branded with their manager's name to help investors identify them easily, but just because a trust carries the name of a particular manager does not mean that manager has any protection. If a portfolio has been underperforming against its benchmark or peer group for any length of time, the manager might echo the words of the former Arsenal football club manager Arsène Wenger, who likened his job to living on a volcano: any day could be your last.

Pulling the Weeds

Corporate action in the investment trust industry usually results from some sort of problem. Serial underperformance, persistent discounts, strained relations with the board, or something else that is undermining the future potential of the trust to deliver a strong investment performance for shareholders. Takeovers, mergers, and management changes all help the process of renewal, to remove underperformance, to refresh the industry for better times ahead. Gardening analogies seem particularly apt, that corporate action is the process of pulling the weeds to ensure a healthy soil. It does not guarantee future growth, but it prepares the ground. The investment trust industry has proved quite adept at reinventing itself and coping with change over a very long period, balancing tradition and innovation to form a sector that evolves steadily over time.

Part 2 - The Players

Chapter 11: The AIC

The AIC, the Association of Investment Companies, is a non-profit-making industry trade body, funded by a large proportion of all investment trusts. It works to assist members, to represent their interests, and to promote the sector as a whole.

The AIC has been in existence for a long time, in one form or another. Those who have been following the investment trust industry for a while will remember when the association was called the AITC – the Association of Investment Trust Companies. A wave of issuance from offshore funds and from AIM-listed investment companies, together with a desire to expand its universe to include Venture Capital Trusts (VCTs) triggered a name change in 2006. Some might also be old enough to remember some of the association's former heads, such as Ernest Fenton, Michael Hart and Daniel Godfrey. It is less likely (though not impossible) that many will remember the formation of the association way back in 1932, making it older than its larger peer The Investment Association, which looks after the interests of unit trusts and investment managers, founded in 1959.

Based at its offices in the City of London, the AIC works on behalf of its members, those being 356 investment companies that collectively manage an impressive £206bn of assets.[104] That number includes around 70 VCTs. There have been some high-profile defections over the years as certain trusts have been disgruntled with the fees or with some aspect of the association's work but it bears testament to the overall quality of the AIC that it can count a large majority of the industry as members. At the last count, the reckoning was that AIC members accounted for 93% of the industry's assets:[105] not bad in view of the increasingly diverse operations of trusts with differing structures and aims. It is unlikely that 100% of the industry would ever be captured. There is no compulsion to join, and there will always be some trusts that are quite different, or committed to minimising costs, or just those with a fierce independent streak.

Each trust that has joined pays a membership fee based on its size, with a minimum annual fee of £3,200 and a maximum of £20,500. The AIC's revenue in 2019 was just over £5.3m,[106] mainly from those membership fees, and most of that was spent on salaries for its 22 staff, including its chief executive Ian Sayers. Ian, who became the head of the association in 2010, is both a technical expert and an articulate advocate for investment trusts.

---

[104] As at 30th November 2020, www.theaic.co.uk

[105] September 2019

[106] AIC Annual Report and Accounts, year ended 30th September 2019

At first reading there is a bit of a clash between the AIC's principal activity, as laid down in its annual report, and its more public mission statement. The AIC's principal activity, first, is described as being "to represent the views and concerns of the members to the UK Government or other government or regulatory bodies on matters including legislation, regulation and taxation which affect the business or professional interests of members in relation to investment companies". This suggests the AIC's role as a lobbyist is paramount, whereas its mission statement is "to help members add value for shareholders over the longer-term". That feels rather different, although the two statements are not incompatible. In reality, the AIC's reach spans several different areas, all of which are pursued at once.

On its website (www.theaic.co.uk), the association describes its activities in six sections: (i) lobbying – working with regulators and government departments to develop the best possible tax and legal environment for the members and their shareholders; (ii) generating interest in investment companies – the AIC's press team works with the media and opinion-formers to engage investors and financial advisers; (iii) technical advice and guidance – keeping members up-to-date with legal and regulatory changes and providing guidance and advice on how to comply with them; (iv) events and training – holding regular conferences, seminars and roundtables for members on key topical issues, as well as running training courses for both members and financial advisers; (v) statistics – the AIC calculates and publishes performance information on its members; and (vi) online presence – the AIC's website is a hub used by thousands of investors, financial advisers and journalists to get reliable and up-to-date information and news about investment companies.

The AIC seems very effective at what it does, but it's important to remember that it is only a lobbyist, a pressure group. It is not a policeman, not a regulator, has no power to make rules or laws, or to enforce its guidelines. Unlike the Football Association it cannot fine members for bringing the industry into disrepute, it does not give advice, and is entirely focused on one sort of financial product to the exclusion of others. It works for its members, not for investors, although happily the aims of the two often coincide.

Lobbying

Lobbying can take many forms, but for financial trade associations it largely means presenting your industry's point of view as persuasively as possible to policy-makers and legislators. Guy Rainbird, a former parliamentary aide to Dr David Steel, joined the AIC in 2004 as its first public affairs director, and now leads the charge to promote the industry's case in the UK and Europe.

In practice, over the years, the AIC's lobbying remit means it has spent a lot of time fighting the industry's corner in battles against excessive regulation, much of it from the European Union. It is understandable that investment trusts do not fit very comfortably into many new financial rulebooks. After all, they are a minority structure representing a tiny part of the overall funds market. They are arcane, purely British, and their long histories mean they have odd elements to them such as revenue reserves that are not replicated by funds of other types. It seems that with each new major revision to financial law there is some clause somewhere that has the unintended effect of threatening the structure, or indeed the very existence, of investment trusts. The AIC's role in making representations and submissions on the industry's behalf has been absolutely crucial, and its importance can hardly be overstated.

There have been numerous examples over the years of the AIC pushing back against regulators with little understanding of investment trusts, and it is hard to imagine the industry being in the same strong position today without some crucial interventions. Before the MIFID II rules were due to be introduced at the start of 2018 investment trusts were initially classified in draft proposals as 'complex', meaning there could be severe limitations on how they could be sold. The AIC vigorously lobbied against this, suggesting alternative ways of defining which financial products were complex, and finally prevailed. More recently the AIC has been very vocal in its criticism of the Key Information Documents (KIDs) introduced under the PRIIPS regulations. Regulatory changes can frequently be a burden, but sometimes an opportunity too. The association was instrumental in ensuring that investment trusts were included in the development of Child Trust Funds when they were introduced in 2005, that the structure was considered appropriate for property investment funds, and that financial advisers would be further encouraged to consider investment trusts after the implementation of the Retail Distribution Review (RDR) at the end of 2012.

Perhaps the association's greatest victory in this realm, in measurable terms at least, was its joint case started in 2004 with the trust JPMorgan Claverhouse (JCH) against HM Customs and Excise, challenging whether investment trusts had to pay VAT on management fees, unlike open-ended funds. A long battle, referred to the European Court of Justice, eventually resulted in a victory for the AIC and JPMorgan Claverhouse. As a result HMRC refunded an estimated £300m wrongly collected since 1990, and the ruling saved investment trusts an estimated £40m a year from 2007 onwards.

Promotion

Investment trusts are the little guy, the underdog, when compared to the larger open-ended fund industry. This makes media work of special importance, since it creates an opportunity to present the sector's case on equal terms. Annabel Brodie-Smith,

Communications Director of the AIC, and her colleagues Elmley de la Cour and William Sanderson are continually trying to engage the press with lunches, briefings, training, and press releases. They often have a hand in many of the articles about investment trusts that appear in national newspapers and in the trade press for financial advisers.

Most of these efforts are low-key, often based on personal contact and away from the public glare, but this has not always been the case. One of the most famous episodes in the AIC's recent history was the "its" campaign of 1999-2001. Masterminded by the association's then-head Daniel Godfrey, a former marketing executive, this was a grand scheme based on the idea that the industry needed to recruit new legions of private investors to replace large institutions who had been selling old positions, forcing discounts to widen. A plan was formulated for a bold advertising campaign centred around a bright red "its" logo. The campaign was extensive and expensive, including TV ads accompanied by the Paolo Conte song 'Via Con Me'. A special levy collected £25m for the campaign, which had some success in disseminating information and raising awareness, but the consensus view was that this dashing initiative was largely unsuccessful in creating a new investing constituency at a time when the industry was quite gloomy about its future.

Technical Advice and Guidance

Take a look at the biographies of the board members of any large trust and you will quickly become aware of how experience is valued in the industry. There is a great deal of expertise around, both on these boards and available to them. Nevertheless, with so much regulatory change, combined with changes to taxation and the law, the AIC fulfils a useful role by providing further assistance to its member companies.

Members gain access to a valuable policy and technical library, where one of the most important documents is the AIC Code of Corporate Governance. This provides guidance on 'best practice' to boards, to assist them in delivering the standards that shareholders want and expect. Amongst other things, the AIC has also published a Statement of Recommended Practice (SORP) setting out its latest guidance on accounting practices for investment trusts and VCTs, and it regularly publishes policy papers that present the case for investment trusts in various ways.

In terms of setting standards and identifying best practice for the industry, one annual set of awards arranged by the AIC stands out. The association's Shareholder Communication Awards identify the best annual reports, marketing and PR campaigns, and websites created by member companies. These set benchmarks for the rest of the industry. The 2020 awards for the best report and accounts went to Merchants Trust (MRCH), Allianz Technology Trust (ATT), and 3i Infrastructure (3IN), praised for their clear language, engaging content, and quality of reporting. The prize for best factsheet went to ICG Enterprise Trust (ICGT), and for best website to AVI Global Trust (AGT).

Events and Training

Organising all kinds of regular events and training sessions has been a part of the AIC's role for a long time, but the axis has shifted a little over recent times, away from private investors and towards advisers. Whereas the association used to arrange a number of large regional conferences for private investors, usually with some presentations by fund managers and other experts who would then form a Q&A panel, those have now disappeared in favour of a whole new range of training events for financial advisers and wealth managers, run by Nick Britton, who joined in 2015. This shift reflects the post-"its" campaign and post-RDR environment in which financial advisers, discretionary stockbrokers, and wealth managers are seen as the accessible sources of new demand. Ian Sayers said in 2019 "the changes RDR put in place were a significant step in the right direction to improve financial advice to retail investors. Purchases of investment companies by advisers and wealth managers on adviser platforms have increased five-fold since RDR, from £219m in 2012 to nearly a billion in 2018".[107]

Financial advisers can tap into their own dedicated section on the AIC website for written material, videos, news of industry developments, and online training. Often these advisers are starting from a low base of knowledge, having not previously considered investment trusts, but the AIC material aims to build sufficient confidence for these advisers to start recommending them to clients or buying them on their behalf.

There are events for industry participants too, at least during non-pandemic times. For member firms and their directors there is the AIC Annual Conference, and for VCT Directors the AIC Annual VCT conference, both providing important forums for discussion and a chance to keep abreast of the key developments affecting each sector. Another formal and celebratory occasion is the AIC Annual Dinner, held in one of the large London hotel ballrooms, with a celebrity after-dinner speaker (there is also a summer reception in the City of London). One largely unspoken benefit of these industry events is that they help to build a sense of community and common purpose that serves to unite different people working for different firms, facilitating a useful exchange of ideas. It is quite notable, when attending one of these events, how many people know so many others. The AIC is instrumental in helping to forge these links.

---

[107] AIC press release 1st May 2019

One area in which this 'community spirit' is both evident and useful is in the composition of various specialist AIC committees and forums. Their members are volunteers and include a whole raft of fund managers, stockbroking analysts, industry executives, corporate brokers, and sector specialists, all helping to shape policy and offer their expertise for the good of the industry as a whole. The financial world is not exactly known for its altruism, so it is no mean feat to attract all of this highly-skilled help.

Statistics

For many years, investors looking for an authoritative and reliable source of statistics covering such matters as historical performance, yields, discounts and charges relied on the association's Monthly Information Service (MIS). The MIS was a must-have printed publication that required a lot of effort to compile and disseminate (the AITC, as it was back then, had a Statistics Manager, a Statistics Executive, and a Statistics Assistant), but the advent of plentiful free data on the internet meant the expensive paper service effectively became redundant and was discontinued.

Now, working with Morningstar, the AIC has a whole section of its website devoted to statistics, which you can search, filter, and rank in numerous ways to suit your particular needs. It is easy to underestimate the depth and richness of the data set on offer here, if you are just browsing quickly through the numbers. There is a whole new level of data available by clicking through to individual trust names, at which point another world opens with huge detail of dividend history, NAV and price charts, company documents, company announcements, and much more. This hidden treasure trove is a very useful source, particularly as it gathers information together in a way that is not replicated elsewhere.

Online Presence

In the interests of modernity, efficiency and economy, the AIC has invested heavily in its electronic capability, and that is how it prefers to interact with investors. Its website is packed with useful information, the association has a YouTube channel, it has podcasts, educational guides, news, and it invites questions by email. It does not give advice, but for self-directed investors wanting to learn more and make well-informed decisions for themselves, the site is a very good starting point.

Chapter 12: Managers

At the very heart of the investment trust industry are the people responsible for the day-to-day management of the assets that can ultimately generate wealth, through capital gains or through income. A few are well known, but the majority of firms and individuals are largely anonymous in spite of their key roles. It's worth getting to know them.

Management Groups

Some names are synonymous with the investment trust industry, like JPMorgan, Aberdeen, Henderson, Invesco, BlackRock, and Schroder. The chances are that most investors with even a fleeting interest in the sector will have heard of at least some of these asset managers who have their names attached to multiple trusts and have remained in the sector for many years. It would be wrong to think of the industry as being in any way static though, and although change may happen gradually, the cumulative effects can be substantial. It is a certainty that any list of management firms will require regular updates over time. Let's start with a look at the top management groups ranked by assets under management, and how the list of the top ten has evolved over the last decade.

30th September 2010	Total Assets £m
JPMorgan Asset Management	7017
3i Group	5800
F&C	4785
Baillie Gifford	4329
Aberdeen Asset Management	4176
Henderson Global Investors	3454
Alliance	3002
Invesco	2933
BlackRock Investment Management	2919
Franklin Templeton	2200

Source: AIC

Ten years is a relatively short period for an industry that has been around since 1868, but there has been quite a lot of change since 2010. Only three of the ten asset managers have stayed in the top ten in the same form, namely JPMorgan, Baillie Gifford, and 3i Group. Aberdeen merged with Standard Life, Henderson Global Investors merged with Janus Capital, F&C was acquired by BMO, and places 7-10 have all been replaced by faster-growing firms. One of those is a hedge fund manager, one is an alternative assets manager, and Frostrow Capital is a full scope Alternative Investment Fund Manager (AIFM) that provides services for a number of client trusts.

30th September 2020	Total Assets £m
Baillie Gifford	24157
JPMorgan Asset Management	11778
Aberdeen Standard Investments	9856
BMO Global Asset Management	9840
3i Group	8924
Janus Henderson Investors	6592
Pershing Square Capital Management	5859
Frostrow Capital	4986
Fidelity	4933
InfraRed Capital Partners	4809

Source: AIC

Edinburgh-based Baillie Gifford is now the largest investment trust management group after experiencing a phenomenal five-fold increase in its investment trust assets under management over the last decade. Led by the huge success of its approach with Scottish Mortgage Investment Trust (SMT), Baillie Gifford has developed its ethos as a management house and has become almost evangelical in its advocacy for growth stocks. There is a consistent ideology across all of the group's trusts, and this is not a new fashionable style created to jump on the growth bandwagon in the wake of technology's renewed pre-eminence. Baillie Gifford has been a growth manager for a long time, and its approach has evolved in a thoughtful and progressive way as the managers have continued to learn over years of daily interaction with their portfolios.

Based on independence of thought and a long-term perspective, Baillie Gifford's active management style has brought the firm and – let's not forget – investment trust shareholders great success, but it has not always been an easy path to tread. In the summer of 2013 the firm added an extra manager to the team for Pacific Horizon Investment Trust (PHI) after the chairman said that results had been unsatisfactory and warned "the board holds regular discussions with the managers about the performance of the company and the potential consequences of future unsatisfactory results". In the midst of the credit crisis in 2008, Scottish Mortgage Investment Trust (SMT) saw its NAV halve over the course of two months and the trust came close to breaching the covenants on its long-term debentures.

Patience has paid off for investors though, and this is a central quality to Baillie Gifford's house style, which permeates all of its investment decisions. Charles

Plowden, senior partner of the firm and the manager of Monks Investment Trust (MNKS) says that two types of asymmetry inform the investment process, the first being that all normal equities have the natural imbalance that you can only lose 100% of your stake, but the upside is unlimited and potentially a large multiple if you are a patient, long-term investor. The second asymmetry is that not all equities are equal. He draws on academic research by Professor Hendrik Bessembinder at the WP Carey School of Business in Arizona, showing that big returns are achieved from just a small number of companies. The conclusion Baillie Gifford reaches is that it is very important to find these winners, to accept risk as part of an 'investing to win' strategy. This style is optimistic, and dismissive of those who worry much more about losses and assume big winners are just lucky. Baillie Gifford's research efforts are directed at hunting for growth outliers, the great businesses that can be held for long time periods as they compound exceptional returns. This is why Scottish Mortgage's largest holdings [108] include Tesla, Amazon, and Alibaba, and Monks holds Alphabet, Microsoft, and Naspers.[109]

Baillie Gifford manages twelve (soon to be thirteen) investment trusts, having been successful in winning mandates from trusts undergoing reconstructions. Baillie Gifford European Growth Trust (BGEU) was European Growth Trust, Baillie Gifford UK Growth (BGUK) was Schroder UK Growth, Baillie Gifford China Growth (BGCG) was Witan Pacific, and at the end of 2020 it also won the mandate for Keystone Positive Change Investment Trust, formerly just Keystone. The firm rarely creates new trusts through IPO. Baillie Gifford US Growth (USA) marked its first launch in 32 years when it raised £173m through an IPO in early 2018, followed in 2019 by The Schiehallion Fund (MNTN).

In terms of the number of different investment trusts, JPMorgan and Aberdeen Standard Investments vie for top spot with a total of 44 between them, split 21 and 23 respectively. JPMorgan is a global powerhouse, a major asset manager with something like US$2.2trn under management,[110] and Aberdeen Standard Investments has assets under management of some £456bn.[111] It is perhaps not surprising that these managers have a less unified approach to their numerous trusts, but both emphasise the depth and reach of their resources and the value of fundamental research. JPMorgan was one of the forerunners of the move into emerging markets and in addition to its global emerging markets trusts it maintains four single-country trusts devoted to the BRICs – JPMorgan Brazil (JPB), JPMorgan Russian Securities (JRS),

[108] Scottish Mortgage Investment Trust monthly factsheet 31st October 2020
[109] Monks Investment Trust top ten holdings 31st October 2020
[110] Data from am.jpmorgan.com website, for 31st December 2019
[111] From aberdeenstandard.com website for 30th June 2020

JPMorgan Indian (JII), and JPMorgan China Growth & Income (JCGI). Its largest trust is The Mercantile Investment Trust (MRC) with £1877m[112] of net assets.

Both Aberdeen Asset Management and Standard Life managed investment trusts at the time of their merger in 2017. Dunedin Smaller Companies was merged into Standard Life UK Smaller Companies (SLS), but otherwise the range was re-branded and continued. Its largest trust is Murray International (MYI) with £1395m of net assets.[113]

For a long time in the industry, most trust launches came with a recognisable brand name in a world where big was better. More recently though, and certainly since alternative asset trusts became the real driver of expansion for the sector, many of the management firms are new to investment trusts, and new to even the most experienced of investors. Very often they are smaller, boutique firms with a specialist area of expertise that suits one or two trusts instead of a global range. Outside of the big five broad managers – Baillie Gifford, JPMorgan, Aberdeen Standard Investments, BMO Global Asset Management, and Janus Henderson Investors – the majority of the remaining managers are much narrower in scope and many manage one investment trust only. This presents more of a challenge to investors and analysts required to examine a larger number of asset managers like Amber Infrastructure Group, Sequoia Investment Management, Dragon Capital, Pharmakon Advisers, and Bellevue Asset Management. In corporate terms, there is far greater dispersion of management activity now in the investment trust industry, a shift that reflects the broader and more varied range of assets under management.

The rise of boutique management houses, able to compete with the large behemoths, has also encouraged some individual fund managers with strong reputations to move on and set up their own management firms, taking the mandate for an investment trust with them. This was the case in 2019 when Alexander Darwall, the manager of Jupiter European Opportunities, established his own firm called Devon Equity Management and kept managing the trust, now called European Opportunities Trust (JEO). Of course Neil Woodford did the same thing, with a different outcome.

Fund Managers

There is not too much of a cult of personality in this sector, but from time to time the media will latch on to particular managers with strong performance records, and perhaps a nice turn of phrase, or just a willingness to engage with the press. Neil Woodford was certainly an example, as was Anthony Bolton, plus perhaps Dr Mark

[112] JPMorgan Cazenove Daily Statistics 24th November 2020
[113] JPMorgan Cazenove Daily Statistics 24th November 2020

Mobius, Terry Smith, and Nick Train. These 'star' fund managers can attract large followings that enable them to raise large sums of money and to maintain high ratings on their trusts, but this can also mean sharper falls when they stumble or when their specialist area falls out of favour. If there is one lesson to be learned from the experience of recent years, it is that star fund managers can fall from grace when they try to expand their realm of expertise and deviate from their past successful methodology. This happened with Neil Woodford most dramatically, but also with Anthony Bolton with his Fidelity China Special Situations (FCSS) trust, and to Terry Smith as well with Fundsmith Emerging Equities Trust (FEET). In June 2019 he acknowledged the trust's lacklustre performance at that time, cut the management fee, and handed over the day-to-day management to two colleagues.

The stockbroker Winterflood warns against blindly buying into trusts on the basis of reputation alone. The broker says "investors often like to follow 'star managers' who have become household names. However, it is important to understand whether or not the outperformance is likely to be sustainable. For instance, a manager who performs well with a small fund, may struggle to do so following a significant growth in assets and in some cases they may have to alter their investment process. In addition, they may have to spend more time marketing and the investment trust may no longer be a priority account if substantial sums are being attracted into other vehicles".[114]

While the existence of a star fund manager can be very helpful for marketing, and these managers have generally become stars for a good reason, many fund management firms prefer to emphasise a team approach, deliberately eschewing a star manager culture. They argue that teamwork ensures a rich debate and believe that a more collegiate atmosphere where perspectives and beliefs can be challenged is better for developing an investment process that moves with the times and has more chance of delivering consistent long-term results. Genesis Emerging Markets Fund (GSS) operates with all ten of its partners as portfolio managers, with shared responsibilities divided by country and sector. The managers say the diversity of culture, background, and experience is helpful, and they can collaborate well within a system of constructive challenge. This approach helps to manage biases and also to smooth generational change.

A career in the City, specifically in the well-paid world of fund management, may have been one of the standard routes for privileged male Oxbridge graduates for many years, and it still is, but managers are a more diverse set nowadays, with more women and people from different backgrounds. The individuals who become managers tend to share certain common characteristics, being highly educated, motivated professionals able to articulate their work clearly. They are aware of league tables of performance and the highly scrutinised nature of their work, and they will generally have served fairly

[114] Winterflood 2020 Recommendations, 8th January 2020

long apprenticeships under the wing of more experienced managers. The majority are career fund managers, whilst others have entered the sector from other professions, perhaps as analysts or from specialist roles in particular industries. Dr Carl-Harald Janson, lead manager of International Biotechnology Trust (IBT) was a medical doctor before becoming a fund manager.

Skin in the Game

Besides the subjective measures of professionalism and dedication, there is one objective way that shareholders can gauge the true connection between a fund manager and their trust. Managers are frequently asked whether they back their own judgement and invest in their own trusts, and whilst there is no legal disclosure requirement as there is for directors, this information can be gleaned and is collated in a renowned annual survey by the stockbroking team now at Investec Securities. Called 'Skin in the Game', the report analyses the shareholdings of directors and managers to judge whether these key participants have meaningful personal investments that align their interests with shareholders. The 2019 report[115] found that 74 management teams had holdings worth more than £1m. The largest investments were from the management teams of Pershing Square Holdings (PSH) at £668m, Tetragon Financial Group (TFG) at £257m, and Apax Global Alpha (APAX) at £194m, but Investec question the link with performance after suggesting that the large stakes held by the management of Boussard & Gavaudan (BGHL) at £129m and JZ Capital (JZCP) at £100m perhaps give the managers too much power in cases where the performance records do not justify the high fees paid.

In terms of individual managers, other large stakes included Christopher Mills at North Atlantic Smaller Companies (NAS), Mark Sheppard at Manchester & London (MNL), Alexander Darwall at European Opportunities Trust (JEO), and Nick Train at Finsbury Growth & Income Trust (FGT). Of course the absolute size of these stakes is not necessarily the best measure, as it depends on the wealth of the individuals concerned. Investec Securities say "we take equal comfort from individual portfolio managers who have a significant portion of their wealth invested; for example we recently met with Simon Barnard, manager of Smithson Investment Trust (SSON), who advised that 90% of his investible wealth is in this fund with the balance invested in the Fundsmith Equity Fund".

It would be easy to overstate the importance of skin in the game, but it undoubtedly provides some extra confidence for other shareholders to know that the experience – good or bad – is being shared by those with direct responsibility. It's like asking a chef

[115] Skin in the Game – 2019, 1st November 2019, Investec Securities

if they eat their own cooking, and if a manager does not want to invest in his or her own trust, then it is not so easy to see why you should.

Management Changes

Whether or not large stakes held by managers make them more difficult to change if performance is poor, there is of course a natural turnover of managers as some reach retirement. This is the most frequent reason for changing managers, and it has usually been signalled well in advance so that management firms can implement a succession plan. Most handovers seem smooth, typically to a junior or deputy manager who has already been involved with the portfolio for a number of years. The new manager may well implement some changes to put their own stamp on the portfolio, but without wholesale changes that change the character of the trust.

The stakes are different if a manager is being changed because of poor performance. Sometimes a manager might be shuffled out in favour of a replacement with a different style, but within the same management firm. In that case the new manager might undertake a more radical re-shaping of the portfolio to position it differently to try to capture better returns.

The third category of manager change is those that come as a surprise, because a manager decides to leave, either to move to another firm or to leave the industry. Will Landers left as manager of BlackRock Latin American (BRLA) in March 2019 and was replaced by Ed Kuczma at BlackRock. Carlos Hardenberg left Franklin Templeton in March 2018 to join a new firm established by Mark Mobius, so deputy manager Chetan Sehgal stepped up as manager of Templeton Emerging Markets Investment Trust (TEM). On these occasions it can be more difficult for investors to assess whether the management has been weakened, and this can be equally difficult for boards to assess, although they will sometimes step in to instigate a change. When Alastair Mundy left as manager of Temple Bar Investment Trust (TMPL) for health reasons in early 2020, the board decided to seek a new management firm and moved the contract from Ninety One to RWC Asset Management.

Managing Multiple Trusts

Managers may be dedicated in the sense of being committed, but few are dedicated in the sense of being specific to solely one trust. In theory, having one manager for one trust might be an ideal situation for investors wanting managers to have a very direct sense of accountability, but the reality is different for managers at most management houses. They will also look after open-ended funds and other institutional portfolios. Whilst in public they will certainly say that the investment trust is very important for them as a public face of their work, and that is probably right, in terms of the assets under management it may be a relatively small part of their overall responsibilities.

Some managers may even have responsibility for more than one investment trust. After Neil Woodford left Invesco, Mark Barnett took over as manager of Edinburgh Investment Trust (EDIN), to add to his existing responsibilities as manager of Perpetual Income & Growth (PLI) and Keystone Investment Trust (KIT). That did not work out well, and eventually he relinquished all three. For many years, BlackRock Smaller Companies Trust (BRSC) and BlackRock Throgmorton (THRG) were both managed by Mike Prentis, with considerable overlap in their portfolios. Sam Vecht is the co-manager of BlackRock Frontiers Investment Trust (BRFI) and was the manager of BlackRock Emerging Europe before it wound up in 2018.

Management Styles

Ask a hundred managers to describe their style and methodology, and you'll likely receive a hundred different answers. Every manager likes to believe they have a USP, a unique selling proposition, that is distinctive and can elevate them above the pack. Most managers will have a defined process that they can explain, providing a framework for a disciplined investment approach that can be consistently applied in different market conditions. Flair, gut feeling, and instinct are not descriptions that appear in any presentations, but there are certain classifications that recur quite frequently, albeit with subtle differences.

A rather blunt way of dividing equity managers is as value or growth managers. Value managers are keenly aware of the price they are paying for stocks, looking for cheap ratings and high dividend yields. They may screen for certain target metrics and may focus on free cash flow ratios, price to book ratios, operating margins, return on equity, and sometimes certain proprietary figures derived from models. This approach will often direct managers towards unfashionable companies that are out of favour or underappreciated, making value managers somewhat contrarian. Growth managers, in contrast, may tend more towards stocks with considerable upward momentum, since the focus for them will be on finding sustainable growth in earnings per share, perhaps from disruptive companies, those with strong market positions and defensible 'moats' that mean they can sustain high profit margins and grow their market share over time. In practice, while some managers will accept one or other of these labels, more commonly they are somewhere in the middle, with elements of both in their methodology.

If a manager's techniques are mainly targeted at finding individual stocks with the right characteristics, this is termed 'bottom-up' investing, where the portfolio is constructed from the bottom up. The emphasis here is on finding the best companies, and the overall shape of the portfolio is the outcome of that process. It may be skewed towards particular areas as a result, but true bottom-up managers will not be striving for a well-balanced portfolio across sectors or applicable geographies. A less strict approach may involve a 'macro overlay' being used to incorporate some macroeconomic analysis and views that may build in some specific underweights and overweights.

A middle path is to have a thematic approach, whereby certain themes are identified as a starting point, such as growing healthcare needs for an ageing population, growing environmental awareness, or growing use of internet shopping, and fundamental analysis is then used to identify the most promising companies in those areas.

Depending on the blend of styles that has been adopted by a particular manager, the methods for achieving the end goals will also vary. Some managers participate in huge numbers of company meetings or like to go out on the road to visit company premises and talk to senior management directly, in situ, in normal non-pandemic times. Third-party research might be added to that, plus industry conferences and interviews with customers and competitors. Other managers will be more content to use financial modelling techniques or screens and to rely much more on numeric data for decision-making – there is no particular right or wrong way, but a colourful spectrum of different analytical approaches that work for different techniques at different times in different markets.

Self-Managed Trusts

For trusts that keep their management in-house rather than awarding a contract to an external manager, there are some key differences. Not all boards choose to outsource their management. Instead, some trusts are run more like companies, with their own internal staff who make the investment decisions. Self-managed trusts include Independent Investment Trust (IIT), Scottish Investment Trust (SCIN), RIT Capital Partners (RCP), Hansa Investment Company (HAN, HANA), Utilico Investments (UTL), Picton Property Income (PCTN), and Caledonia Investments (CLDN). Some of these are fairly heavyweight trusts, so this is not a small backwater that can be ignored. Indeed, 3i Group (III) is self-managed. Having its own staff means that a trust can exercise more direct control, adapting its capabilities as it sees fit, and these managers are both committed and dedicated to this single trust. They may also feel more freedom to pursue long-term goals that have been agreed within the trust, even if these underperform for a while, whereas an external fund manager may well feel more pressure to chase short-term performance to keep the contract. On the negative side, it may be harder to change the managers if they are underperforming, and the depth of resources may not be as great as that of a large asset management group.

Multi-Manager Trusts

Witan Investment Trust (WTAN) broke new ground in 2004 when it switched to a multi-manager format, meaning that it outsourced the bulk of its assets not to a single manager, but to several. Rather than allocating 100% of assets to a sole manager, Witan sliced up its portfolio and allocated portions to different specialist managers, arguing that the trust became an umbrella for the best specialist talent in the fund management industry. The trust does not chop and change these managers too frequently, but will adjust the proportions and sometimes switch a manager as different styles become more or less effective at different stages of the market cycle. The structure is flexible, as it is easier to change 10% of the portfolio than to make the massive board decision to move the management contract for the whole lot. Essentially this amounts to a top-down allocation by the trust, and a bottom-up stock selection by the active managers chosen.

This is a quite different approach to management, but one that has since been adopted to a greater or lesser degree by a number of other global trusts, most notably Alliance Trust (ATST). The private equity funds of funds like HarbourVest Global Private Equity (HVPE) arguably take a similar approach, delegating the work of finding good private equity investments to a number of different fund managers. Approaches to multi-manager selection differ, but there is a common belief in the benefits that come from diversification and the greater flexibility to change not just the balance of the assets, but the style as well.

Chapter 13: Directors

Much is made of the independence of investment trust boards – the men and women who are responsible to shareholders for the most fundamental aspects of how trusts function. Yet most of their work is in the shadows and they generally receive much less attention than the managers. Famously described in 2010 by Peter Hargreaves (the co-founder of Hargreaves Lansdown) as "fuddy-duddies", the nature of investment trust boards has been changing, as has their more regular intervention in radical actions to change managers or structure.

Non-Executive Responsibilities

Self-managed trusts can be run much like normal companies, but for the majority of trusts that outsource the daily activities of management, accounting, administration, and company secretarial services, there is no need for full-time executive directors. Instead, a board of non-executive directors (NEDs) takes on the critical role of providing oversight of all of these services. In very simple terms, directors have formal and informal tasks to keep their trusts running smoothly, in compliance with regulations and with the stated objective. They will sign off the report and accounts, decide on the dividend, set policies and limits for gearing and share buybacks, and consider whether the managers are performing as expected.

At each board meeting, due diligence will be carried out to ensure that the manager is adhering to the restrictions and limitations set by the board, and the fund manager will report on a wide range of other matters. F&C Investment Trust (FCIT) says the manager "reports on the investment portfolios; the wider portfolio structure; risks; compliance with borrowing covenants; income, dividend and expense forecasts; errors; internal control procedures; marketing; shareholder and other stakeholder issues, including FCIT's share price discount or premium to NAV; and accounting and regulatory updates".[116] Boards will also consider the trust's position in its peer group, discuss what other trusts might be doing, they may provide support and encouragement to the manager, and perhaps add industry insight in specialist areas, look at ESG issues, examine the costs of all services, review the need for the manager to seek board approval for certain actions, and take into account the views of shareholders. The management of conflicts of interest is an important part of the role, especially in terms of the fees payable to the manager.

There has been an increasing trend towards the professionalism of boards, with more accountants and solicitors used to dealing with the technical aspects of company administration. More recently, though, triggered by the need to encourage greater

[116] F&C Investment Trust Report & Accounts 31st December 2019

diversity – and there are far more women on boards now - the AIC launched a website called 'Pathway' which is designed to encourage a broader range of candidates to consider becoming investment trust non-executive directors. The website[117] suggests that a NED for a typical investment company might require about 15-20 days work in an average year. Many NEDs have multiple positions, and current guidance is that up to five is acceptable in terms of the time commitments. There are a couple of directors with six positions, but five seems to be the current limit by consensus. In terms of gathering wide experience and for the cross-pollination of ideas, it can of course be valuable to have NEDs with existing board seats elsewhere. This is a point highlighted by Brunner Investment Trust (BUT), which says its board "is particularly experienced as its directors also sit on the boards of a number of large companies. So as well as providing shareholders with the reassurance of a diligent environment of checks and balances, they also provide the trust with invaluable knowledge and economic insight".[118]

Pen Pictures

As there are, conveniently, two directors at the top of the list of those with multiple directorships, we can take a small detour and provide a couple of pen pictures of what a director may look like.

Jon Bridel, aged 55, has six directorships, on the boards of Sequoia Economic Infrastructure Income Fund (SEQI), The Renewables Infrastructure Group (TRIG), Fair Oaks Income Fund (FAIR), Starwood European Real Estate (SWEF), SME Credit Realisation Fund (SCRF), and DP Aircraft 1 (DPA). He is a resident of Guernsey, which gives him an advantage because while Guernsey-registered investment companies are not required to have directors resident in Guernsey, it does ease some administration. All six of these trusts are domiciled in Guernsey. Mr Bridel, a chartered accountant previously with Price Waterhouse, was Managing Director of Royal Bank of Canada's investment businesses in the Channel Islands. He also has an MBA and a number of other professional qualifications.

Sue Inglis did have six posts as a director, but has shed one, retaining Bankers Investment Trust (BNKR), BMO Managed Portfolio Growth/Income (BMPG/BMPI), Seneca Global Income & Growth (SIGT), Baillie Gifford US Growth (USA), and NextEnergy Solar Fund (NESF). She has over 30 years' experience in advising investment companies and financial institutions. Sue is a qualified lawyer, and was a partner, and head of the funds and financial services group, at Shepherd & Wedderburn, a leading Scottish law firm. In 1999 she was a founding partner of Intelli

---

[117] http://www.theaic.co.uk/pathway

[118] www.brunner.co.uk, Meet The Team, October 2020

Corporate Finance, an advisory boutique firm focusing on the asset management and investment company sectors which was acquired by Canaccord Genuity in 2009. Before embarking on a non-executive career, Sue's executive roles included Managing Director – Corporate Finance in the Investment Companies teams at Cantor Fitzgerald Europe (2012-2018) and Canaccord Genuity (2009-2012).

You will find descriptions like these in the annual reports of trusts, to help you evaluate the board members and to understand exactly who these guardians of the assets are. There are accountants and lawyers aplenty, equipped with good core skills for the tasks required, but they may be surrounded by a greater variety of experienced people in the future if current trends persist.

Skin in the Game

Part of the joy of analysing investment trusts rather than open-ended funds is the greater range of public information and disclosure, and directors' dealings are a part of that additional material. Directors are required to disclose all changes in their shareholdings, and whilst there may not be very much to be gained from following director buying, it can be an expression of confidence when boards add meaningfully to their shareholdings.

The annual 'Skin in the Game' Investec Securities study of shareholdings[119] includes those held by directors, and also reveals some other useful findings. The stockbroker finds that 27.9% of directors are women, up from 8% in 2010; that 50 directors have holdings worth more than £1m, but that excluding 2019 appointments, 10% of directors have no personal investment at all; and that 94.6% of directors are independent. It does stand out when boards have no investment, and five are highlighted where there is no investment at all by any board members, namely Carador Income Fund (CIFU), Ground Rents Income Fund (GRIO), Axiom European Financial Debt (AXI), Honeycomb Investment Trust (HONY) and Boussard & Gavaudan (BGHS).

Independence

In view of the sometimes difficult decisions that must be made about managerial fees, limits and restrictions, and on occasions, managerial changes, the need for board members to be independent of the manager is of great importance. This is a weakness of the self-managed model, where the board members are executive and are effectively overseeing their own work. For NEDs though, there are guidelines laid down by the AIC's Code of Corporate Governance that lay down exactly what independence means,

[119] Skin in the Game – 2019, 1st November 2019, Investec Securities

and the code says that a majority of directors for each board should be independent. Some of the criteria are obvious, so an employee or recent employee of the manager would not be independent, nor would an adviser providing services to the trust, nor someone representing a significant shareholder. Perhaps less obvious is the point that whilst directors can sit on the board of more than one company managed by the same manager, they will not be regarded as independent if they do. A director serving for more than nine years from the date of their first appointment is not considered independent either, presumably because they are at risk of having forged too close a relationship with existing managers and service providers, and with the status quo more generally.

Boards in Action

Whilst a lot of work by boards is routine and is about keeping the trust shipshape and moving in the right direction with little friction, boards do sometimes take difficult decisions that can even mean voting themselves out of a job. Many boards have negotiated management fees lower over recent years, some have decided to wind-up, others have accepted mergers or takeovers, and of course a number have broken the news to their managers that they are losing the contract. At the really critical flashpoints in a trust's history it is the board that is responsible for the most important decisions, even if they are referred to shareholders for approval. Clare Dobie was a director of Alliance Trust (ATST) as it navigated its way through a period of change, and told an AIC roundtable in 2018[120] "the board of Alliance Trust has completely transformed the £3bn trust. It has introduced a new investment approach, changed the manager, streamlined the corporate structure, seen off an activist investor and more. It has set a demanding performance target for the equity portfolio, which it is in line to meet. In summary it has undertaken a radical overhaul of a 130-year-old investment trust for the benefit of shareholders. The board has led this work and continues to oversee progress." This was recognised when Alliance Trust won the 'best board' award in the Citywire Investment Trust Awards 2019.

When Perpetual Income & Growth Investment Trust (PLI) decided in April 2020 to seek a new manager, it was the chairman of Murray Income Trust (MUT), Neil Rogan, who immediately saw the potential for a merger to reduce costs and benefit his shareholders. In an interview with Rob Murphy of Edison Group,[121] Neil Rogan explained how he worked with the managers of his trust, Aberdeen, to approach PLI and join the 'beauty parade' of managers pitching for the business, with of course this different element, suggesting a merger rather than taking over the mandate. The result, once the merger proposal was accepted, was the management fee coming down from

---

[120] The role and impact of investment company boards, AIC roundtable 2nd October 2018

[121] Chairman's insight: Murray Income Trust, Edison, 20th November 2020

about 0.50% to 0.38% of assets, and of course with extra liquidity and qualification for entry into the FTSE 250 Index to attract larger investors. One interesting aside from the same interview was that revenue reserves cannot be transferred in a merger, so those were instead paid out as a special dividend to the shareholders of PLI before the transaction was completed. The dilution of revenue reserves for MUT was a disadvantage of the arrangement, but the chairman believed this was outweighed by the cost-saving benefits.

Most of the time, boards seem to do a good job of protecting shareholder interests. Very occasionally there is news of some technical breach of company law or an accounting issue that causes a problem with the investment trust tax status, but this is rare. As an extra layer of governance, it is perhaps the 'soft' skills of boards that are least appreciated: directors can work to encourage better performance and to act as a guide for the manager, challenging them and keeping them accountable for their actions and performance.

Chapter 14: Stockbrokers and Third-Party Research Firms

Stockbrokers perform a dual role in the investment trust world, and there is a well-established community of firms that provide corporate broking services to the industry and publish regular research on trusts as well. Much of this work is effectively hidden from private investors though, who are frozen out by regulators more than commercial concerns. More accessible is a new breed of service provider paid by trusts to promote them through written profiles and videos. These firms have opened up new channels of communication between trusts and investors, and as a result there is probably more in-depth information available to all potential buyers than ever before.

Corporate Broking

Trusts will have an arrangement with one or more stockbrokers to perform corporate actions on their behalf and to advise them on market-related matters. If the trust is raising money, whether through an IPO or a secondary fund-raising, the stockbroker will play an important role in advising on the structure of the offer and its likely success, and then helping the trust reach the relevant clients. The broker will make a market in the trust's shares, to ensure liquidity for investors. If a trust is buying back shares, that is the job of the broker. If trusts are thinking about share splits or consolidations, or if a major shareholder wants to exit, or a new institution wants to take a big stake, or there is a monthly savings scheme to buy shares, or the trust is involved in any kind of merger or takeover, these are all times when the corporate broker is an important adviser and a link between the trust and investors. Importantly, because the corporate broker will have inside information on the intentions of trusts, this side of the business must be entirely separate from the research side, which provides information to the market, details on the trust's structure and approach, and an opinion on its likely future performance. This level of communication can be vital in helping to maintain a liquid two-way flow of trade in the shares.

Research

The sell-side research provided by stockbrokers has traditionally taken the form of a research note, which may be devoted to a single trust, a sector or theme, or the whole industry. Varying in length from a couple of pages to 50 or more for a really detailed analysis, it will typically outline the case for a trust, with a critical examination, and end with a buy, hold, or sell recommendation (sometimes classified as overweight, neutral, and underweight). Research output may also take the form of manager interview notes, news round-ups, analysis of discounts or price movements, or specialist reports on certain aspects of the industry, including a hefty annual review. Most of this work is of a high quality, produced by serious-minded and experienced analysts. If you are not an early riser, or you like the idea of skipping a day's work every now and then, the bad news is that you are probably not suited to the job of investment trust analyst. Every working day of the year, without fail, stockbrokers produce and despatch statistics and news summaries to their client lists, with much of it landing in email boxes before the working day begins for many.

It is useful to note when reading a research item whether the trust involved is a client of the broker concerned. If so, the conclusion is highly unlikely to be negative – that is just the nature of the business, but it does mean that some material needs to be read with an educated eye. Information on the distribution of ratings, as well as the history of ratings for any given share is now part of the statutory disclosures that form part of a lengthy appendix to all brokers' notes. Other information includes the name of the analyst, whether their remuneration is linked to the advice, and whether the broker provides services to the trust(s) concerned.

Stockbrokers also organise regular conferences during non-pandemic times, at which several trust managers may present to the audience of industry professionals. Brokers may also take some managers out on the road, to tour major conurbations and meet regional wealth managers, discretionary brokers, and advisers.

Getting access to this broker research and the ancillary services is not easy. Generally you will need to be a client of these large broking firms, and that means having a very large portfolio, and even then the MIFID II rules may mean you are required to pay a hefty fee. If you are an influential adviser, perhaps you will be lucky enough to get on a distribution list or two. As a private investor you don't get a look-in. The only way you are likely to see this research is if it happens to be disseminated by a third party. Occasionally the AIC will send round a particularly interesting sector note to its distribution list, and it has long been a popular section of the Investment Trust Newsletter, which provides a short monthly précis of some of the research. The stumbling block here is not so much the brokers themselves, who see the benefit of their research being more widely distributed as long as their key clients still get to see it first. It is more of a regulatory issue, as brokers classify the documents as being for professional investors only, with a specific set of disclosures and risk warnings that are suitable for that audience, and not for retail investors where the bar is set much higher. There is no real reason for these brokers to engage with private investors, where they open themselves up to the risk of research being misunderstood and misapplied, with scope for messy complaints, so the limited circulation is a form of self-protection. Some research is digitally watermarked with the name of the recipient to ensure it is not circulated surreptitiously.

Stockbroking Firms

Broking is a fluid, dynamic sector in which firms regularly enter and exit market segments, merge and take over others, and where teams of analysts move firms when the music stops. The major stockbrokers in the sector have changed almost completely over the years, and it seems nostalgic now to mention names like BZW, Merrill Lynch, SBC Warburg, Credit Lyonnais Laing, James Capel, Arbuthnot Securities, UBS, and NatWest Securities. In a fast-moving segment, the following thirteen firms may not constitute an exhaustive list, but some of the main players in the sector are very well established.

Alvarium Securities is a newcomer to the sector, launched in June 2020 and headed by Mark Thompson and Eddie Nissan, formerly at Peel Hunt and JPMorgan Cazenove. They have been involved in raising in excess of £4bn over the previous five years, launching investment trust IPOs and being ranked by Extel as the top salespeople for investment trusts. They successfully launched Home REIT (HOME) in October 2020, raising £240m at a tricky time for new launches.

Cenkos Securities is a UK securities business that provides a full suite of services to investment companies from corporate finance through to sales, trading, corporate broking and strategy. Its sector team was formed in 2006, and since then has raised over £7bn for clients through a combination of both primary and secondary fund raises. Cenkos is corporate broker to about twenty investment companies including a number of FTSE 250 constituents. Cenkos does not produce written research, but organises contact between client trusts and institutional investors through meetings and seminars.

Next up, finnCap's listed-funds team has expertise in the emerging market and alternative funds sectors, especially real estate, debt and private equity, and complex transactions. It sponsors a wide range of corporate transactions, including fundraisings, changes of structure and changes of policy. It makes markets in investment companies' shares and is one of the largest RSPs (Retail Service Providers) providing electronic quotes for shares. finnCap's research director for investment companies, Monica Tepes, also provides some individual stock or thematic written research, primarily focused on the alternative funds market.

The team at Investec Securities is a seasoned collection of professionals who moved over from Canaccord Genuity in June 2019, having previously been together at Collins Stewart Europe, Dresdner Kleinwort, and NatWest Securities. They cover corporate broking, sales, trading, market-making, and research, the latter written by Alan Brierley and Ben Newell. Their annual 'Skin in the Game' report is a well-known piece of research, and it is just a small part of the regular research output covering trusts across the sector.

Jefferies International is part of a US diversified financial services company that acts as corporate broker and financial adviser to a number of mainly US-related or alternative asset investment companies, including SDCL Energy Efficiency Income Trust (SEIT), Sequoia Economic Infrastructure Income Fund (SEQI), US Solar Fund (USA), RTW Venture Fund (RTW), and Gresham House Energy Storage Fund (GRID). It arranged the asset swap for AVI Global Trust (AGT) in relation to its holding in Pershing Square Holdings (PSH).

JPMorgan Cazenove is wholly-owned by the huge US bank JPMorgan, having initially been a joint venture between JPMorgan and the UK investment bank Cazenove. It offers services to institutional clients across the range of corporate finance, sales and trading, market making, and a detailed research offering. Christopher Brown and his team produce daily research notes and detailed statistics, plus a model portfolio, a detailed annual review, individual trust notes, and useful links to other JPMorgan analyst research. Meetings and seminars are also organised for, and offered to, institutional clients.

Liberum Capital was formed in 2007 as a wholly staff-owned business and has carved out a niche for itself in an alternative assets space, working with trusts like Merian Chrysalis Investment Company (MERI), The Renewables Infrastructure Group (TRIG), Real Estate Credit Investments (RECI), and AEW UK REIT (AEWU) to raise capital. The broker's research team of Conor Finn and James Shields releases daily updates on alternative asset trusts and occasional detailed notes.

N+1 Singer has a dedicated investment funds team of five professionals that focuses on equity raising and market intelligence, helping to match trusts with the right investors. Over the last twelve years the team has helped to raise over £4bn for new funds and has advised boards on capital raisings, M&A and restructurings. It is joint corporate broker to Hipgnosis Songs Fund (SONG) with JPMorgan Cazenove, and includes Artemis Alpha Trust (ATS), Atlantis Japan Growth Fund (AJG), Augmentum Fintech (AUGM), The PRS REIT (PRSR), and Urban Logistics REIT (SHED) on its client list. Paul Glover and Markus Jaffe write regular notes on client trusts and are active in promoting trusts through direct contact with investors around the country.

An investment bank that proudly claims to have the largest client base by number of corporates in the UK, Numis Securities has a sizeable investment companies business. Twenty professionals provide a full range of services comprising research, sales, trading and corporate broking/finance. Numis says its research-driven approach focuses on investment companies with specialist or differentiated mandates, including quoted equity, emerging markets, private equity, hedge funds, property and other alternative assets. Its research (classified as marketing communications) includes a daily data sheet covering all UK-traded funds as well as regular fund-specific and broader-based research offering insight into individual companies and specific asset classes. It also organises lunches, conferences and seminars for clients. Following the retirement of Charles Cade in 2019, the research team is headed by Ewan Lovett-Turner. Numis makes markets in around 300 trusts traded on the London Stock Exchange, including all funds in the FTSE 350 Index, and also offers an electronic dealing service which provides access to order flow from retail brokers. The corporate team is retained as broker/adviser by 44 investment companies and has raised around £3.8bn primary and secondary capital for clients over the past three years.

Panmure Gordon's closed-end funds team focuses on primary and secondary distribution (contact with investors) supported by in-depth research, plus corporate finance advice. The broker produces what it calls 'sponsored research' on its client trusts, including Polar Capital Global Healthcare (PCGH), The Diverse Income Trust (DIVI), Civitas Social Housing (CSH), Gresham House Strategic (GHS), European Assets Trust (EAT), BMO Real Estate Investment Trust (BREI), and Alternative Income REIT (AIRE).

Shore Capital was the financial adviser and sole book runner for Nippon Active Value Fund (NAVF), the last IPO to get away in the investment trust sector before the start of the pandemic lock-down in 2020. It also raised money for Gore Street Energy Storage Fund (GSF), LMS Capital (LMS), and was the broker for the Buffettology Smaller Companies Investment Trust that tested the waters for an IPO in November 2020 before deciding there was insufficient demand. Other clients include Canadian General Investments (CGI), Downing Strategic Micro-Cap (DSM), and NextEnergy Solar Fund (NESF). Its main focus is on distribution, with reports on its house stocks, plus regular roadshows and events during non-pandemic times.

One name not that well known in the UK, but a staple of the investment trust industry now is Stifel, a US financial services firm founded in St Louis. The firm is corporate broker to more than 20 investment trusts, including BlackRock Throgmorton (THRG), Fidelity Japan Trust (FJV), GCP Student Living (DIGS), Murray International (MYI), Polar Capital Technology Trust (PCT), and TR Property (TRY). It is also well endowed with four research analysts, Iain Scouller (formerly at UBS and Oriel Securities), Anthony Stern, Sachin Saggar, and Max Haycock, who produce a lot of written research through daily update notes and more detailed papers. They also organise seminars and conferences for industry professionals.

Winterflood has a high profile in the industry and claims to be the largest dedicated investment trusts team in the sector offering a full range of services and with the strength and depth to provide trading, sales, research and corporate advice. Winterflood Securities, a subsidiary of Close Brothers Group, is an international capital markets firm based in London, covering more UK stocks as a market maker than any other firm. Winterflood says its strengths lie in a combination of traditional trading values and the performance of its own proprietary cutting-edge technology. The trust team has been an integral part of the firm since 2002. The analyst team of four led by Simon Elliott provides broad sector coverage, with daily data feeds, monthly sector reports, a model portfolio, plus major annual conferences in London and Edinburgh. They published 142 research notes in 2019, and Simon features regularly in podcasts, videos, and on awards committees.

Third-Party Research Firms

Needing to report concrete figures for the number of meetings with potential investors and the number of published reports on the trust, managers have stepped beyond the boundaries of traditional stockbrokers in their quest for additional coverage and distribution at a time when increasing regulation has become a burden under the MIFID II regime. Other firms have sprung up to service this new need, writing paid-for research and taking managers around the country to meet prospective shareholders, and then adding video conferencing once the Covid-19 pandemic struck.

Founded in 2008, Kepler Partners produces non-independent marketing communications in the form of broker-style research notes, together with conference calls, webinars and presentations by fund managers. It acknowledges that its commercial relationship with its client trusts may impair its objectivity, but this does not mean that its reports are without value. They are often written in close liaison with the trusts themselves, meaning they are well fact-checked and can contain valuable insights about the managers' approach and latest views. They are available online[122] and are free to access. There are two versions of the site, for investors and for wealth managers, but apart from the ability to request meetings and sign up for the direct access to managers that is restricted to professionals, the written material seems much the same, with some tweaked risk warnings. This has never been the case for broker research, so the introduction of this third-party material has played an important role in democratising the sector and going some way towards levelling the playing field for private investors. Counting the number of clients on Kepler's website[123] indicates that it has gone a long way to providing broad coverage of the sector, with reports on 189 trusts. Some of these are branded with a 'Kepler growth rating' or 'Kepler income rating' that labels them as outstanding options for investors seeking growth or income, so there seems to be an element of advice here too. Using quantitative screens, they

[122] http://www.trustintelligence.co.uk
[123] As of 27th October 2020

have selected what they regard as the twenty best trusts in their classes over the past five years. Kepler also maintains a 'discounted opportunities shortlist' with a collection of trusts they believe are trading on attractively wide discounts in double figures with the potential to close.

There's little doubt that Kepler has brought something valuable to the industry, adding an extra layer of analysis and relationships to help investment trusts reach new buyers or to encourage existing shareholders to build their holdings.

Edison Group is another research firm, this time with a broader reach across different industries and geographies, but with a large core rooted in investment trusts. The industry accounts for more than 15% of its overall client list, with 67 trusts signed up.[124] Like Kepler, Edison produces paid-for research reports that are detailed and regular, and the company also arranges roadshows for managers, taking them to meet prospective shareholders and their advisers. As part of its admirably detailed disclaimer, Edison says that its standard fees are £49,500 per year for the production and broad dissemination of a detailed note followed by regular updates, with separate payment for roadshows and other investor relations services. That's a not insignificant fee, but one that underscores the growing importance of research firms and their well-developed reach into the wealth manager, stockbroking, family office, and adviser communities. Both Edison and Kepler work hard to foster relationships with these groups to ensure their distribution is up to scratch.

Slightly different is Marten & Co, a boutique advisory business that specialises in research, investor relations and asset-raising. It trades as QuotedData and through its website[125] it provides news, research and information on the sector, free of charge to all investors. The portal has some depth to it, with statistics and educational guides to back up the news and analysis. It is a more explicit aim here to spread the information to all, and the company says "today, seasoned investors are finding it harder to access reliable research as traditional investment banks scale back their research output". The same commercial model is applied, with the notes all being paid-for research, again written by experienced industry individuals. Heading the investment company research is James Carthew, a former investment trust manager who writes articles and hosts interviews and presentations from managers. The company also supports trusts with distribution.

Hardman & Co is another research provider that works with investment companies to help them communicate with investors. Clients include ICG Enterprise Trust (ICGT), Oakley Capital Investments (OCI), Pantheon International (PIN), Real Estate Credit

[124] As of 27th October 2020; http://www.edisongroup.com
[125] http://www.quoteddata.com

Investments (RECI), and Volta Finance (VTA). The research analyst Mark Thomas produces detailed notes and updates.

So whilst private investors may not be able to get hold of analyst research from the leading stockbrokers in the sector, they can reach out and obtain thorough and in-depth information on trusts from these third-party providers, all at the click – or a few clicks – of a mouse. The two-tier system is still in play though, and professional investors or advisers fortunate enough to be able to tap into all of the available research are still in a superior position. And in our strange regulatory world where certain regulations seem to apply haphazardly to some types of firm and not to others, all stockbrokers have a variation of the same disclosure as Investec Securities, that "this report may only be issued to professional clients, eligible counterparties and investment professionals, as described in S19 of the Financial Services and Markets Act 2000 (Financial Promotions) Order 2005 and is not intended for retail clients".[126] The information advantage may have narrowed, but it seems unlikely to disappear.

[126] Investec Securities research note, 8th October 2020

Chapter 15: Shareholders

When you buy shares in an investment trust you own a small slice of the company and its assets. This gives you certain rights, including the right to vote on certain proposals and to attend an Annual General Meeting (AGM). Your fellow shareholders might be your neighbours or they might be large institutional investors with different aims to yours, but this anonymity does not shroud their importance. From their decisions to buy and sell, to their votes on crucial changes and their influence on future investing policy, shareholders are at the centre of this industry.

Who Owns Investment Trusts?

This simple question has been the subject of a lot of navel-gazing over many years as those who seek to shape the future of the sector consider who the next generation of buyers is likely to be. To understand how to fine-tune the appeal of investment trusts and their characteristics, there needs to be a target market.

In the 1980s the holders of investment trusts that mattered were mainly institutions like pension funds and insurance companies. Their large stakes dominated share registers, but as the investing world became more sophisticated and these shareholders began to realise they could replicate most of these investments themselves, without paying fees and costs, so they began to step away, sell their stakes, and discounts widened. The industry fretted at length about who might step in to restore equilibrium, and the 'its' campaign was born at the turn of the century to attract private investors. That may not have worked particularly well at the time, but the ship righted itself as wealth managers moved into the sector. More recently, private investors have returned as well, encouraged by greater media attention, problems with open-ended funds, and – critically – the aftermath of RDR which has seen many individual investors abandon expensive financial advisers to become 'self-directed' investors making their own decisions.

Investment trust management groups are sometimes fairly tight-lipped about exactly who owns their shares, although stakes over 3% must be declared to the stock exchange. Shareholder registers are no longer the treasure trove they once were, either. The problem is that as electronic share trading through platform stockbrokers has grown in popularity, so more and more holdings are held through nominee accounts (for speed, cost, and simplicity), which means the individual holdings are no longer recorded. In times past, private investors would have executed the deal with their stockbroker and their names and addresses would be entered on to the shareholder register. Some time later, a paper certificate would arrive in the post, and that would need to be returned when the shares were sold. The trust would have access to the share register and to the details of all shareholders. Now, when clients of a large platform broking firm like Hargreaves Lansdown deal, all that happens is a small adjustment to the large number of shares held by Hargreaves Lansdown Nominees Limited. Individual owners who trade shares in this way are no longer identified, making them hard to reach for marketing purposes.

A detailed study[127] by Richard Davies Investor Relations (known as RD:IR) and the consultancy Warhorse Partners has examined share register data for over 220 UK-listed investment companies, reaching the conclusion that sophisticated retail investors are emerging as the driving force behind a resurgence in demand for investment trusts. The study found that private investors, mostly investing directly through online platforms, are putting new money into investment trusts more than three times as fast as the largest wealth managers are cutting back on their holdings. Direct to consumer shareholders – individuals – now account for an estimated 35% of the market capitalisation of the sector, their largest ever percentage after buying a net £6.7bn of investment trusts in 2019. Many invest through Hargreaves Lansdown, Interactive Investor, and AJ Bell. Institutions account for around 29%, with just ten institutions accounting for half of that amount. Wealth managers are next at 28%, after reducing their exposure to investment trusts by £1.8bn during 2019. Independent regional brokers account for 6%, and adviser platforms 2%.

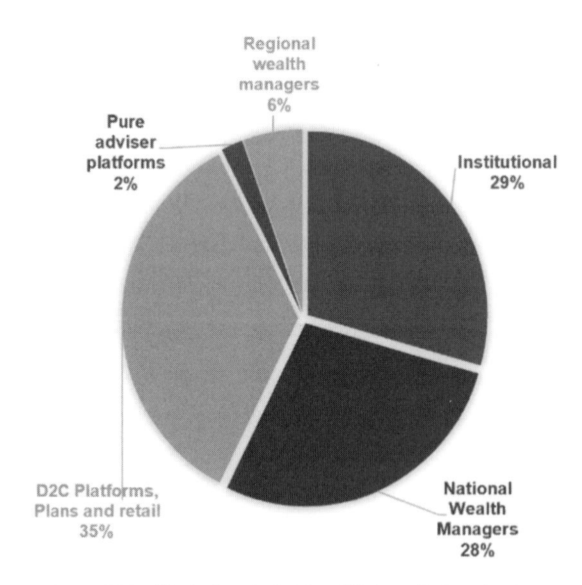

Investment trusts ownership by shareholder type, end 2019; source Richard Davies Investor Relations and Warhorse Partners

[127] Investment Trusts: changing ownership trends 2019, Richard Davies Investor Relations Limited and Warhorse Partners, June 2020

When reporting that only 31 investing institutions remain now with more than £50m in the sector, way down from the figures from twenty years ago, when there were 200 institutions, the RD:IR/Warhorse study refers to the AIC's Colson Liquidity Report 2012[128] and the fact that this group has different needs and expectations. That report, from Dr Simon J Colson, was about demand, supply, and trading of investment trust shares on the secondary market, and was an update to an original report from 2002. Dr Colson actually reached many insightful conclusions on quite a wide range of matters, and said that institutional investors were quite different from all other groups in welcoming discount volatility as a chance to exploit pricing anomalies.

Back to the RD:IR/Warhorse report, it said that the institutional owners of investment trusts are now dominated by index funds that are required to hold those trusts that are constituents of the major FTSE indices. The traditional institutional investors, the local authorities, pension funds, and insurance companies, have largely left. Thankfully, private investors have stepped in to take up the slack and now form the largest single cohort of shareholders by type. This renaissance of investment by individuals is supported too by broader data from the Office for National Statistics, which also notes that individuals' shareholdings have begun to rise in recent years after a long decline. In 1963, the ONS says that individuals owned approximately 54% of UK quoted shares in terms of total value. This dropped to a low of 10.2% in 2008, since when it has risen modestly to stand at 13.5% at the end of 2018.[129]

The ONS does also release some data on shareholdings in investment trusts that allow some comparison over time, although the categories have changed a little.

	2018	2010
Individuals	38.3%	20.6%
Charities	1.3%	0.9%
Insurance companies	2.4%	5.7%
Pension funds	1.3%	1.8%
Investment trusts	4.2%	1.1%
Unit trusts	0.4%	0.2%
Banks	0.6%	0.9%
Other financial institutions	3.4%	9.9%
Private non-financial companies	1.2%	0.2%
Rest of the world	1.8%	1.8%
Multiple ownership pooled nominees	45.0%	43.9%
Excluded	-	12.8%

Shareholdings in investment trusts, 31st December 2018 and 31st December 2010; source ONS

[128] Secondary liquidity in the investment company sector, a report by Dr Simon J Colson on behalf of the AIC, 2012
[129] Ownership of UK quoted shares: 2018, Office for National Statistics

This data again confirms the rising importance of individuals investors to the investment trust sector, and it also reveals one other salient yet often unspoken truth. The percentage ownership outside the UK is very low at 1.8% - investment trusts are very much a British structure that appeals to British investors. Amongst this group though, there remains an exclusivity that is hard to explain in a world of free information and easy access. For a large chunk of the British population, the stock market generally and investment trusts more specifically are never likely to even be considered. Research by Alliance Trust (ATST) in December 2020[130] found that 56% of respondents thought that investing was "too much of a gamble", and 20% said that investing was too complex for them. More than a third said that nothing would make them more likely to invest their cash, in spite of rock-bottom returns on savings left in interest accounts. It is frustrating that so many minds are closed to the possibility of sensible investing.

Generally though, the growth of the retail segment is very welcome for the industry, and private investors are usually a positive addition to a shareholder register. Individuals are often more loyal and long-term in outlook, and their trades are less likely anyway to cause discount volatility than a larger investor moving in and out. They can also help investment trusts to stay on the right side of the regulators – in mid 2020 the Aberdeen Emerging Markets Investment Company (AEMC) ran into an issue because of the concentrated nature of its shareholder register, with most shares held by larger investors with stakes of more than 5%. Under the listing rules, investment companies must have at least 25% of shares as a free float, in public hands, to ensure sufficient liquidity for market transactions.

Differences Across Sectors

Aggregate figures and generalisations across an industry can obscure considerable variation and differences between trusts. The big traditional global equity investment trusts like Alliance Trust (ATST), Bankers Investment Trust (BNKR), F&C Investment Trust (FCIT), Monks Investment Trust (MNKS), and Scottish Mortgage Investment Trust (SMT) will naturally be used much more by private investors who use these trusts as long-term savings vehicles. Sadly, it is much harder now to get accurate figures for who owns individual trusts without trawling through individual share registers and getting stuck into some detective work. Shareholder analysis provided by trusts can be opaque too – Monks Investment Trust (MNKS) says in its latest annual report[131] that institutions own 16.9% of the shares, intermediaries 77.1%, individuals 5.8%, and market makers 0.2%. Presumably, that broad and vague classification of 'intermediaries' includes platforms, but it is hard to tell. Scottish Mortgage Investment

[130] Alliance Trust press release 8th December 2020

[131] The Monks Investment Trust Annual Report and Financial Statements 30th April 2020

Trust (SMT) uses a similar classification,[132] although it clarifies that 'intermediaries' (77.9% ownership) includes both wealth managers and execution-only platforms.

UK equity trusts are likely to be largely of interest to individuals too, and Fidelity Special Values (FSV) provides a useful analysis of shareholders in its annual report,[133] indicating that private shareholders, including Fidelity platform investors, account for 86.5% of the shares, with 8.6% institutions, 2.5% pensions, 1.8% insurance companies, and a small tail of others.

For more specialist trusts there is probably a middle path, where these are attractive to private investors but also to professionals who need to outsource the management in these areas. BlackRock Frontiers Investment Trust (BRFI), which invests in some out-of-the-way markets around the world, provides some analysis of its 884 shareholders in its annual report.[134] Again, the breakdown by type is not helpful, listing "banks or nominees" as 76.8% of the share ownership and individuals at 20.4%, but the breakdown by type of client might perhaps be inferred by the breakdown by size of holding. Under the rough and ready assumption that most of the holdings under 100,000 shares (worth around £132,000 at the 30th September 2019 closing price of 132p per share) are probably private investors and those larger than that are probably institutions, the split is 80.7% smaller, 19.3% larger.

There is also a category of investment trust (more properly here, investment company) that is most likely to be held by mainly professional investors. Complex and sophisticated trusts, particularly those listed on the specialist fund segment of the London Stock Exchange, are not targeted at retail investors and will try to restrict the availability of information accordingly. Some of these shares may not be available to trade on popular platforms. The investment companies listed on the specialist fund segment in September 2020[135] are Africa Opportunity Fund (AOF), Alpha Real Trust (ARTL), Amedeo Air Four Plus (AA4), Biopharma Credit (BPCR), CATCO Reinsurance (CAT, CATC), Ceiba Investments (CBA), Chenavari Capital Solutions (CCSL), Chenavari Toro Income Fund (TORO), Doric Nimrod Air One (DNA), Doric Nimrod Air Two (DNA2), Doric Nimrod Air Three (DNA3), DP Aircraft 1 (DPA), EJF Investments (EJFI), Fair Oaks Income (FAIR), Gabelli Merger Plus+ (GMP), Gresham House Energy Storage Fund (GRID), Honeycomb Investment Trust (HONY), JZ Capital Partners (JZCP), Life Settlement Assets (LFAA, LFAB), Marble Point Loan Financing (MPLF, MPLS), Marwyn Value Investors (MVI, MVIR), NB Distressed Debt (NBDD, NBDG, NBDX), NB Private Equity (NBDG, NBDX), Nippon Active Value Fund (NAVF), Oakley Capital Investments (OCI), The PRS

[132] Scottish Mortgage Investment Trust Annual Report and Financial Statements 31st March 2020

[133] Fidelity Special Values Annual Report 2020

[134] BlackRock Frontiers Investment Trust Annual Report and Financial Statements 30th September 2019

[135] London Stock Exchange, SFS Instrument List 30th September 2020

REIT (PRSR), Riverstone Credit Opportunities (RCOI), RTW Venture Fund (RTW), Secured Income Fund (SSIF), Stenprop (STP), Supermarket Income REIT (SUPR), Tetragon Financial Group (TFG, TFGS), The Schiehallion Fund (MNTN), Trian Investors 1 (TI1), Tufton Oceanic Assets (SHIP), UIL (UTL), and UK Mortgages (UKML).

Votes and Rights

Substantial efforts have been made to try to overcome the problems created by the development of platform stockbrokers in relation to voting rights. In times past, when private investors were identified separately on shareholder registers, they could easily be sent a notice of the AGM and the relevant voting slips. When platforms first arrived with their nominee accounts, shareholders using these services were effectively disenfranchised, and it has been a struggle since to persuade private investors to vote on board appointments, authorise share buybacks or share issuance, approve the dividend, or approve the trusts' remuneration policies. Much of this is down to apathy and the routine nature of the majority of these votes, but there are occasions when votes can be important, and marginal. Continuation votes are an obvious example, where it is not just the outcome that is important, but the numbers themselves as a vote of confidence (or not) in the trust. A narrowly-passed continuation vote can sometimes result in a further consultation and reconstruction. Platforms such as Interactive Investor have improved their mechanisms and enabled shareholder voting through a separately flagged 'voting mailbox' which provides alerts and the opportunity to vote with a simple click. It has never been easier to get involved and to participate fully as a shareholder.

Members satisfying the thresholds in section 338 of the Companies Act 2006 – essentially meaning shareholders representing at least 5% of the total voting rights – may request a trust includes a resolution which those shareholders intend to move at the Annual General Meeting (AGM). Such requisitions are usually related to a disgruntled shareholder or an activist or arbitrageur trying to shake things up with board changes or perhaps force an exit at NAV. When Invesco Enhanced Income (IPE) could not agree revised terms with its managers in mid-2018, a group of shareholders proposed the removal of two directors from the board. Requisitions are usually a last resort once other lines of communication have broken down, but they can be used to ask shareholders to vote on important changes.

Chapter 16: Other Cogs in the Mechanism

In any old, complex, evolving industry there are a lot of moving parts, and in the investment trust industry there are many other market participants who help the whole sector to keep ticking over. There are administrators and registrars, accountants and solicitors, and some people who may be largely invisible to most shareholders while they fulfil important roles.

Public Relations

Making connections between investment trusts and influential advisers and the media is the job of public relations consultants, sometimes known as communications consultancies. They work hard to make contacts, form connections, provide access to managers, deliver supporting material, and act as a conduit to positive press coverage. Companies like Buchanan, Camarco, FTI Consulting, Lansons, Maitland/AMO, and Quill are engaged by trusts to help them communicate their message to the wider world, although some larger trusts and management houses also have their own PR staff. These consultants are instrumental in arranging and hosting meetings, and providing feedback to managers and trusts to help them hone their arguments and understand exactly what potential shareholders may be seeking, or may be worried about. The people working day-to-day on a trust can easily lose sight of how their trust is perceived by the outside world, and it is vital to keep the signals to the market as clear as possible. In this time of growing private investor influence too, articles in newsletters, magazines, newspapers, and on websites, carry greater power than they have for some time.

Valuers

The spotlight does not shine very brightly yet on valuers, but that may change as their central role in setting reliable net asset values for alternative asset trusts is more fully appreciated. Unlike equity trusts, where the assets can be valued easily, based on public prices, the valuation of privately held assets that may not have a price in a publicly-traded market is more of an art. Some trusts value their own assets, while others engage third-party valuers to provide an independent assessment.

Private equity assets are most often valued by the trusts themselves, who will all say they are very conservative in their methodology. 3i Infrastructure (3IN) says that the movements in its portfolio value for the year to 31st March 2020[136] were driven principally by the realisations during the year at prices considerably above opening valuation, plus changes due to new investments and the delivery of planned cash flows and other asset outperformance. Breaking that down into its constituent parts, when

[136] 3i Infrastructure Results for the Year to 31st March 2020

a private equity investment is sold, that crystallises its value and a profit or loss is realised against the previous valuation – the 'book value' as it is known. The majority of private equity realisations do tend to be at a premium to the previous book value, supporting the premise that the valuations are if anything undercooked.

In the case of 3i Infrastructure and many other private equity trusts, the task of valuation lies with those who know the investments best, the managers, but with a review by the board. Valuations are conducted within industry guidelines, generally using a discounted cash flow (DCF) methodology, checked against earnings multiples, recent transactions, and quoted market comparables. It is in the trust's interest to provide accurate valuations that do not create large swings in value as assumptions change, but most importantly to gain the market's trust. It is understandable that for self-valued portfolios that naturally have less transparency than public equities, the market may generally apply a discount to the share price. If for any reason that valuation is seen as unreliable or too optimistic, of course the applicable discount could be much wider, perhaps threatening the future existence of the trust.

Property trusts will generally use an independent valuer to estimate a fair market value for their buildings, someone with recognised professional qualifications and recent experience of the location and category of the investment property being valued. For a domestic UK REIT like Picton Property Income (PCTN) this is fairly straightforward and they use CBRE, a firm of chartered surveyors.[137] The REIT notes that CBRE's fees from Picton are less than 5% of its total UK revenue – relevant because CBRE needs to be independent and free from influence, which it might not be if it were overly reliant on the REIT as a continuing client. CBRE's quarterly valuations are reviewed by the REIT's property valuation committee, which reviews the underlying assumptions and models used. In the immediate aftermath of the Covid-19 crisis, the valuers included a 'material valuation uncertainty' clause to make it clear that less certainty could be attached to the valuations at that time. This underlines the importance of accurate valuations to professional reputations and also to the confidence with which shareholders can receive this information in normal times.

For property trusts with more widespread assets, the task is more onerous and the range of expert firms they can ask to undertake the valuation must either be limited to large firms with sufficient reach, or it must be spread amongst different valuers, in which case consistency is a key issue. In the case of Schroder European Real Estate Investment Trust (SERE),[138] it uses Knight Frank, a well-known large international property company. Trusts investing in specialist types of property also need to ensure

---

[137] Picton Property Income Annual Report 2020

[138] Schroder European Real Estate Investment Trust Annual Report and Consolidated Financial Statements for the year ended 30th September 2019

their valuers are sufficiently well qualified to undertake the task. Civitas Social Housing (CSH), which invests in social housing and healthcare, uses a large firm called JLL, perhaps better known as Jones Lang LaSalle.[139] Again here, there is a nod to the need for independence in that JLL has a rotation policy in place whereby the signatories on the valuations rotate after seven years. That's quite a long period, but in principle it again illustrates the need for separation between the trust and its valuer: if they were to get too cosy, this could in theory impair the need for impartiality. It helps too that Civitas Social Housing lists the principal assumptions in its annual report, recognising that while any valuation is subjective and open to judgements, the basis is clear and transparent for shareholders to gauge for themselves.

Debt trusts similarly need to use independent valuers, as do infrastructure and renewables trusts. GCP Asset Backed Income (GABI) uses a valuation agent called Mazars, who use a discounted cash flow methodology.[140] The valuations are discussed with the investment manager and the board, and the auditor also evaluates the competency of the valuation agent by assessing their professional qualifications, experience, and independence from the company. Valuation experts from PwC UK assess the reasonableness of the methodology and key assumptions, so there are checks and balances in place to ensure as much as possible that the valuers are producing fair results. This could come under greater scrutiny if a period of rising interest rates ushers in a period of sharply falling valuations.

One interesting point about the whole process is that the discount rates used to produce the DCF valuations do vary between fairly similar trusts as their valuers take slightly different views on what rate is applicable to their particular portfolio assets. This is not something that receives a lot of attention, but it does highlight the differing assumptions made in relation to valuations that are generally accepted fairly easily by the market as precise and accurate. The daily statistics collated by the stockbroker JPMorgan Cazenove include a column for the infrastructure sector for the 'average discount rate' used by each trust, and it does vary considerably (the lower the discount rate, the higher the present value). There may of course be completely justifiable reasons for each rate differential, based on the type of assets, the contracts secured, the valuable lifespan of the assets, recent market transactions, and all kinds of other factors that play into the valuation model. Again though, the use of a particular discount rate and the impact of any change is something that potential investors should take into account when assessing these trusts, and the role of the valuer is not to be underestimated.

---

[139] Civitas Social Housing Annual Report 2020

[140] GCP Asset Backed Income Annual Report 2019

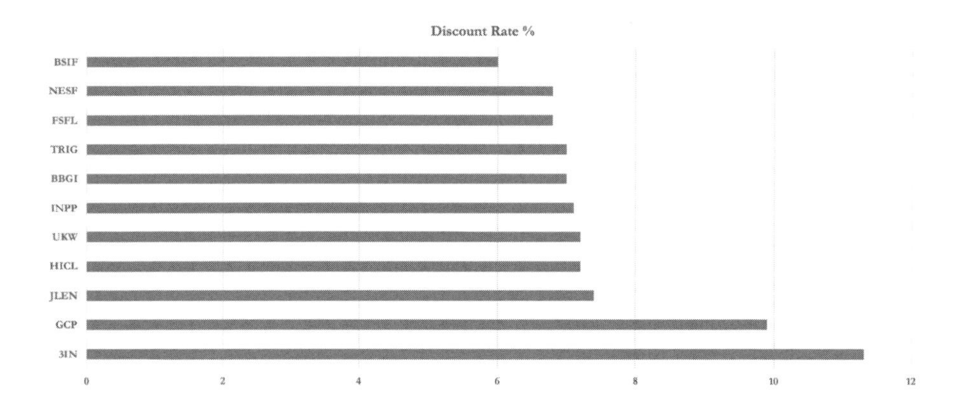

Discount rates used by infrastructure trusts; JPMorgan Cazenove Daily Statistics 29th October 2020; chart created by The McHattie Group

One other reason for taking note of what valuers are doing is that sometimes investors may be able to note an adjustment for one trust and 'read across' to what this means for another. The Hipgnosis Songs Fund (SONG), which invests in song catalogues, uses a specialist New York-based valuer called Massarsky Consulting, and the Round Hill Music Royalty Fund (RHM) is using the same valuer. If the valuer changes the discount rate that it is using for one catalogue, it may be a reasonable assumption (though not a guarantee) that it may change it similarly for the other trust, which may be on a different calendar cycle for its results.

Nick Greenwood, the experienced fund-of-funds manager of Miton Global Opportunities (MGO) made the point at a Kepler Partners virtual seminar[141] that investors used to equities would naturally want to use the stated NAVs as the basis for their investment decisions. As they become more sophisticated with their analysis of alternative asset trusts though, they may begin to question the assumptions of the valuers and do their own work on what the assets might be worth, particularly if there is a chance of those assets being bought. A 'fair value' model may not be answering quite the same question as a 'current market value' model, and there is certainly scope for investors to reach different conclusions from the official valuers on exactly what underlying assets may be worth.

Financial Advisers

The Retail Distribution Review (RDR) was the greatest shift in fund regulation over recent years, and the great hope for adviser engagement with investment trusts. Many

[141] Presentation to Kepler Partners clients, 'Now that's what I call a discount 2020' event, 5th November 2020

observers felt that once open-ended funds were no longer able to pay commission to advisers, a level playing field would mean that financial advisers would look much more closely at investment trusts and recommend them to clients, increasing demand. Anecdotally, this does not seem to have happened in any broad sense across the industry. Advisers have stuck to what they know, citing the additional complexity of investment trusts, with gearing, discounts, and liquidity limitations as reasons to steer clear. Of course there are exceptions, but on the whole the financial adviser community has not been quick to embrace the benefits of investment trusts.

The AIC published the findings of a research survey by Research in Finance at the start of 2020,[142] noting that while the use of investment companies since the RDR has increased, with purchases on advised platforms in excess of £1bn annually, the majority of advisers still do not use investment companies. Six main barriers to greater use were identified, namely (i) the knowledge gap – many advisers acknowledged they did not have a good working knowledge of investment companies; (ii) inertia, as open-ended funds are simply the path of least resistance; (iii) limited contact with the managers of investment companies; (iv) network-wide policies meaning that investment companies do not appear on centralised buy-lists, or all being classified as high risk; (v) research constraints, that investment companies are not part of the research tools commonly used; and (vi) platform-related issues including the availability of investment company shares, trading costs, and model portfolio functionality.

The AIC has a separate section of its website dedicated to advisers, with guides, articles, case studies, data, a portfolio watch list feature, and CPD structured training. There are IFAs with a positive attitude towards investment trusts, such as Blyth-Richmond Investment Managers, Pigott Investments, Birkett Long, Smith & Williamson, Milestone Wealth Management, Master Adviser, and certainly some others, but they probably still find themselves in a minority. There is scant evidence of any real upturn in practical adviser engagement on investment trusts. Product sales data collected by the Financial Conduct Authority indicates that in the year to June 2019[143] there were 1,477 sales of investment trusts recorded, compared to 91,856 sales for OEICs over the same period.

[142] Research reveals barriers to investment company use by IFAs, AIC 30th January 2020
[143] Annual PSD RI data, July 2018 to June 2019, Financial Conduct Authority

Part 3: The Practicalities

Chapter 17: Dealing

Most of the time, the majority of investors will use a stockbroker for buying and selling their investment trust shares. There are exceptions – and some interesting alternatives - but this is most common. Whereas it used to be a daunting experience to find a suitable stockbroker, open an account, and detail your instructions very carefully by telephone, technology means that this is all very much easier than it used to be, and no longer a meaningful hurdle. With a debit card and a phone or a computer, anyone over the age of 18 can be up and running within minutes. There are options for younger investors too.

The Rise of Platform Stockbrokers

Now that you can shop online, watch TV online, hold business meetings online, even find a partner online, it should come as no surprise at all that the majority of investors choose to execute their stock market deals this way. It is cheap, simple, and works well for many people. You can hold open-ended funds, ordinary shares, bonds, gilts, and investment trusts all together in one account, without any issues with transfer payments or certification, and it makes for a straightforward proposition at a time when so many matters of administration are becoming more complex. Dealing charges are low too.

This is why Hargreaves Lansdown has over 1.3 million clients.[144] Interactive Investor, which has been a consolidator in this market, acquiring the European business of TD Direct Investing, Alliance Trust Savings, and The Share Centre, says it has more than 350,000 users.[145] Size, reputation, the quality of customer service, the ease of use of the technology, and the range of different investment products available through the platform are all elements to think about when choosing a provider, as is if course the cost of the services. Many charge a fixed fee to maintain an account, with dealing charges on top, but there are different service plans available, and of course these change regularly as competing platforms vie for new clients.

The Edinburgh-based consultancy 'the lang cat', which specialises in the analysis of platforms, has produced a useful table of charges, hosted on the AIC website. The chart reproduced on the next page is for 100% investment in investment companies, in an ISA, and assumes four trades per year. The blank lines indicate that Aviva and Santander do not offer investment companies, and the columns along the top are for the size of portfolio.

---

[144] Hargreaves Lansdown website, 30th October 2020

[145] Interactive Investor website, 30th October 2020

	£5,000	£15,000	£25,000	£50,000	£100,000	£250,000	£500,000	£1,000,000
AJ Bell Youinvest	1.05%	0.47%	0.28%	0.14%	0.07%	0.03%	0.01%	0.01%
Aviva Consumer Platform								
Barclays	1.44%	0.48%	0.29%	0.15%	0.12%	0.11%	0.10%	0.10%
Bestinvest	1.00%	0.60%	0.52%	0.46%	0.43%	0.41%	0.31%	0.25%
Charles Stanley Direct	1.40%	0.66%	0.53%	0.44%	0.29%	0.11%	0.06%	0.03%
Close Brothers A.M. Self Directed Service	0.97%	0.49%	0.39%	0.32%	0.29%	0.26%	0.26%	0.23%
EQi	1.09%	0.36%	0.22%	0.11%	0.05%	0.02%	0.01%	0.01%
Equiniti Shareview	1.50%	0.83%	0.56%	0.28%	0.14%	0.06%	0.03%	0.01%
Fidelity Personal Investing	1.70%	0.57%	0.34%	0.17%	0.09%	0.03%	0.02%	0.01%
Halifax Share Dealing	1.25%	0.42%	0.25%	0.13%	0.06%	0.03%	0.01%	0.01%
Hargreaves Lansdown	1.41%	0.62%	0.37%	0.19%	0.09%	0.04%	0.02%	0.01%
iDealing	1.19%	0.40%	0.24%	0.12%	0.06%	0.02%	0.01%	0.01%
IG	0.64%	0.21%	0.13%	0.06%	0.03%	0.01%	0.01%	0.00%
Interactive Investor (Investor Product)	2.40%	0.80%	0.48%	0.24%	0.12%	0.05%	0.02%	0.01%
iWeb	0.90%	0.30%	0.18%	0.09%	0.05%	0.02%	0.01%	0.00%
Santander								
Sharedeal	0.76%	0.25%	0.15%	0.08%	0.04%	0.02%	0.01%	0.00%
Strawberry	1.56%	0.67%	0.54%	0.45%	0.35%	0.29%	0.27%	0.26%
The Share Centre (standard)	1.80%	0.80%	0.64%	0.52%	0.46%	0.42%	0.41%	0.41%
The Share Centre (frequent)	3.72%	1.24%	0.74%	0.37%	0.19%	0.07%	0.04%	0.02%
Willis Owen	1.00%	0.60%	0.52%	0.46%	0.38%	0.27%	0.21%	0.18%
X-O	0.48%	0.16%	0.10%	0.05%	0.02%	0.01%	0.00%	0.00%

Charges heatmap for platforms, AIC/lang cat, November 2020

Platforms are not for everybody though, and some investors still prefer to use a traditional stockbroker that offers a much more personal service – at a higher cost. It's a trade-off, and it depends on whether you are prepared to pay more for a non-internet service. For people who distrust electronic communications or who have concerns over cyber-security, an old-fashioned service can still be the right choice. Sometimes as well it can be reassuring to give your dealing instructions to a person who can spot any obvious errors.

Minimum Dealing Size

One of the nagging worries for newcomers to investing is that they might not have enough money to start investing on the stock market. A question frequently asked is how little you can invest. Technically, the glib answer is that you can buy one share, so you could spend 17.9p on a share in Geiger Counter (GCL)[146] or 26.6p on a share in Schroder UK Public Private Trust (SUPP),[147] but of course this would not be an efficient dealing size once you have paid a fixed dealing charge. If we take the standard dealing fee of £11.95 charged by Hargreaves Lansdown[148] (reducing if you deal regularly), then perhaps £400 is a reasonable minimum, implying a 3% hit from the dealing fee. If you are investing for the long-term, perhaps a figure closer to a 5% dealing charge is acceptable, reducing the acceptable minimum lump sum investment

[146] Closing price 26th November 2020, Geiger Counter Ltd, 17p-17.9p

[147] Closing price 26th November 2020, Schroder UK Public Private Trust, 25.95p-26.6p

[148] Hargreaves Lansdown website 30th October 2020

to around £240. As dealing charges have come down fairly sharply over recent years, so this minimum has fallen, making stock market investment more accessible to smaller investors than ever before. The hurdle to getting started is set quite low.

Regular Saving

In fact, the hurdle can be much lower still. There is a way to invest much smaller amounts efficiently, through a regular monthly savings scheme. These first came into existence in the 1980s and were administered by most large management groups seeking regular flows of buyers to help support valuations. Investors could sign up to invest as little as £25 per month, and trusts would convert this into share purchases very cheaply, with some even allocating fractions of shares to make it more efficient, and with dividends reinvested for free. You could still sell at any time, and stop and restart payments, but every six months a statement would arrive in the post to show you how many shares you owned and what the value was. The discipline instilled by the monthly payments meant these schemes, effectively subsidised by the other shareholders or the management companies, were a tremendous way to save into a sensible investment trust, and it also meant that market fluctuations became opportunities rather than reasons to be fearful. If prices moved lower, your regular payment would buy more shares that month, so continuing investors benefited from volatile markets as long as values went up eventually.

Scenario A: no movement in share price; £50 per month
Month 1: share price 100p; buys 50 shares
Month 2: share price 100p; buys 50 shares
Month 3: share price 100p; buys 50 shares
Month 4: share price 100p; buys 50 shares
Month 5: share price 100p; buys 50 shares
Month 6: share price 100p; buys 50 shares
Closing price: 100p, 300 shares worth £300

Scenario B: volatile movement in share price; £50 per month
Month 1: share price 100p; buys 50 shares
Month 2: share price 110p; buys 45 shares
Month 3: share price 90p; buys 56 shares
Month 4: share price 75p; buys 67 shares
Month 5: share price 90p; buys 56 shares
Month 6: share price 100p; buys 50 shares
Closing price: 100p; 324 shares worth £324

For encouraging a long-term mentality that is unflustered and unburdened by doubt when markets get sketchy, a monthly savings plan into a solid trust with a long history that has weathered many storms before can help to overcome doubts by turning temporarily weak markets into a way of buying more shares. This is sometimes called 'pound-cost averaging'. As many investors only want to buy after prices have been rising for some time, and shun markets when they are low, this mechanistic contrarian investing can have real benefits over the long term. The stockbroker Hargreaves Lansdown comments on its website,[149] "it's good discipline – it takes the emotion out of your decisions, and you won't be tempted to try timing the market". Similarly, Interactive Investor says "if the market goes through a rough patch, regular investing helps to cushion the impact".[150]

The development and popularity of platform stockbrokers has sounded the death knell for most of these management schemes, with another one closing just as this book was being written, but three still remain and you can also set up similar arrangements through the platforms. For any investor just starting out with investment trusts and intending to use them as a long-term savings plan rather than for short-term speculation, monthly payments can work extremely well, although saving into an ISA is also worth considering if you have tax considerations or want to simplify your paperwork.

Aberdeen Standard Investments offer the Aberdeen Standard Investment Trusts Share Plan[151] with a minimum monthly investment of £100 per trust, or a minimum lump sum of £250 per trust, with no upper limit. There is no commission charge and no annual plan charge – just the stamp duty and the usual dealing spread on the shares. There is an exit fee of £10+VAT per sale. It is not tax efficient like an ISA. With Aberdeen Standard's wide range of investment trusts, 22 eligible for this scheme, there is plenty of choice and flexibility.

The BMO General Investment Account[152] offers a way to invest in BMO's ten investment trusts, including F&C Investment Trust (FCIT), from £50 per month per trust, or a minimum lump sum of £100 per trust to start, and £250 thereafter, with no maximum. Like the Aberdeen Standard plan, this is not an ISA, but could appeal to investors who have already invested the maximum amount in their ISA, or for whom tax is not an issue. This account carries an annual charge of £40+VAT, and whilst there is no fee for monthly instalments or for dividend reinvestment, other deals are charged at £12 by post or £8 online.

Troy Asset Management offers schemes for its two trusts. Personal Assets Trust (PNL) has an arrangement with Interactive Investor whereby the trust will cover the annual

[149] http://www.hl.co.uk
[150] http://www.ii.co.uk
[151] Details correct as at 30th October 2020; http://www.aberdeenstandard.com
[152] Details correct as at 30th October 2020; http://www.bmogam.com

fee, online dealing costs and dividend reinvestment costs if you only hold this trust in the account. Troy Income & Growth Trust (TIGT) has a scheme through Equiniti, with no annual charge and no commission on purchases. Sales are charged at £10.

All three of these managers also offer regular saving into an ISA, and monthly saving plans are also available from the main platform providers. They are not subsidised, so the overall charges will be higher, but of course there is the big compensating factor of being able to invest in many more trusts across the whole marketplace, not just with one manager. Hargreaves Lansdown has a regular investing scheme with a minimum of £25 per month, and maintains a list of eligible investment trusts, mostly those in the FTSE 350 Index. The list is fairly extensive, running to 180 trusts,[153] and the dealing charge is only £1.50 per trade. The broker can offer such a cheap rate because it is able to bundle the trades together and execute them on the same day. The shares will need to be held in a trading account or an ISA or SIPP though, and that will attract monthly account charges. Interactive Investor goes one better and offers free regular investing from £25 per month in a large number of popular investment trusts. Again, the underlying account will attract its own monthly charges.

Other platforms may also offer regular investment schemes – you will need to check this with your preferred firm. Even if you struggle to find lump sums to invest, and we don't all have spare cash to invest throughout our lives, you can still participate in the investment trust market in a modest way by keeping your hand in the market and maintaining a monthly investment scheme or two, tweaking the amounts to match the income you can spare. Monthly savings plans can also perform a tremendously useful function if they can get young people to start investing sooner, drip-feeding a small sum into the market, hopefully to benefit from the magic of long-term compounding, rather than waiting to have a lump sum of a certain size that might never arrive or be prioritised over competing needs.

Young Investors

You must be 18 years of age or older to open a stockbroking account, but this does not mean that children cannot participate in investment trusts. There are a variety of ways to get started, and for parents and grandparents to fund investments for under-18s. This can make a great deal of sense, to benefit from the long-term compounding effect of a low-cost investment, to encourage a savings habit and ethos, and to build a nest-egg to be used for university fees or as a deposit on a first home. At a time when many young people are finding it harder than ever to overcome these financial hurdles, even a small starting investment can be of value.

---

[153] Hargreaves Lansdown website 30th October 2020

Simplest of all, it is possible to open an account with a stockbroker in the form of a 'bare trust', effectively a dealing account that is run by a parent or grandparent, but with the child's initials attached to indicate they are the beneficiary. There is little extra paperwork involved, besides providing some identification for the child and self-certificating the arrangement. You can access the money at any time, without investment or withdrawal limits, and remain the account holder beyond the child's 18th birthday, although the investments are legally theirs from that moment. This is a simple, flexible choice.

Child Trust Funds, Junior ISAs, Junior SIPPs, Lifetime ISAs

Child Trust Funds were a Labour Party wheeze that did not really work. Introduced in 2005, the tax-free scheme provided a minimum of £250 of government funds for children born between 1st September 2002 and January 2011, and this small lump sum could be put into a variety of schemes – including some investing in investment trusts. Families and friends could add funds, currently with a limit of £9,000 per year, and the scheme matures when the child reaches 18, at which point the scheme can be cashed in or converted to an adult ISA.

About six million CTFs were set up, and the first ones began to mature in September 2020, but there was criticism of the relatively high charges for investing such a small sum, the opportunity to add funds was not widely taken up, and the scheme was superseded by Junior ISAs.

Junior ISAs work very much like adult ISAs, for under 18s, although the limits are different, and there are also Junior SIPPs and Lifetime ISAs, with different characteristics. These products may develop and you should investigate them for yourself to determine which, if any, is most appropriate, depending on the amount to invest, the ultimate purpose of that capital, and the length of time it is likely to be left to grow. The main point here is that there are numerous sensible ways to invest for young people and to get them started with investment trusts well before their 18th birthdays.

In terms of types of investments that might be the most relevant, age is clearly a factor to take into account. With many years ahead of them to make up for any losses and to earn income, growth investments in areas such as technology, biotechnology, and emerging markets may be most appealing, along with some specific trusts that may engage their interests, such as Impax Environmental Markets (IEM) or Hipgnosis Songs Fund (SONG). The idea of owning songs and being paid to listen to them on Spotify or other streaming services might appeal, and effectively makes the link between the idea of buying assets and then receiving income as a direct result.

Liquidity

Moving from age to size, liquidity can be a factor in determining which investment trusts are suitable for dealing at a particular level. If you have £10,000 to invest, your decisions may be different to someone with £10m, not least because with closed-end funds the market must function well to ensure you can, within reasonable limits, buy when you want to, and sell when you want to, in both cases at a price that is at or close to the quoted market price. The largest investors cannot invest easily in the smallest investment trusts, because it would take days or weeks to build or dispose of what for them would be a normal-sized position. It is a common criticism of investment trusts when compared to open-ended funds that for institutional investors they are more difficult to trade, and this seems fair. Although open-ended funds can also place limitations on very large trades, they will generally be able to create and cancel units without too much difficulty.

Ensuring you can deal in a timely fashion is a key consideration for larger investors, who can examine the daily trading data that is in the public domain to gauge whether certain trusts are suitable. As one would expect, there is considerable variation between a trust like Scottish Mortgage Investment Trust (SMT) with a market capitalisation of £15.5bn[154] and average daily volume of shares traded of £32.8m,[155] and one like Majedie Investments (MAJE) with a market capitalisation of £115m and an average daily volume of shares traded of £66,000. There is a reasonably strong link between market capitalisation and daily trading volume, but other factors can come into play such as the structure of the shareholder base, the frequency of newsflow, the size of the discount and any buyback policies, the public profile of each trust, and whether one happens to be in a period of change.

A quiet six months when a trust is simply plodding along with its usual investment process can be completely different to one in which a trust is seeking to raise money, is changing its manager, perhaps tweaking its investment remit, or making other changes that cause a shift in the shareholder base. When Keystone Investment Trust (KIT) made the decision to hand over the managerial reins to Baillie Gifford in late 2020, shifting to a radically different geographical balance with most assets moving outside the UK, and reducing the income, it had to expect significant turnover on its shareholder register as a result. Unsurprisingly, this news stimulated a burst of much higher trading volume. From 77,314 shares traded on the trading day before the announcement, the volume jumped to 472,579 shares on the day and 734,442 shares the next day as investors repositioned themselves.

---

[154] JPMorgan Cazenove Daily Statistics 24th November 2020

[155] Average over six months; JPMorgan Cazenove Daily Statistics 24th November 2020

Volume data can be presented in absolute form across the whole market, allowing you to see which trusts are actually the most traded on any trading day. For larger investors this can create a handy shortlist, and it's also a quick way of getting some idea about which trusts are the big guns of the sector, or at least those that are currently receiving more attention. It is no great surprise in the list below to see both Scottish Mortgage Investment Trust (SMT) and 3i Group (III) at the very top, followed by a list of other familiar names.

Top 20 most liquid funds on an absolute basis (previous business day)

Name	Sector	Mkt Cap	Yesterday's traded value	1yr avg daily traded value
Scottish Mortgage Investment	Global	£15,514m	£37.0m	£27.5m
3i Group	Private Equity - Direct	£10,461m	£16.5m	£17.0m
Greencoat UK Wind	Renewable Infrastructure	£2,371m	£11.7m	£3.4m
Primary Health Properties PLC	Healthcare Real Estate	£1,873m	£8.0m	£5.0m
HICL Infrastructure Co Ltd	Infrastructure	£3,320m	£7.5m	£4.5m
Renewables Infrastructure Group	Renewable Infrastructure	£2,212m	£7.3m	£4.0m
Pershing Square Holdings Ltd	Hedge Funds	£4,500m	£7.1m	£2.8m
Smithson Investment Trust	Global Smaller Companies	£2,142m	£6.4m	£6.0m
Polar Capital Technology Trust	Technology	£2,939m	£6.0m	£5.0m
Tritax Big Box REIT	UK Real Estate	£2,794m	£5.9m	£8.0m
Templeton Emerging Markets	Global EM	£2,159m	£5.8m	£3.1m
JPMorgan Emerging Markets	Global EM	£1,480m	£4.9m	£2.7m
Assura	Healthcare Real Estate	£1,978m	£4.7m	£4.0m
Worldwide Healthcare Trust	Biotechnology & Healthcare	£2,159m	£4.7m	£4.0m
Monks Investment Trust	Global	£2,847m	£4.5m	£3.9m
Finsbury Growth & Income Trust	UK - Equity Income	£1,875m	£4.5m	£4.1m
RIT Capital Partners PLC	Flexible	£3,080m	£4.4m	£3.6m
Pacific Horizon Investment Trust	Asia Regional	£508m	£4.3m	£1.2m
HarbourVest Global PE	Private Equity - FoF	£1,378m	£3.8m	£1.5m
Civitas Social Housing	Specialist Property	£639m	£3.8m	£1.4m

Source: Liberum, Bloomberg

Trusts ranked by trade on an absolute basis, Liberum Alternatives Daily note 26th November 2020

Trusts can also be ranked on a relative basis, showing what percentage of their shares have been traded. This is more dynamic and provides some insight into money flows, to identify which trusts are 'hot' and attracting most trade for their size. At the time of the snapshot on the next page, both Baillie Gifford China Growth (BGCG) and Pacific Horizon Investment Trust (PHI) were in great demand and trading on premium ratings in the market.

Top 20 most liquid funds on a relative basis (previous business day)

Name	Sector	Mkt Cap	1d vol (% of share capital)	1y vol (% of share capital)
Majedie Investments	Global	£117m	2.8%	21%
Baillie Gifford China Growth Trust	Asia Regional	£242m	0.8%	160%
Pacific Horizon Investment Trust	Asia Regional	£508m	0.8%	85%
Ranger Direct Lending Fund	Direct Lending	£10m	0.7%	31%
Civitas Social Housing	Specialist Property	£639m	0.6%	57%
Blackrock Throgmorton Trust	UK Smaller Companies	£603m	0.6%	75%
Gresham House Energy Storage	Renewable Infrastructure	£254m	0.6%	19%
BlackRock World Mining Trust P	Resources	£773m	0.5%	74%
Greencoat UK Wind	Renewable Infrastructure	£2,371m	0.5%	35%
Bluefield Solar Income Fund	Renewable Infrastructure	£480m	0.5%	36%
Fair Oaks Income Ltd	CLOs	£205m	0.5%	39%
City Natural Resources High Yield	Resources	£67m	0.5%	61%
BlackRock Latin American Investment Trust	Latin America	£143m	0.4%	33%
Primary Health Properties PLC	Healthcare Real Estate	£1,873m	0.4%	64%
Fidelity Special Values	UK All Companies	£680m	0.4%	55%
Henderson Alternative Strategies	Flexible	£108m	0.4%	72%
Polar Capital Global Financial	Japanese Smaller Co's	£167m	0.4%	69%
JPMorgan Asia Growth & Income	Asia Regional	£441m	0.4%	58%
Henderson International Income	Global Equity Income	£287m	0.4%	38%
JPMorgan China Growth & Income	Asia Specialist	£459m	0.4%	97%

Source: Liberum, Bloomberg

Trusts ranked on a relative basis, Liberum Alternatives Daily note 26th November 2020

For private investors, dealing size is less of an issue and does not require constant monitoring at all, although you might still trip up occasionally if trying to deal in an esoteric second-line trust that has not attracted very much attention. It can come as a shock, and is certainly a frustration, when you try to execute a fairly small trade and the system won't process it because the stock is not available at that time. Usually in such cases, a little patience pays off and deals can be executed successfully, but the liquidity is still worth bearing in mind, particularly in relation to the moment when you want to sell and exit. It may be reasonable to exercise patience and wait when buying, because if the price moves up you can just shrug your shoulders and move on to something else, but that is not the case when selling, when you might have an urgent need for the capital, particularly in a market crisis. For that reason it is probably prudent to have at least one very liquid trust in your portfolio that you are likely to be able to sell quickly and easily in even the worst market conditions to raise emergency cash.

More liquid trusts usually command higher valuations than less liquid trusts, as they are more desirable for a wider range of investors, and larger investors do not need to demand a reverse 'liquidity premium' to justify a purchase. There are some odd exceptions though, in cases where the shares are tightly held by loyal shareholders who are generally reluctant to sell, and it can be hard therefore to find willing sellers. In such cases, market-makers may mark the shares up to large premium ratings to entice some sellers, and this can produce curious and temporary market anomalies that are much larger than you might expect.

The most obvious example here must be Lindsell Train Investment Trust (LTI), which has a consistently strong performance record over a good number of years, but a chequered share price return record, dominated by massive swings in the valuation. This has been so extreme at times that the trust's own board has warned investors against buying its shares. With the half yearly report released in November 2013[156] chairman Donald Adamson said "the directors repeat their caution to potential new investors from buying shares at such an elevated premium. A general fall in markets could impact the value of our quoted equities and, perhaps more significantly, the value of the 21% we have invested in LTL. Together these could quickly eliminate the premium, and potentially translate into material capital losses for such investors in the short term. The effect could be further magnified if the company's share price were to trade at a discount to NAV, which has been the case for significant periods since the company's launch". Further warnings have followed from Julian Cazalet, the trust's next chairman.

In January 2017 the Investment Trust Newsletter highlighted the 56.1% premium to net asset value and said "we cannot recommend the shares at this level in spite of their sparkling performance record", and a year later noted that a NAV total return of 37.3% delivered only a single penny of return, 0.1%, to shareholders as the premium reduced. In early 2019 the premium spiked again to extraordinary levels that caused the Investment Trust Newsletter to comment, on its front page, that the 74.7% premium to net asset value "makes us very uncomfortable, so while we have watched the trust's marvellous ascent wistfully from the sidelines, without having recommended the shares, we can't help but feel the risk-reward trade-off looks unfavourable in anything other than bullish conditions, and we cannot be sure of those continuing".[157] Five months later, the trust's shares dropped by more than a quarter in a single month. Such extreme discount volatility – translating into share price volatility - can result from illiquidity, and is less likely to occur when a trust is being traded actively every day by a large number of market participants.

---

[156] Lindsell Train Investment Trust Report for the Half Year ended 30th September 2013

[157] Investment Trust Newsletter April 2019

Share price performance compared to the Net Asset Value and the Benchmark for ten years to 31 March 2020

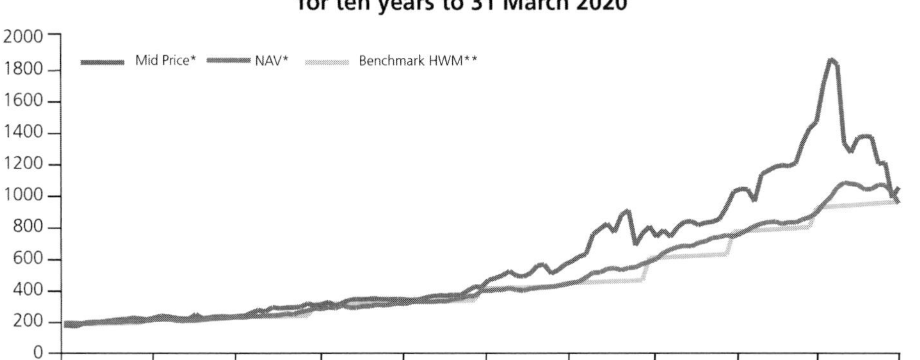

The Lindsell Train Investment Trust share price performance compared to the net asset value and the benchmark for the ten years to 31st March 2020[158]

Dealing Spreads

Many investors immediately think of stockbrokers' commission and perhaps stamp duty when considering the cost of dealing, but in many cases the largest cost by far is the dealing spread on the shares. This is the difference between the selling price and the buying price, and is similar to when you exchange currency at a bureau de change. The dealing spread is the market-maker's profit and compensates them for the risk of holding shares and providing market services. It differs markedly between trusts, it can also change at different times or throughout the day, and in any event, maybe the quoted spread that you can see on the screen isn't really the effective spread anyway. There is more to explore here.

First of all, let's take a look at a couple of spreads and introduce some more market jargon. For Empiric Student Property (ESP) the dealing spread is 73.3p to 73.6p,[159] meaning that if you are selling, you can in principle sell at 73.3p; and if you are buying you can buy at 73.6p. The selling price, 73.3p, is also known as the bid price, because it is the price at which the market is bidding to acquire your shares. The buying price,

[158] The Lindsell Train Investment Trust Annual Report and Financial Statements for the year ended 31st March 2020. Note: the chart is based on monthly raw data. When a performance fee is paid, the Benchmark is adjusted up to the high watermark ("HWM") at that point. This only occurs annually, if at all, on 31 March. * The NAV and share price are unadjusted for dividends. ** The Benchmark is adjusted for inclusion of the HWM. Please note that the inclusion of the HWM means that, at the financial year end, if a performance fee has been paid, the Benchmark is adjusted to the same level as the NAV or the share price whichever is lower. If the Benchmark performs better than the NAV and/or the share price, or a performance fee has not been paid, no adjustment is made.

[159] Closing price, London Stock Exchange, 26th November 2020

73.6p, is also known as the offer price, or ask price, because this is the price at which the market is offering shares, asking if you want to buy them. For River & Mercantile UK Micro Cap Investment Company (RMMC), the dealing spread is 183p-190p.[160]

The percentage spread is the amount that the share needs to move for you to cover the cost of the dealing spread, and this will generally be greater for less liquid shares. For ESP, above, the percentage spread on 73.3p-73.6p is equal to the difference between the two prices, divided by the bid price, so 0.3/73.3, multiplied by 100 to make it a percentage, in this case 0.41%. For RMMC the spread is considerably wider, at 7/183, 3.83%, so it is a far costlier trade to deal in RMMC than it is to deal in ESP.

On a typical day, the range of dealing spreads may be very wide, from perhaps 0.2% or 0.3% at the low end, to between 5% and 10% at the top end (occasionally more for low-priced shares). It is something to take into account when examining trusts, although perhaps of most relevance for active traders rather than for long-term investors who might hold the shares for many years. Spreads will vary through the day as well, as the quoted spreads are the best bid and offer prices in the market, and may be from different market-makers. Let's say there are two market-makers in a share who currently agree that the price should be 100p-105p, then that is the quoted price. If one market-maker sells some shares to buyers and finds themselves short of stock, they might respond by raising their price to 102p-107p, and that will make the overall market price 102p-105p – so the spread has narrowed in this case because of the dynamic nature of the market. When the market first opens in the morning, spreads will often appear wider because one market-maker opens before the others, but even when the market is up and running fully, spreads will naturally change throughout the day, and perhaps in response to market conditions as well. During sudden bouts of volatility, when market-makers find their own risk rises sharply, they have been known to widen their spreads. This happened during the initial Covid-19 lockdown in the spring and summer of 2020. Many dealing spreads widened to multiples of where they were prior to the crisis, particularly for the less liquid trusts.

Normally, when discussing or specifying prices, these are based on the 'quoted' spreads, the public spreads that make up the prices for the London Stock Exchange, relayed to various price feeds. To complicate matters though, the quoted spread may not be the price at which you actually deal. More often than not, you will find you can obtain a better price – sometimes a much better price – when it is actually time to deal (although the reverse can also be true if you are dealing in larger size). If the market-maker has enough shares on their book to satisfy your requirement, you can frequently deal 'inside' the spread, at a better price. This is not merely anecdotal – trading data that is all recorded by the stock exchange can be checked and verified.

[160] Closing price, London Stock Exchange, 26th November 2020

Taking the example of Gore Street Energy Storage Fund (GSF) on 9th November 2020, when the price remained stable all day at 105p-110p, the data shows that none of the 18 trades were actually executed at 105p or 110p. The first two trades of the morning, before 8:30am, were very small trades, deemed to be buys at 107.95p. Most of the trade thereafter was on the buy side, with all deals struck at prices between 108.75p and 109p. One sell order, in the late morning, was dealt at 105.25p. So the 'real' price was more like 105.25p-108.8p, a narrower dealing spread than the quoted figure, and it is quite normal for automated trades to include some element of 'price improvement'. A skilled dealer may be able to do even better. It is worth bearing this in mind if all of your analysis points towards a particular investment trust trade, and then the quoted dealing spread is off-putting. It may be worth checking to see if it is possible to deal well inside the public price.

Num.	Price	Size	Type	C	T	Bid	Offer	Time	Buy	Sell	?	Buy %	Buy Vol.	Sell Vol.
18	108.75	10000	O			105.0	110.0	16:24:44	10,000				79,424	19,009
17	108.75	4000	O			105.0	110.0	16:22:21	4,000				69,424	19,009
16	108.75	603	O			105.0	110.0	15:32:10	603				65,424	19,009
15	108.75	2683	O			105.0	110.0	14:36:40	2,683				64,821	19,009
14	108.8	11000	O			105.0	110.0	13:35:39	11,000				62,138	19,009
13	108.8	1714	O			105.0	110.0	13:23:34	1,714				51,138	19,009
12	108.8	5400	O			105.0	110.0	13:18:21	5,400				49,424	19,009
11	105.25	19009	O			105.0	110.0	13:17:36		19,009			44,024	19,009
10	108.8	10000	O			105.0	110.0	13:04:13	10,000				44,024	
9	109.0	18363	O			105.0	110.0	12:07:40	18,363				34,024	
8	108.8	436	O			105.0	110.0	11:51:08	436				15,661	
7	108.9	6000	O			105.0	110.0	11:41:50	6,000				15,225	
6	108.9	4564	O			105.0	110.0	11:22:48	4,564				9,225	
5	109.0	1500	O			105.0	110.0	10:20:40	1,500				4,661	
4	109.0	2000	O			105.0	110.0	09:30:21	2,000				3,161	
3	109.0	917	O			105.0	110.0	09:30:03	917				1,161	
2	107.95	129	O			105.0	110.0	08:29:08	129				244	
1	107.95	115	O			105.0	110.0	08:10:17	115				115	

Gore Street Energy Storage trades 9th November 2020; source ADVFN/London Stock Exchange

The Online Mechanism

Prior to the internet age, dealing used to be a somewhat daunting experience for less experienced investors. Telephoning the stockbroker, making sure you identified yourself and gave your instructions very clearly, waiting for a quote to come back from the market-maker and then deciding whether to proceed, could be nerve-wracking. Although digitalisation can certainly bring its own stresses, particularly when systems are not working as intended, it is generally a much easier and more relaxed method of dealing. There is no need to be intimidated by it, and it does not require any deep knowledge or use of jargon.

Once you have logged in to your account, you can ask for a quote at any time, without commitment. So, between 8am and 4.30pm, London time, simply typing in a ticker code and the amount you would like to trade, and whether you want to buy or sell, will obtain an indicative price. You then have a short period of time, typically 15 seconds, to decide whether to accept the price by clicking a button, or you can by default let it lapse. It is a simple process to check prices and dealing spreads, which you can do multiple times, without any pressure at all to deal until you are absolutely comfortable and certain.

Problems with PRIIPS

Dealing is not usually problematic, but at the start of 2018 it became more difficult, thanks to an unintended effect of new regulations for packaged retail investment and insurance products (PRIIPS), intended to make trading more orderly for all participants. It had the opposite effect as some investment trusts did not make the right documents available to all stockbrokers, meaning they could not deal in those trusts for clients. Most of these issues have since been ironed out, but on the fringes of the industry there are still problems, with esoteric trusts that may or may not appear on dealing platforms. Tetragon Financial Group (TFG, TFGS) has two sets of shares, the standard dollar-denominated shares and the sterling shares, which are effectively the same, just quoted in sterling. This is a large trust, but off the beaten track and not widely dealt, and stockbrokers seem to have had difficulty adding it to their systems. In November 2020, Interactive Investor clients can deal in the dollar shares, but not the sterling shares, as the broker says there is no KID document available; with Hargreaves Lansdown you cannot deal in the dollar shares, but you can deal in the sterling shares. This sort of confusion only exists for a certain number of less popular investment trusts, but it is still a considerable source of irritation and market disorder that should not exist. It is nonsensical.

One possible response for private investors is to open trading accounts with different stockbrokers. This can be prudent anyway, to spread your funds in case of technical problems, or worse, fraud or other criminal activity, but also to ensure the best access to the full spectrum of investments available. There seems to be very little consistency across platforms – some esoteric shares can be traded on one platform, but not another. Whilst having all of your investments in one place, under one umbrella, wins in terms of keeping things simple, markets can be more complex than that.

Chapter 18: Tax

As with most forms of investment there can be tax implications for you to consider before you invest. If you are using a standard dealing account for your transactions, you may be liable for capital gains tax and for tax on dividend income. Using an ISA or a SIPP is a popular and effective solution for many personal investors in investment trusts, effectively sidestepping tax in an efficient and completely legal way, but there may be additional tax issues to consider in relation to offshore trusts and REITs. Investment trusts and REITs themselves are exempt from UK corporation tax, so there is no double-taxation.

Books are not an ideal format for taxation information, as tax structures, rules and allowances change regularly, and text that seems quite definitive can quickly date. Individual circumstances will also vary widely and mean that generic statements may not apply to your financial arrangements. Tax is best considered individually, with professional advice if necessary when matters become complicated, and for that reason this chapter is a short overview only.

ISAs

Individual Savings Accounts, known universally as ISAs, came into being in April 1999, introduced by the chancellor of the time, Gordon Brown. They replaced PEPs – Personal Equity Plans – as the government's preferred product for encouraging saving, and they have stood the test of time. There are cash ISAs and stocks and shares ISAs, and the major benefit of using this wrapper for your investments is that there is no tax to pay on ISA investments. Capital gains are free from tax, and so is income, whether from dividends or from interest. From an initial limit of £7,000 per year, the maximum contribution per year for each individual has steadily risen to reach £20,000, which seems generous. Companies that administer ISAs, whether those are platforms or other stockbrokers, or individual management companies, need to levy an annual fee to cover their costs, but these are not generally high. For the majority of people, investing in an ISA makes complete sense, and that remains true even if you do not really expect to incur any tax. ISA investments also save on paperwork, since you do not need to include them on a tax return, so there is no need to keep contract notes every time you deal, or to maintain a list of dividend payments to detail on an annual tax return for the government. ISAs sweep away cost and complexity, and this can be a massive benefit, whether you are an active trader wanting to keep things simple, or a long-term investor hoping to harness the power of compounding growth to create a large capital sum for later in life that can be used without any tax implications. Introducing tax considerations into investment judgements almost always muddies the waters and leads to sub-optimal decisions, so avoiding (not evading) tax makes sense on many levels.

According to research by the Financial Conduct Authority,[161] 17% of UK adults have a stocks and shares ISA, around 8.8m adults. Some investors have grown large portfolios within their ISAs. An article in The Sunday Times in 2019[162] quoted Rebecca O'Keeffe of Interactive Investor, saying that a typical ISA millionaire's portfolio held with her platform had 59% in shares, 23% in investment trusts, and 7% in unit trusts, with the balance in cash, ETFs, and bonds. Investment trusts, as securities listed on a recognised stock exchange, are eligible for inclusion, including most esoteric trusts. In a general 'self select' ISA with a platform stockbroker, you can choose your own investments and freely mix investment trusts with other shares and securities, with few limitations.

SIPPs

Self Invested Personal Pensions are another popular tax shelter for up to £40,000 per year for most taxpayers, although one that works in a different way to an ISA. With an ISA, the tax benefit is at the end, when hopefully your investment has grown and you can either cash out some or all of the capital without any tax to pay, or perhaps take an income from the dividends, again free of tax. SIPPs are structured differently, so that the main tax benefit comes up front instead, in the form of a tax relief contribution from the government that can turbo charge your early returns, potentially growing a larger portfolio over time, again free from UK income and capital gains tax whilst in the SIPP. SIPPs are less flexible than ISAs though, in that you cannot access the money before age 55, and then you can only take out a quarter of the value tax free. The remainder of withdrawals will be taxed as income.

If you are choosing between an ISA and a SIPP, you can perform some calculations based on your age, contributions, tax rates, likely need to withdraw funds, and growth assumptions. Using this number of variables over a long period though creates a great deal of uncertainty about the outcome, and for many investors the distinction is not clear. There is no reason why you should not have an ISA and a SIPP, and that is the way forward for many investors who may have their entire investment portfolios within these tax shelters.

Ordinary Trading Accounts

If you have reasons to eschew the attractions of ISAs or SIPPs, or you have already maximised your contributions to those tax wrappers and have more to invest, a standard trading account is also a perfectly acceptable home for investment trusts. In

---

[161] The financial lives of consumers across the UK, published 20th June 2018, updated 29th July 2020, Financial Conduct Authority

[162] A brief history of ISAs in facts and figures, The Sunday Times 20th March 2019

this case you may be liable for capital gains tax on annual gains in excess of £12,300 for an individual in the 2019/20 tax year, and you may have to pay tax on your dividends as well. For 2019/20 there is a personal dividend allowance of £2,000, and above this, your dividends are added to your other income for the purpose of income tax. At the time of writing, changes to the capital gains tax rules seem highly likely.

REIT PIDs

Before leaving the subject of taxation on dividends, real estate investment trusts (REITs) typically pay out most or all of their income as property income distributions (PIDs). These are different from dividends in that they incur withholding tax of 20% unless investors are exempt and qualify for gross payments (such as UK resident companies, public bodies, charities, pension funds, ISAs, and child trust funds). They must be declared on tax returns, and higher rate taxpayers may then be liable for a further tax charge. For this reason, anyone transferring assets from a standard trading account to an ISA or SIPP may find that moving holdings in REITs becomes a priority.

Stamp Duty

Most ordinary shares that are traded on the London Stock Exchange, and that includes investment trusts, are liable for stamp duty reserve tax (SDRT) – the 0.5% charge you must pay when you make a purchase (not a sale). This is added automatically by stockbrokers when you deal, so there is no extra administration, but it's a cost that can become significant if you are seeking to benefit from a short-term trade that might offer a relatively small profit margin.

The good news is that there is a reasonably long list of offshore-registered investment companies that are exempt, as are those listed on the Alternative Investment Market (AIM). Working through the daily Issuer List from the London Stock Exchange[163] and separating these out manually produces a fairly lengthy list of around 120 trusts where no stamp duty is payable on purchases. These include a number of billion-pound-plus trusts such as 3i Infrastructure (3IN), HarbourVest Global Private Equity (HVPE), International Public Partnerships (INPP), Pershing Square Holdings (PSH), Princess Private Equity Holding (PEY), Sequoia Economic Infrastructure Income Fund (SEQI), Syncona (SYNC), The Renewables Infrastructure Group (TRIG), and Vietnam Enterprise Investments (VEIL). Combining their stamp duty-free status with narrow dealing spreads means that these may be amongst the very cheapest trusts to deal for active traders looking to make quick trades with small profit margins. Also on the list are a variety of AIM-listed investment companies and REITs, including Crystal Amber Fund (CRS), Globalworth Real Estate Investments (GWI), Gresham House

[163] London Stock Exchange Daily Issuer List, 10th November 2020

Strategic (GHS), and Secure Income REIT (SIR). Others are Channel Islands registered companies, such as Aberdeen Latin American Income Fund (ALAI), Bluefield Solar Income Fund (BSIF), India Capital Growth Fund (IGC), Real Estate Credit Investments (RECI), and The Schiehallion Fund (MNTN).

Inheritance Tax

Some AIM-listed shares have become extremely popular because they can qualify for inheritance tax relief, but the bad news is that AIM-listed investment companies do not meet the requirements. It is only commercial companies that can qualify, and not companies whose activities are wholly or mainly focused on dealing in land, buildings, or in investments.

Chapter 19: Analysis

There isn't a manual for analysing investment trusts, and no right or wrong way to make your choices. To pick from a large number of competing trusts though, and perhaps to decide how to blend those trusts together, some sort of process is necessary, particularly when investment trusts are run by highly articulate managers backed by clever marketing departments that can provide convincing figures to show historic outperformance and make a strong case for the future. Fortunately there are plenty of ways to make that assessment for yourself. This discussion won't be a blueprint, and it won't be complete, but it should provide some pointers and some interesting angles on how to get started.

Defining Your Aims

Investors often just want a simple answer to a simple question – which trust should I buy now? Alas, the answer is rarely straightforward: forecasting would be easy if it didn't involve the future. It also involves unknown factors, risk levels, the actions of others, judgement calls about skills and characters, and – crucially – a determination of just what counts as a good trust for each investor. A volatile go-go growth trust might be fine for a speculative investor looking for a flutter with some spare cash, but another investor seeking a steady retirement income without putting their capital at severe risk of loss is going to be looking for something entirely different. Figuring out what blend you are seeking is a big first step. Or maybe several steps, covering (i) risk tolerance; (ii) time; (iii) desire for income; (iv) diversification; (v) the purpose of the investment; and (vi) your knowledge and level of involvement.

Starting with risk tolerance, this is really about the downside and the chance of significant capital loss. Depending on your circumstances, a capital loss might be something that causes you to grumble about your lack of judgement or luck for an hour or two, or it may have much more serious consequences that prevent you from fulfilling your future plans. Thinking about how painful a loss might be can help to develop your views on what is actually a very difficult question, if we are being asked to self-evaluate. It is easy to define ourselves as tolerant of high risk until a market collapse occurs and we feel the burden of a heavy loss. To this small degree at least, episodes like the sudden bear market caused by the Covid-19 pandemic in March 2020 can help us to understand the question by living through the experience, even if we still struggle for an answer. Many firms have tried to develop risk questionnaires to tease out more reasoned responses, sometimes including an objective quantitative element that includes elements of proportionality and the ability to recover investment losses with other sources of income. It is a mistake as well to think that it is only overoptimism that is a potential problem, causing investors to take on too much risk. Risk aversion can also mean investors take on insufficient risk to generate the sort of returns they require, perhaps fearing the gearing. This is at the root of much apparently irrational allocation behaviour by less sophisticated investors with a lack of knowledge and too much fear of loss to accept modest risk in exchange for much higher returns. It has been estimated by many that losses are twice as painful as profits are enjoyable, and loss aversion can lead to negative behaviour that causes missed profits and poorly judged short-term actions, such as selling at the first sign of a bearish phase that may well be temporary. Trying to match your investment choices to your true risk tolerance can avoid many problems later on.

The second factor in determining your aims, and which trusts might be most suitable for meeting those aims, is time. Investors willing to commit long-term capital that they are unlikely to need or withdraw in the near future can adopt riskier strategies because their capital has ample time to recover from near-term setbacks that might be more problematic for those needing access to their capital sooner. Investment trusts are often pitched as long-term savings vehicles that can target capital growth over periods from five years to five decades or more, and it seems reasonable to suggest that the longer the time period, the more likely it is that the real qualities of a trust and its managers will deliver expected returns. There are wrinkles in this approach though, for example taking into account the age of the lead manager. If you are intending to invest for 20 years, then picking a trust with a 65-year old manager and expecting consistent returns might be a flawed strategy. There is an argument for selecting managers reasonably close to your own age or younger if you are making investments that you are intending to leave untouched for a long time.

Third, in choosing investment trusts you will often be choosing between the potential for capital growth or a high level of dividend income. There are certainly numerous trusts that offer a portion of both, but again to avoid major errors that reduce your total returns, this is something to bear in mind. Younger investors in the early or middle parts of their careers when the future earnings stream should be long and growing probably have little need for income from a portfolio and can concentrate more on capital growth to build their savings pot for the future. Investors approaching retirement may wish to dial down the capital risk and start to blend in more income-producing trusts, which are naturally less risky on the whole, with an eye towards taking that income in retirement and perhaps moving towards a high dividend portfolio. Those are of course sweeping generalisations, and it is your own need or preference for income that will inform your own personal investment decisions.

If you already own lots of UK smaller companies trusts, or just lots of individual UK smaller company shares, then buying another UK smaller companies trust might not make sense for you. The overall balance of your portfolio, ensuring it is diversified sufficiently across industry or geographic sectors, can help to reduce your risk level and the chance of serious underperformance or loss. Whilst it is tempting to build up a large holding in one big 'core' trust that seems to be a solid performer and is considered reliable, spreading your investments between a few different trusts to achieve a broader exposure with less correlation may be a better approach that smooths out performance peaks and troughs as different investment techniques swing in and out of vogue. At certain times in the past, growth managers, or value managers, or contrarians, or emerging markets managers, or small cap managers, or multi-asset managers have been top of the charts, but no trend lasts forever, and cycles turn. In November 2020 there was a dramatic example of exactly this, when the pharmaceuticals firm Pfizer announced some very good trial results for a Covid-19 vaccine, to the massive relief of global stock markets that had been weighed down by localised and periodic economic lockdowns for several months. A select group of technology growth stocks had been buoyed during the lockdown period as investors paid up for the rarity of growth and for exposure to trends towards online activity that had been accelerated by the virus, but the extremely welcome news of the potential vaccine caused a very quick rotation out of growth and into value trusts that had previously been depressed. Having a balanced portfolio made sense at this time, and seeking to have a richly diversified portfolio that can keep the ship steady in rough waters means seeking investments to achieve and maintain that equilibrium.

Fourth, it is useful to remember the purpose of your investment, whether that is specific or rather vague. It may be to fund a particular project or lifestyle target, or to pay for future expenses such as university fees or a house deposit for yourself or your children, or it may be more general, to provide for a comfortable retirement, or to act as a reliable custodian for inherited family wealth. Different reasons are likely to lead to different risk preferences and investment choices, and if a specific amount is required at a specific future date, then financial modelling can help determine a suitable path for achieving that goal without taking unnecessary risk.

Finally, be realistic about your level of knowledge and the time you want to spend on your investment portfolio. An industry professional with great information flows and contacts, immersed in the sector every working day and ready to watch a portfolio closely and react to events might well be prepared to take on some more spicy or developing trusts with bumpy short-term prospects, playing valuation changes and grabbing opportunities as they arise in an attempt to find the biggest winners. A lay investor with a busy home and working life in a different profession, perhaps armed with only a basic understanding of investment trusts, is more likely to want to opt for something mainstream, steady and long-term that can provide decent returns without too many nasty surprises. Overestimating your knowledge level can mean that you are taking on investments that are too esoteric, perhaps with hidden risks that you have not really understood; overestimating the time you can devote to your portfolio can mean that you buy trusts that need too much attention with capital-raises, changes of manager, and swings in performance that can be costly if ignored.

By defining these aims as carefully as possible, you may develop some parameters for your investment trust choices, whether you are seeking relatively low-risk mainstream branded trusts with a reasonable level of income and revenue reserves, likely to sit somewhere in the middle of performance tables; or whether you are seeking pure capital growth in whatever form that might take, with specialist trusts run by managers with high conviction and concentrated portfolios; or perhaps something specific to fill some gaps, such as a Japanese trust or some exposure to renewable energy. Once you know what you are looking for, it is much easier to start the hunt.

Risk Levels

Before moving on to the more exciting topic of returns and potential profits, the flip side of the chase for higher returns is the risk that must be assumed. There are several specific elements to risk profiling for investment trusts, meaning that a detailed analysis must range quite widely.

One place to start is with the self-classification that investment trusts must now provide to all investors as part of their Key Information Document (KID). Trusts must rate themselves on a scale of one to seven, calculated according to complicated guidelines laid down by the regulator. For equity trusts without any credit risk, this is based on past volatility of the share price; for trusts exposed to credit risk in their portfolios it is a blend. Many of the figures in the KIDs make reasonable sense – so the big global multi-manager generalist Alliance Trust (ATST) is medium risk, rated a four, as are its peers F&C Investment Trust (FCIT) and Witan Investment Trust (WTAN). It doesn't take too much digging around though to find some that don't seem to tally with general perceptions of where trusts lie on the risk spectrum. Tetragon Financial Group (TFG), which carries dollar risk and invests in some less transparent parts of the US market, is also rated a four, as is Crystal Amber Fund (CRS) in spite of a 57% decline in its share price in the year to November 2020,[164] and so is Baillie Gifford China Growth Trust (BGCG), a single-country fund with a concentrated portfolio that has exhibited some strong price movements. For this to have the same moderate risk rating as HICL Infrastructure (HICL), a large income-producing infrastructure trust where the cash flows are mainly paid by the government, really doesn't make much sense. It seems unwise to rely on these documents for definitive risk screening.

One of the obvious places to start for a more nuanced and multi-faceted analysis of risk is with the underlying investment objective and target assets. Single country trusts focused on individual countries such as Vietnam, China, India, Russia, Brazil, or Thailand are likely to carry a higher risk than a trust with regional or global diversification. Trusts investing in smaller companies are likely to carry a higher risk

[164] Investment Trust Newsletter November 2020

than all-cap trusts or those investing mainly in more established businesses. Trusts with exposure to unlisted companies are higher risk again. In the world of alternative assets it can be much harder to generalise about asset classes, but if trusts like Civitas Social Housing (CSH) own physical assets that produce cash flows paid by governments or major companies, those seem less risky than a portfolio of opportunistic credit investments in the technology-enabled lending sector that is the focus for VPC Specialty Lending Investments (VSL). REITs with higher exposure to retail properties at a time of considerable change and disruption in that sector are generally considered riskier than those with warehouse assets to serve online customers. Taking a common-sense approach should work most of the time in this sector, where there are some fairly evident distinctions to be made between asset classes.

Next, the size of the trust, the quality of the management firm, the depth of resources available to the manager, and the management style should contribute towards a largely qualitative judgement about the scope for mistakes or for sudden unexpected changes, or unexplained underperformance. Smaller operations that rely on the judgement of one or two individuals may experience greater variability in the returns than a more structured firm with a well-defined process, as Neil Woodford perhaps demonstrated. The style of the portfolio is relevant as well – a trust with a manager striving aggressively for top performance from a high-conviction portfolio of 30 shares is likely to be more volatile and riskier than one that is focused on steady and reliable income from a more widely diversified list of stocks.

Of course the variability of returns may be exaggerated by gearing, and this is a simple quantitative measurement of the additional risk that a trust has in its structure. The higher the net gearing (accounting for cash balances), the greater the risk level. The range of gearing levels can be quite wide, causing significant differences in performance. The five-year performance of Fidelity Japan Trust (FJV) with 26% gearing[165] against Aberdeen Japan Investment Trust (AJIT) with 13% gearing[166] illustrates that the trust's shares have experienced more movement in both directions, although the gearing level may not explain the whole of this difference.

Trusts that exhibit greater volatility, like Fidelity Japan Trust (FJV) are likely to have a less consistent record of historical returns. Whilst performance tables are extremely useful, they are only providing a single snapshot in time, so it can be valuable to build knowledge incrementally by regularly examining these tables and developing a picture of whether top-performing trusts are able to sustain their advantages when market

[165] JPMorgan Cazenove Daily Statistics 24th November 2020

[166] JPMorgan Cazenove Daily Statistics 24th November 2020

conditions change, or whether they yo-yo from the top to the bottom of the sector, indicating greater risk.

Fidelity Japan Trust and Aberdeen Japan Investment Trust, one year share price performance to 24th November 2020

Discount volatility brings greater risk, too, of share price changes that are greater than expected, exacerbated by the 'double-whammy' effect in falling markets of declining asset values and widening discounts or evaporating premiums. Trusts that have a wide range of discount ratings and currently stand at the high end of the range, perhaps at a premium, will generally be at greater risk of a major price fall than a trust on a steady discount rating. The same is true for less liquid trusts, where the emergence of a small number of sellers could push the share price down more rapidly during a sell-off and there is the additional risk here of a widening of the dealing spread that prevents you from selling out at a reasonable price when you want to.

The list goes on, but one final factor here is the level of complexity and transparency. A straightforward equity trust might be considered to have less risk of a negative surprise than a trust with more complicated unlisted assets that are valued on a periodic basis, and where the valuation is difficult to judge independently. Some trusts with highly specialised assets can find themselves in situations with binary outcomes, where events will cause sudden and major adjustments to the quoted net asset value. Trusts in sectors such as insurance, aviation, loans, and legal funding have found themselves the victims of unexpected developments that caused major impairments to previous valuations. Potentially, too, trusts that are more innovative and investing in new sectors that are perhaps less well understood than more traditional asset classes are at greater risk of negative shocks from unforeseen circumstances.

Looking Backwards: Historic Performance

The standard risk warning that past performance is no guide to the future does not prevent investors from examining tables of historic performance as a gauge of relative quality. There is an argument in favour of trusts that have delivered good results in the past being more likely to do so in the future, and used sensibly this can have some predictive power. It is in the more flippant and simpleminded interpretation of performance tables that danger really lurks. Simply buying last year's great performers is unlikely to be a recipe for success. The temptation is very real for investors who lack understanding and the patience to acquire it, and simply want to buy the 'best' trusts at the top of their game. They read about an investment trust in a newspaper, or see what is top of the performance tables, and put in their buy order in haste. Very often, a year later, they can repent at leisure.

As with all statistics, the importance of interpreting them sensibly cannot be overstated. They can be tremendously useful when used well to compare like with like, and when combined with other information that explains the position, high or low, of individual trusts. If a trust has been the beneficiary of a fair wind specific to their sector, or a one-off boost from a major item of news that could not have been foreseen, or if the manager simply had an aggressively positioned and highly geared, concentrated portfolio at the start of a bull run, then a lofty position in the performance tables really provides no particular insight into the management quality and likelihood of continuing the strong performance. If, conversely, a trust consistently beats its peer group over a period of years, without using excessive gearing or a riskier portfolio structure, then this may yield some confidence in the managers that can be taken forward. Context is all-important, and that context is something gained over time, by following investment trusts and getting to know them better.

One particular aspect of the data that rears its head regularly is whether it is trustworthy and can be taken literally. For equity trusts, the bulk of the valuations are likely to be accurate, based on daily data. For trusts with significant unquoted holdings or alternative asset trusts though, where assets are valued periodically, it is vital to know whether the NAV being used is from the last official valuation point or whether it is a more recent estimation, adjusted for subsequent market movements. Depending on which figure is used, and in which direction it is moving, positions in performance tables might be over or understated. There are valuation lags for private equity, property, and for other physical assets.

Manager Meetings and Presentations

One of the very best ways of getting to know a trust, its style and methodology, its successes and failures, is by meeting the manager. For private investors this is difficult, as not only do managers have limited time, but they also have to answer to compliance departments that are often very nervous about direct contact with private investors and the chances of some comments or information being misunderstood and leading to complaints or regulatory conflict. They feel on safer ground talking to other investment professionals and intermediaries, where their 'counterparty' status means that a certain level of knowledge can be assumed. This is the main reason – along with pressures on their time - why most managers will not speak directly to individual investors, although the increasing use of video material online and also the existence of certain intermediary firms that shoulder the regulatory burden and carry hefty disclaimers, means that private investors can occasionally gain access.

For professionals, like wealth managers, stockbrokers, IFAs, analysts, institutional fund managers, and some journalists, though, regular meetings are a standard part of the marketing apparatus for trusts that are always keen to attract new buyers. These fall into four main categories, whether or not these meetings are face-to-face or online. The first type is a manager presentation, conference-style, followed by a short question-and-answer session. Typically the manager will explain their objectives and why they believe their particular investment approach is best for capturing the potential of their market effectively. They will talk about recent trades, about the outlook for the sector and how they see the future, run through the largest holdings, maybe use a case study, and then speak about the structure of the trust and why the gearing, dividend level, and other policies are all appropriate. Managers are nearly always articulate and passionate, and they make their cases well. The drawback with these kind of meetings is that the managers are very much 'on message' and delivering their standard pitch, which they have rehearsed many times. Investors looking for a new angle, a new way of understanding a trust, may not find it here.

One to one meetings, which are also regular and typically last for an hour, may also be loosely based around a presentation, but investors can much more easily direct the conversation, wander into allied areas, dig in to certain issues, and perhaps ask some very basic or even impertinent questions that would not be appropriate in a group. Managers can be more relaxed in these situations and more likely to be frank, and these meetings are a great way to resolve any unanswered queries about why a trust does something in its own way, perhaps different to others. Analyst briefings are a bit different, as a high level of knowledge is assumed and the questions tend to be much more technical in nature, perhaps about specific holdings or accounting issues, or buyback policies, gearing limits, new share issuance, and more detailed concerns.

Regular follow-ups are sometimes offered by trust managers, particularly after results announcements. These will include a summary of the returns for the period, and what went right and wrong, but because both parties assume a certain level of familiarity with the trust, these conversations can delve straight into problem areas - the portfolio imbroglios – or into new developments, or actions that might be innovative or different from how the manager previously reacted to certain market conditions. These can be a great source of market intelligence about what is really going on in markets, information that analysts can sometimes cross-reference and apply profitably elsewhere.

Understanding Trusts

Some trust names give you an immediate steer as to what the trust is all about, like Aberdeen Smaller Companies Income Trust (ASCI) or BlackRock World Mining Trust (BRWM), but when it comes to Monks Investment Trust (MNKS), Manchester & London (MNL), Temple Bar Investment Trust (TMPL), and a whole host of others, it is not obvious at all. Finding out what assets are in each trust, and exactly what makes each trust tick, is central to being able to make an assessment of their prospects. And each one is subtly different – the managers know that they must have a unique selling proposition, a USP, to justify their existence. Just because trusts may be grouped together conveniently in a sector does not mean they are particularly alike.

In the global emerging markets sector, Templeton Emerging Markets Investment Trust (TEM), managed by Chetan Sehgal and Andrew Ness, is the largest trust in the sector with a long track record since its launch in 1989. The managers follow the philosophy of trying to buy sustainable earnings power at a discount to the market, using Templeton's global footprint to meet company executives and make judgements, and they try to mitigate risk through diversification. The trust has 83 holdings[167] across the capitalisation spectrum, and roughly half the assets in larger companies over US$50bn market cap, with some familiar names such as Alibaba, Taiwan Semiconductor, Tencent Holdings, Samsung, Naspers, and Unilever. By country, the trust has around a third of assets exposed to China and its territories, 19% in South Korea, nearly 15% in Taiwan, and 7% in Russia. It is underweight India.

There are good reasons to think that Mobius Investment Trust (MMIT) might be very similar, as it is managed by two former managers of the Templeton trust, Dr Mark Mobius and Carlos Hardenberg. They share much of the same philosophy of investment, and there is some overlap in terms of the importance of ESG (environmental, social, and corporate governance), but actually it is quite different. It is a far more concentrated portfolio with only 30 holdings,[168] and a key plank of the managers' approach is to engage with these companies and to work with them to improve their ESG standards and to develop in such a way that will be attractive to other international investors, thereby raising their ratings. The country weightings are

[167] All figures to 30th September 2020; http://www.temit.co.uk

[168] All figures to 30th September 2020; http://www.mobiusinvestmenttrust.com

completely different, being 24% in India, 15% in Brazil, and 14% in China, plus 5% in Turkey and 4% in Kenya. The focus is on dynamic small and mid-sized companies, and none of the top ten are widely recognised names.

This is not unusual, to find that superficially similar trusts actually have very different characteristics once you start to look at them properly, to drill down into their underlying propositions and the stock or asset selections that result from that. In this case, investors looking for fairly mainstream emerging markets exposure may find that TEM more closely matches their needs, whilst MMIT is a much more specific bet on the skill of the managers to extract additional value from their activist methodology.

These types of distinctions exist everywhere in the investment trust sector, and they make for fascinating comparisons as different managers present different arguments and beliefs about how the future will take shape and which trends will be most influential, and about how they can find assets at the right price to take advantage of their views.

From the alternative assets sector, it is instructive to look at the two REITs devoted to student property, GCP Student Living (DIGS) and Empiric Student Property (ESP). Both have acquired portfolios of properties that are used to house students, and they receive rents and pay out dividends from that income stream. As is immediately evident from the two share prices though, something is very different. In 2019 in particular, the pair moved in completely opposite directions.

GCP Student Living has an investment thesis based on a structural shortfall of student accommodation in and around London, although it has subsequently branched out a little. Prior to the Covid-19 pandemic of 2020 that caused a major interruption to its plans and its revenue streams, the trust had been providing a modestly growing dividend and had expanded at a steady pace. To understand why Empiric Student Property, which always had a more regional approach, has underperformed so badly it is necessary to go back to the turn of 2017/18, when after a change of chief financial officer the trust realised its administration expenses were out of hand, cut its dividend and removed its chief executive. It has struggled to reset itself operationally since that time, and has been regarded as a lower-quality proposition at a time when income investors have not generally been disposed to forgive disappointments lightly. This is crucial context that investors should understand when comparing these two REITs: simply comparing the discounts and yields and buying the one with the more attractive metrics is insufficient analysis, and a qualitative judgement is essential.

The core message here is that every trust has a story. This is not an industry dominated by cold, hard figures and ratios, instead it is about ideas, about people, and about the future of our changing world.

GCP Student Living and Empiric Student Property share prices, five years to 24th November 2020

Differing Management Styles

Part of understanding how a trust works is to examine how the manager or management team structures their own analytical framework. There are different style factors to bear in mind. Investment management is a rich subject with a myriad of different legitimate techniques, and different managers will deploy a range of methods just as football teams have different tactics and play to the strengths of their squad. Some of these seem to be in direct opposition to each other, such as growth versus value, bottom-up versus top-down, specialised versus flexible, and concentrated versus diverse, and different techniques will work better at different times. What matters more is that the approach is applied consistently so that potential investors can judge its efficacy. One criticism sometimes levelled at managers is that they can be subject to 'style drift' when they respond to underperformance by slowly moving away from the investment process that was promised.

The growth versus value debate is probably the greatest one of recent years, something of a grudge match in the equity market that has been won spectacularly by growth investors. Growth investors aim to find the most successful companies of tomorrow, believing that most additional value is generated by long-term compounded growth from a small number of big winners, most notably the large US technology companies, the so-called FAANG stocks, Facebook, Apple, Amazon, Netflix, and Google (Alphabet). Of course there are also examples from China in the form of Alibaba and Tencent, and in the UK from companies like boohoo.com and Fevertree Drinks. The search here is for innovative companies that can capture market share in fast-growth segments of the economy, and managers focus naturally on dynamic sectors where there is considerable disruption, like technology and financial services. They will generally be less exposed to traditional parts of the economy that are no longer developing at a fast rate, such as mainstream banking, or oil and gas, or tobacco. There will not typically be much focus on dividends or on finding stocks with low P/E ratios. This approach has been most famously espoused by the Edinburgh-based management house Baillie Gifford, which has a standardised growth style across all of its mandates.

Value investors come at the market from an entirely different angle, seeking to buy quality companies on cheap ratings, with good dividend yields, and this will often mean they are contrarian, alighting on unloved companies that they view as being temporarily out of favour. This style of investing has a long heritage, from Benjamin Graham to Warren Buffett, and it carries the badge of being sensible – buying decent stocks with real cash flows at good prices, in a disciplined way that avoids falling for an optimistic narrative and a rosy vision of the future. Many investment trust managers have been trained to have a full-on value approach, or a value tilt, including Nitin Bajaj at Fidelity Asian Values (FAV), Simon Gergel at Merchants Trust (MRCH), Fran Radano at North American Income Trust (NAIT), and Joe Bauernfreund at AVI Global Trust (AGT).

The reason for dwelling on this particular division is that this particular style difference has accounted for much of the performance differentials over recent years. Growth has been hugely in demand as investors pay up for scarce growth opportunities in a low-growth world, while value investing has languished and been dismissed as 'old economy' by those who believe that technological change has accelerated the pace of disruption massively. Not all trusts are one or the other – there are plenty in the middle with all sorts of processes that could not be clearly defined as growth or value – but this has been a major factor to bear in mind and a really key determinant of relative performance. If you can find it, the information provider Morningstar has an 'Equity Style Box' that assesses each trust's value or growth style bias.

The majority of equity managers will describe themselves as stock pickers, trying to find the best individual shares that meet their criteria. Those who make their selections purely on this basis are known as 'bottom-up' investors, where the shape of the portfolio is determined from the bottom up, by those individual stock selections. In theory, the resulting sector and, if applicable, country selection, is an outcome of the process rather than an input. Few managers are completely 'top-down', using macroeconomics and political judgements to make asset allocation calls and then finding the stocks to fit that model, but many will use a 'macro overlay' to inform their decisions and create a shape for the portfolio that reconciles all of the information they have available. In this case the resources of the management firm may be important, as the larger asset managers have a potential advantage in the intelligence they can share with their managers at a macro level.

Specialist managers for trusts that have a narrowly-defined mandate can develop huge expertise in their areas, whether these are in equities or in alternative assets. There is little doubt that these smart, educated managers with real focus on niche areas can develop information advantages over other investors and that it makes sense to delegate investments in these realms to dedicated professionals. Listening to the manager of a biotechnology trust, or a Chinese investment trust, or a logistics property REIT, or a solar and wind farm operator is always an education. It is hard to imagine a generalist investment manager having quite the same depth of knowledge, and that makes it tempting to create a portfolio of specialist trusts that provide uncorrelated exposure across asset types. One problem though is that the same narrow mandates that provide such useful definition can also become straitjackets if the prospects for a particular sector turn sour. For the best part of at least fifteen years after 1990, being a Japanese equity manager must have felt like you had drawn the short straw, and it is difficult for even the best managers to buck the trend if there is a secular problem for a specialist sector like airline finance or Latin America or global financials. Trusts designed to exploit a particular opportunity in one age cannot necessarily adapt and thrive in different circumstances.

Strategic Equity Capital (SEC), a small cap specialist managed by Gresham House Asset Management, had just 20 holdings at the end of September 2020,[169] with its largest holding accounting for 11.8% of assets. At 30th March 2018, a single stock – IMImobile – accounted for 44.6% of the assets of another trust managed by the same firm, Gresham House Strategic (GHS).[170] These are just two examples of concentrated portfolios where managers want to back their convictions. Herald Investment Trust (HRI), meanwhile, has 318 holdings of UK smaller companies in the communications, multi-media and technology sector, and its largest holding accounts for 3.5% of assets.[171] The manager Katie Potts says the long tail of holdings is there because of liquidity, and the trust can start a stake with a very small sum. The nature of the sector means it is hard to pinpoint exactly where the next multi-bagger will come from.[172] The Bankers Investment Trust, a global trust, had 171 holdings at the end of September 2020, with Microsoft the largest holding at 2.8% of assets.

All of these different approaches are perfectly valid, but they may not be equally appropriate for individual investors. The two Gresham House concentrated portfolios are much more punchy and more likely to feature at the top or the bottom end of annual performance tables, whereas highly diversified trusts like Herald and Bankers are far less likely to be outliers.

---

[169] Strategic Equity Capital quarterly factsheet for 30th September 2020

[170] Gresham House Strategic Report and Accounts 2018

[171] Herald Investment Trust factsheet 30th October 2020

[172] Investment Trust Newsletter November 2016

Quirks

Look out for odd features in trust structures and in their portfolios that make them non-standard – these can very often be important. There are the trusts that use derivatives, occasionally with a meaningful result, as has been the case for Pershing Square Holdings (PSH). Diverse Income Trust (DIVI) uses FTSE 100 puts occasionally, and BlackRock Throgmorton (THRG) is unique in its use of a CFD portfolio as a differentiator. Canadian General Investments (CGI) habitually trades on a wide discount with limited liquidity because it is majority-owned by the Morgan family, who hold the position of chair and CEO, and own the management company. North Atlantic Smaller Companies (NAS) is run by Christopher Mills, chief executive and investment manager, who also owns the management company and 26.6% of the share capital.[173] Tetragon Financial Group (TFG, TFGS) has high charges and its shares are non-voting shares, which must contribute to its wide discount to net asset value. Lindsell Train Investment Trust (LTI) has a very large holding in its unquoted management company, accounting for more than 47% of assets.[174] It also prices its shares in pounds rather than pence, along with Personal Assets Trust (PNL). Law Debenture (LWDB) has its independent professional services business. River & Mercantile UK Micro Cap Investment Company (RMMC) has 10% of its assets invested in gold miners, which proved a useful insurance policy against market falls in 2020.[175] Similarly, the UK-focused Keystone Investment Trust (KIT) has the Canadian gold miner Barrick Gold as its largest holding at the end of September 2020, at 5.7% of assets.[176] Ashoka India Equity Investment Trust (AIE) has no fixed annual management fee and pays a performance fee only.

There are many more individual features that might not be obvious at first sight, but which shape the potential returns and the risk levels inherent in a particular trust. Knowing which trusts have peculiarities is partly a function of experience, but these factors can all be unearthed by following a basic research process that includes key public documents, some manager access if available, and perhaps some third-party research.

Currency

Another wrinkle that needs to be considered on occasions is the impact of currency. For the majority of investment trusts that are sterling-denominated, with shares priced in pence, the primary issue comes from those trusts holding overseas assets that may create a headwind or tailwind for their returns in sterling. After the unexpected Brexit

[173] North Atlantic Smaller Companies Investment Trust Annual Report for the year ended 31st January 2020

[174] Lindsell Train Investment Trust monthly factsheet 31st October 2020

[175] Investment Trust Newsletter September 2020

[176] Keystone Investment Trust monthly factsheet 30th September 2020

vote in June 2016 that caused a severe drop in the value of the pound, it came as a surprise to many that the UK stock market subsequently performed well, in considerable part due to this currency effect that boosted exporters and meant that assets held in foreign currencies became more valuable in sterling terms.

The investment trust sector is highly international in nature, meaning that changes in exchange rates crop up frequently as a factor. Adverse swings are an additional risk for any trust investing outside the UK, a risk that is sometimes mitigated by hedging policies, but most often not. The majority of managers say they are not currency experts and do not want to take on the additional cost and complexity of hedging, so that is left up to individual investors. That is all very well, but it is not realistic to expect retail investors to create hedging programs for their portfolios, so on the whole the currency risk is taken head on, although perhaps not always well understood. A period of sustained sterling strength could be bad news for returns from international investment trusts.

There are also a number of investment trusts, in fact mainly investment companies, where the shares are priced in US dollars, or less commonly, in euros. This need not be a major complication, particularly with modern stockbrokers who will execute trades seamlessly for sterling investors, making the currency exchange automatically, but there could be additional charges involved. That is something worth checking before you deal. There are also a few trusts with multiple share classes in different currencies. In general it makes most sense for British investors to keep things simple and to deal in the sterling class, but in some cases these shares are less liquid and may have a wider dealing spread, so again it makes good common sense to check before you deal and make sure you are investing with your eyes open.

ESG

It may not be very obvious at first why you might want to build environmental, social and corporate governance considerations into your investment trust analysis, but this has become an increasing part of virtually all manager presentations and is a growing factor that investors want to talk about. It's a reasonable assumption that trusts with strong ESG policies, both internally and in their portfolios, are more likely to appeal to large institutional investors and therefore achieve higher ratings. There has been a quick expansion of direct environmental investment, into clean energy in particular, but good ESG policies extend way beyond that, to REITs using modern LED lighting to reduce costs as well as energy consumption, to BlackRock World Mining Trust (BRWM) discussing ESG with investee companies to ensure their social license to operate, and some trusts such as Mobius Investment Trust (MMIT) targeting ESG improvements with their stocks to achieve re-ratings. You can even see annual reports detailing the type of water – tap, rather than bottled – served at board meetings. It is something to watch out for, as is the trust's own governance.

Discounts and Valuations

One of the big and vexing questions for investors is just how much importance to place on valuations in the sector. The very broad range of share price ratings against NAV, stretching from some 60%-70% discounts all the way through to premiums of 30%+ means it has to be a factor, but as always there is not really a simple answer to how central it should be to your decisions. Success is not just about buying wide discounts and selling trusts on premiums.

How much notice you take of valuations depends on a whole range of factors, and the best approach seems to be to examine each case on its merits. There are times when ratings reach extremes and the 'right' reaction seems obvious, but of course the market is composed of many different types of investors with different opinions and motivations, and the market price is the aggregate of their combined views. As such, market prices are not to be dismissed too readily – there is usually some sort of rationale for the existence of ratings that seem out of line. A widening discount may be the result of problems not yet widely appreciated in the market, or a big seller working their way through a disposal. A growing premium may be the result of analysts looking ahead to potential revaluations, or a marketing drive by the managers.

Your timeframe is relevant, as a starting point. For long-term investors, discount volatility plays a diminishing part in investment decisions as their time horizon extends far into the future. If you are looking to buy a core investment trust holding that you expect to hold for a multi-year period that might extend into decades, then getting hung up on the rating probably isn't worthwhile. The impact of a change in the rating is likely to fade into insignificance against the long term returns delivered by a successful manager, so if your favoured trust for long-term savings happens to be on a slightly higher rating than you would like, but that is the only reason preventing you from buying, it might not be a good reason to hesitate. There was a time when only a few trusts would trade on premium ratings, so it was an easy mantra to say you should never buy a trust on a premium, but times have changed and many high ratings have been sustained by quality trusts for lengthy periods.

Taking a speculative approach and value-hunting for wide discounts is a difficult game to play. It is tempting, and there is something wonderful about knowing you can buy assets for much less than their intrinsic value, but that does not necessarily mean there are easy speculative gains to be had from quick corrections and mean reversion. Wide discounts often reflect some underlying issues, and can persist for years, even yawning far wider over time. Value can certainly exist in some of these situations, but it is important to assess whether there is some sort of catalyst for positive change. Many frustrated investors have bought the cheapest trusts in a sector, only to watch with growing ire as the expensive, quality competitors forge further and further ahead as they exploit some sort of edge in their structure, management approach, or market positioning.

If experience suggests that discount-hunting per se is a dangerous pursuit, a more profitable tactic may be to think about ratings in relative terms, keeping a close eye out for short-term anomalies against a trust's average discount over recent periods and against peers. Such movements occur fairly regularly, when a premium or discount will suddenly gape in one direction or another, providing an opportunity to trade before other investors also move in to seize the opportunity. Turning yet again to Lindsell Train Investment Trust (LTI), where persistent demand for the managers' expertise, allied to a widely held view that the large unquoted holding in the management company was becoming more valuable, meant that a premium rating was quite normal, it looked like an opportunity to buy when the shares dipped to a rare discount in August 2020. The discount was only small, but in relative terms the rating had shifted away from its normal level without any apparent explanation besides the general market dislocations of the time, during the Covid-19 pandemic. Within a few days the premium had returned and did not take too long to return to double-digits.

Witan Pacific provides another example of a profitable strategy, this time based on a discount level of 10%. As with LTI, the background is essential - the opportunity was again all about context. In this case, after a disappointing period, the trust's board had effectively issued an ultimatum for the managers to beat their benchmark by the end of January 2021 or else it would advance proposals that would include a full cash exit. In November and December 2019 the shares dipped and offered a discount of just over 10%, which looked like an arbitrage opportunity. By April 2020 the discount had halved, and then it halved again when a change of management firm was announced in July 2020, before eventually moving to a premium.

Civitas Social Housing (CSH) provides a third example of where a discount opportunity arose because of a market circumstance, and whilst the discount was never massive in headline terms, a shift in the normal rating did herald a chance to profit. This social housing trust had been a conservatively-managed steady income producer before a new regulator arrived on the scene in 2019 and made some noise, causing concerns about the viability of CSH's business model, and the discount widened out as a result to 18.3% at the end of 2019. The trust had previously traded at a premium, and it seemed as though the shares had been marked down too harshly. The management kept on with business as usual, and within a year the shares were back on a premium.

In each of these cases there were discount misalignments rather than discounts that were wide in absolute terms, and that seems a key distinction for investors seeking extra growth from discount plays. It is a completely legitimate and useful way to turbo-charge your returns from skilful judgement in the market, but it requires more finesse than simply ranking trusts and buying those with the largest discounts. The same applies to trusts with very high yields. These can make good purchases on occasions, but sometimes the high yield is a warning sign that something is wrong or the dividend may be cut.

Using the Structure

The benefits of the investment trust structure from a management viewpoint are considerable, and it is valid to judge whether each trust is making the most of its capabilities. Assessing the directors under normal circumstances is difficult, but if the board has been tested when a trust has been through a period of stress or has hit a problem, their independence, leadership, and willingness to act can all be scrutinised, as of course can their shareholdings. The same is true for policies such as discount controls and share buybacks, which occasionally seem to be more of a promise than a reality. More broadly, if a trust is not making the most of gearing, revenue reserves, the ability to hold illiquid instruments, share issuance at a premium, derivatives to boost income, and is not getting any analyst or press coverage then it is reasonable to question whether it is behaving in an optimal manner that makes it a good choice to own.

On occasions, the capacity to flex the structure can be a potential negative too, particularly if a trust trading on a sizeable premium issues new shares closer to NAV. That can be an excellent move in the long-term for all shareholders, but in the near-term it can serve to mop up demand in the market and reduce the share price. This has been a repeating pattern in some alternative assets sectors that have been in high demand, such as infrastructure and renewables, as well as specialist property, where a manager with a big pipeline of investment opportunities may return to the market numerous times for additional capital, effectively keeping a lid on the premium.

Chapter 20: Sources of Information

This should be a golden era for self-directed investors wanting to conduct their own research and make their own investment decisions. Far from the world of the 1980s when Extel cards in a public library might have been a key resource, or annual reports that you waited for the postman to deliver, the limiting factor now is no longer the breadth of information available; it is the time you have available to process it. Faced with a mountain of PDFs, online tables, videos, presentations, factsheets, guides, articles, opinion pieces, recommendations, podcasts, and news feeds, it has become more important than ever to be discerning and to make qualitative judgements about the information you can access. As an aside, you should also be aware of the smaller corpus of information you probably can't access.

Investment Trust Websites

A decent website is a standard requirement nowadays for investment trusts, although the quality varies. Many supplement the basic documents and information with additional material to inform existing investors and attract new ones, so these websites are an obvious first port of call for primary research.

Annual Reports

The annual reports of investment trusts are probably still the single greatest resource in the market. Some are full of colour pictures, snazzily designed with graphics and in-depth profiles of portfolio investments, whilst others are low-budget black and white text documents, but all have a defined structure that provides detailed insight into each trust. Whether it's the 122-page Polar Capital Technology Trust (PCT) 2020 Annual Report, or the 49-page Personal Assets Trust (PNL) 2020 Annual Report, these documents should form the cornerstone of much basic investment trust research.

After a few introductory highlights, the first chunk of the annual report is made up of the chairman's statement, which can be bland or illuminating, depending on the chairman and their level of insight and frankness. Some are must-reads, to see whether Julian Cazalet has any more exasperated comments on the market valuation of The Lindsell Train Investment Trust (LTI) shares; or the reflections of the experienced Douglas McDougall, a former senior partner of Baillie Gifford and chairman of the AIC, in his role as chairman of Independent Investment Trust (IIT). Next comes the manager's report, and there is a dizzying array of styles here, from the matter-of-fact to tracts of advocacy by managers that are so relentless in their beliefs that they seem almost semi-religious, as well as brilliantly educational.

An extraordinary place to start might be the Polar Capital Technology Trust (PCT) annual report, which for the year ended 30th April 2020 contains a 14-page tour de force explanation of market and technological trends by Ben Rogoff and his team. As a way of quickly gaining real insight into what is really happening with technological change it is recommended reading year after year. Many others can be commended with equal warmth. Nick Train is always thoughtful and perceptive in his reports for Finsbury Growth & Income Trust (FGT). Bruce Stout, the manager of Murray International Trust (MYI) challenges standard thinking in his own acerbic style. For a detached analysis of macroeconomic trends and how these affect the construction of an all-weather portfolio designed to withstand market calamities, Ruffer Investment Company (RICA) provides some cool-headed reflections. More specifically, Joe Bauernfreund of AVI Japan Opportunity Trust (AJOT) writes perceptively about the changes in mindset and culture in corporate Japan, Evy Hambro and Olivia Markham of BlackRock World Mining Trust (BRWM) dig into the performance and outlook of commodities from gold to iron ore, copper, and lithium, and for something completely different, Merck Mercuriadis of Hipgnosis Songs Fund (SONG) explains the new economics of music streaming, royalty changes and synchronisation activity.

Of course there are many others of a high quality. It is easy to dismiss annual reports as old-fashioned constructs, outdated documents that look in the rear-view mirror in a fast-moving world, but for gaining an overview of the thinking behind each trust they remain the place to find the real set-piece expositions. Non-specialists may not want to carry on through the governance and accounting sections, but as a place of reference they remain useful for checking figures such as revenue reserves and borrowing costs.

Monthly Factsheets

If annual reports are the main meal, then monthly factsheets are the on-the-go snack of choice, with enough information to keep you up to date, or reasonably so, once you have a working knowledge of the trusts you want to follow. It is slightly frustrating that monthly factsheets generally take quite a while to become available, which may be due to a compliance lag, but they are still very useful documents. As well as basic factual information with figures for the NAV, premium or discount, yield, gearing, and fees, there will usually be performance information with a chart, and figures of the share price and NAV returns against the benchmark, a portfolio breakdown with a listing of the top ten holdings, and perhaps some commentary from the manager (sometimes separate).

Media Reporting

A good starting point when searching for good media reporting and intelligence on investment trusts is the AIC's annual media awards, designed to recognise the journalists who have best educated private investors and financial advisers. Richard Evans, who writes the Questor column for The Telegraph, won the award for 'Best National Journalist' in 2020. He covers investment trusts regularly, as do a number of other national newspaper journalists, including Merryn Somerset Webb and David Stevenson in The Financial Times, Mark Atherton and Ian Cowie in The Times and The Sunday Times, and Jeff Prestridge in The Mail on Sunday. Financial advisers can also read David Brenchley in Investment Week, winner of the 'Best Trade Journalist' prize, although generally the coverage of investment trusts in the financial adviser trade press seems fairly minimal. Articles by Cherry Reynard, 'Best Freelance Journalist', appear in a variety of places, including the Interactive Investor platform (along with Fiona Hamilton) and in the Investors Chronicle, where articles are also written by 'Best Financial Consumer Journalist' Leonora Walters and by Algy Hall, who also worked on the Investment Trust Newsletter in its early years. The AIC's 'Best Online Journalist' for 2020 was Gavin Lumsden of Citywire, which provides extensive in-depth coverage of the sector and is a good site to bookmark. The award for 'Best Broadcast Journalist' went to Holly Black of Morningstar, whose regular snappy video interviews with investment trust managers are well worth watching.

Overall, there is plenty of coverage of investment trusts in the mainstream media, although much of it is fairly introductory. Investors wanting to delve a little deeper have less choice, and long-time sector devotees probably miss both Money Observer, which ceased publication in August 2020, and the old Investment Trusts Magazine, a quarterly glossy that used to rub shoulders with more mainstream publications on the shelves of WH Smith and other newsagents. It was published by a national newspaper journalist called John Davis and ran from 1986 to 2014. When it was no longer able to continue, it left Investment Trust Newsletter as the only independent periodical devoted to investment trusts. The newsletter has been published continuously since 1996 and is available in both print and electronic form. Online, the paid-for research by QuotedData, Kepler Partners, Hardman & Co, and Edison Group is generally available to all, but the door remains fairly firmly closed when it comes to the best broker research. The platform stockbrokers have been making some efforts to create their own investment trust hubs, but these seem unlikely to deliver research of the same calibre.

Statistics

Most investors want to study performance tables at some point, whether considering new purchases or checking on existing holdings. The existence of these league tables, very much in the public domain, works as a motivation for managers, who all like to be well placed, and of course for boards as well, aware that criticism could be coming their way if a trust languishes at or near the bottom of a peer group for too long. For investors they are a great resource, subject to the usual caveats, and there are quite a number of online sources of regularly refreshed information. Many professionals will use daily spreadsheets provided by leading brokers such as JPMorgan Cazenove and Winterflood, but most of that information is readily available to all, free of charge, from websites like Morningstar, Citywire, Trustnet, QuotedData, Money Marketing, or from the AIC, or from platform stockbroking sites. This information is not hard to find, as long as you are prepared to look at a screen. If you prefer printed information, there is the annual Investment Trust Newsletter statistical supplement, but the inexorable truth is that the majority of dynamic information is in digital form, like it or not.

Awards

As is the case for most industries, there are annual awards events that cynics might say are largely for the benefit of marketing departments, and there is something in that argument, but they also serve to highlight trusts that have done well across the whole sector. If some of these were not previously on your radar, then the awards have done their job of alerting you to a trust that might be worthy of more investigation.

These awards tend to be based on historic performance, perhaps risk-adjusted and sometimes with a small quality or subjective overlay so they don't duplicate all of the prizes. Even so, the same names crop up frequently. Money Observer sponsored a series of annual awards until its demise, but in late 2020 there are two main sets of awards that are both announced in November, from the online service Citywire and the trade newspaper Investment Week.

The Citywire Investment Trust Awards 2020 were broken down into 18 sector categories. Starting with Asia-Pacific equities, the winner was Pacific Horizon Investment Trust (PHI), and for emerging market single country trusts it was JPMorgan China Growth & Income (JCGI), joined by JPMorgan Emerging Markets (JMG) for broader global emerging market equities. For European equities, Montanaro European Smaller Companies (MTE) took the prize. Scottish Mortgage Investment Trust (SMT) was chosen for global equities, and its Baillie Gifford stablemate Scottish American Investment Company (SAIN) for international income. JPMorgan Japanese (JFJ) was the pick for Japanese equities, Jupiter US Smaller Companies (JUS) for North America equities, and TR Property (TRY) for specialist equities. In the UK all companies sector, Baillie Gifford UK Growth (BGUK) came out on top, Murray Income Trust (MUT) for UK equity income, and JPMorgan Smaller Companies (JMI) for UK smaller companies. Lindsell Train Investment Trust (LTI) took the global multi-asset award. 3i Infrastructure (3IN) won by virtue of its strong performance in the infrastructure sector, HgCapital Trust (HGT) was the winner for private equity, Phoenix Spree Deutschland (PSDL) in the property specialist category, and AEW UK REIT (AEWU) for UK property. Rounding it off, VPC Specialty Lending Investments (VSL) won the award for specialist debt.

The Investment Week Investment Company of the Year Awards ran to 19 sectors plus four special awards. Running through the sectors first, for UK all companies the prize went to Mercantile Investment Trust (MRC), for UK income to Finsbury Growth & Income Trust (FGT), and for UK smaller companies to JPMorgan Smaller Companies Investment Trust (JMI). Pacific Horizon Investment Trust (PHI) picked up the prize for Asia-Pacific, and BlackRock Greater Europe (BRGE) for Europe. The overseas award went to Scottish Mortgage Investment Trust (SMT), for overseas income to Scottish American Investment Company (SAIN), and for overseas smaller companies to Edinburgh Worldwide Investment Trust (EWI). JPMorgan Emerging Markets (JMG) took the emerging markets award, and its sister trust JPMorgan China Growth & Income (JCGI) was chosen as the best single-country trust. In the flexible investment category, BMO Managed Portfolio Growth (BMPG) was the winner. Moving on to the specialist categories, for private equity and growth capital, the prize went to HgCapital Trust (HGT), for debt to BioPharma Credit (BPCR), for property to LXi REIT (LXI), for biotech & healthcare and technology to Allianz Technology Trust (ATT), and for commodities and natural resources to Baker Steel Resources Trust (BSRT). The hedge funds award was won by BH Macro (BHMG). In the infrastructure sector the winner was BBGI Global Infrastructure (BBGI), and finally in the environmental and renewables sector the judges were unable to separate two equally deserving trusts, so the joint winners were Impax Environmental Markets (IEM) and The Renewables Infrastructure Group (TRIG). The best new issue was judged to be Octopus Renewables Infrastructure Trust (ORIT). The management group of the year was Baillie Gifford after a spectacular run of performance, and a new award for the 'rising star of the year', awarded to a person with a maximum of six years' experience in the industry went to Claire Dwyer, the associate director of investment trusts at Fidelity International. Last but not least, the Jackie Beard award for an outstanding contribution to the industry was won by Matthew Dobbs, the long-serving fund manager of Schroder AsiaPacific (SDP) and Schroder Oriental Income (SOI), preparing for retirement.

Even if these awards do not necessarily help to inform your judgements on future investments, they can help to validate choices already made, and perhaps provide some extra comfort that you have picked some winners. It must be a good thing too for the industry to publicly recognise the achievements of some of its very best performers, whether those are trusts, management houses, or individuals.

Books

If bookshops were awash with great works on investment trusts, this one would not have been written to be added to the pile. There have been a number, but most are quite out of date and of limited value now: practical investment books about specific sectors do not generally stand the test of time as well as those on broader investing theory. The FT Guide to Investment Trusts by Anthea Masey was written in 1988; and The Investment Trust Industry in the UK by Paul Draper a year later. The weighty tome called Put Not Your Trust in Money, a history of the industry by the wise industry veteran John Newlands came out in 1997; The Split Capital Investment Trust Crisis, edited by Andy Adams, was published in 2004.

More recently, John Baron has updated his 2013 version of The Financial Times Guide to Investment Trusts; John Newlands has been busy writing detailed histories of some of the grand old investment trusts; and Jonathan Davis, a well-connected journalist, author, and investment trust enthusiast edits what has become an annual book on investment trusts published by Harriman House. The Investment Trust Handbook 2021, published in December 2020, is the fourth in the series, containing a collection of very useful articles by investment trust practitioners. It is sponsored by a group of investment trust managers, allowing the electronic copy to be distributed for free (the printed version costs £29.99).

Conclusions

There are technicalities to investment trusts, and you can delve into them if you wish, but you can also be a successful investor using common sense and people skills, judging the talent behind some of the finest trusts that have delivered exceptional returns. Arguably, assessing whether a manager has a good eye for which assets are most likely to prosper in tomorrow's world is at least as important as gearing ratios, z-scores, revenue reserves, and covered call writing strategies. Combining some broad predictive quality with a deepening knowledge of the structure and capacity of investment trusts is probably the best of both worlds. Please don't ignore the history either. There are so many lessons to be learnt from the summary of the last 25 years in the Appendix that follows, from both the adventures and the misadventures. This is a richly endowed sector in so many ways, heavy with history, bristling with bright minds, and still pregnant with potential for the future.

Investment trusts can be great products throughout lifetimes and perhaps even generations, as investors shift from capital growth to income and adjust their risk tolerance to meet their own changing circumstances. ISAs and SIPPs are becoming ever-more sensible holding accounts with pressure building to tax capital gains more heavily, and regular monthly saving is a wonderful way to start.

It seems a great pity that investment trusts have spent so long in the shadow of open-ended funds, and just as long fighting against a cultural resistance to getting involved with the stock market in any way at all. Yet in terms of the practicalities, the amazing flows of information and the ease of dealing, it has never been a better time to take those first steps. Building knowledge over time can be very rewarding, and taking a small stake in a trust is a great incentive to learn more and see if you can find the confidence to scale up your holding. Often it can take a while to get to know trusts and to establish the right level of conviction and belief.

The sector has been through some tough times in the past – certainly the split capital crisis, but also when the industry struggled to find new buyers to replace departing institutions, leaving trusts labouring under some persistently wide discounts. If there is a single issue that seems worrying at present, it is perhaps that many of the younger market participants have only ever known low interest rates, and trusts have been constructed to flourish in that environment. Yet the long-term chart of Bank of England base rates still indicates that this is a strange anomalous period that will likely end. If and when it does, there is a risk that a significant rise in interest rates and discount rates causes massive reductions in value and a liquidity squeeze in the alternative assets sector that has been such a success for the industry.

Undoubtedly there will be more challenges to meet in the future, but the investment trust sector is a proven British construct that has successfully evolved and endured. The considerable market turbulence and troubles caused by the Covid-19 pandemic in 2020 served to hammer home many of the great advantages of the sector, certainly as a home for illiquid assets and for the use of revenue reserves to support dividend payments during difficult times. The sector seems healthy, and it would be nice to think it plays a part in making its investors both wealthy and wise.

Appendix: History

Originally written as a trio of guides for subscribers of the Investment Trust Newsletter, these snapshots of each year of the newsletter's publication from 1996 onwards provide a great deal of background and context for the industry today.

1996 – The Very Beginning

Investment Trust Newsletter launched in November 1996, aiming to provide well-researched advice and to uncover much of the useful information not made easily accessible to investors. The first issue looked in detail at **Electric & General Investment Company** and **Electra Investment Trust,** both of which we recommended. The stockbrokers' research section contained research from Merrill Lynch, SBC Warburg, Credit Lyonnais Laing, James Capel, BZW, and NatWest Securities, none of which exist in the same form now. In December we met Brian Ashford-Russell, the manager of the new **Henderson Technology Trust** that was just being launched, and we also talked to Colin McLean of **Undervalued Assets Trust** and Andy Steel of **Ivory & Sime Enterprise Capital.**

1997 – Arbitrageurs and Vultures: Lots of Corporate Activity

In January we tried to pick some trusts reasonably immune from worries over the forthcoming UK general election. We looked at **British Empire Securities & General Trust,** emerging markets trusts, **Kleinwort Development Fund, Abtrust Scotland, TR Property,** and **East German Investment Trust.**

Investment trusts started the year well and we noted good gains from several of our early recommendations. Using director buying as a signal we examined the attractions of **Latin American Investment Trust, Glasgow Income Trust,** and **Brunner Investment Trust,** amongst others. We also looked at the specialist trust **Voyageur European Smaller Companies. Kleinwort Second Endowment Policy Trust's** 'S' share issue was oversubscribed.

In the early part of the year there was a burst of corporate activity with a bid for **Pilot Investment Trust,** a proposed merger between two Henderson income trusts, and US arbitrageurs buying into UK trusts sitting on wide discounts. There were also rumours of the imminent launch of two 'vulture' funds to target trusts, although they actually failed to arrive until closer to the end of the year. We made our first recommendation of the capital shares of a split capital trust, **Fleming Income & Growth.**

The UK stock market was unfazed by the new Labour government, elected in May, and there were some strong performances from emerging markets trusts. These helped the newsletter to get off to a strong start, with 26 of our first 30 recommendations in profit as at June 1997, with an average gain of 9.95%. We were making a lot of recommendations at this point, in tune with the prevailing bull market mentality that was also manifest in other ways. **Edinburgh Investment Trust** was one of several trusts to issue debentures to boost its gearing. The Trustnet website indicated a lot of interest in the **First Russian Frontiers** trust. The launch of **Mercury Retirement Investment Trust** flopped and was scrapped though, and several trusts left the sector, including **Paribas French, Govett Global Smaller Companies,** and **Matheson Lloyd's Investment Trust.**

In September we revealed details of our Meet The Managers conference, to be held in November. The **Cairngorm Demutualisation Investment Trust** was launched with the aim of profiting from the change in status of building societies, although it did not raise as much capital as it had hoped. Harvard College built stakes in a number of emerging markets trusts. In the second half of the year there was a further flurry of corporate activity, with liquidations, changes of manager, buybacks and strategic stakes all in the news. **TR European Growth** took an 8.6% stake in **Continental Assets Trust.** The Liverpool Partnership, a US arbitrageur, bought a 3.2% holding in **Healthcare Reform Trust** and Regent Fund Management bought 6.5% of **Gartmore Emerging Pacific. Mercury European Privatisation** bought back more shares; **Voyageur European Smaller Companies** and **Kleinwort Overseas** restructured. **European Smaller Companies, BZW Convertible,** and **Saracen Value Trust** decided to wind-up. **Scottish National** issued rollover proposals.

In October 1997 stock markets had a sell-off and Asian trusts tumbled in value. We looked at some income trusts, **Fleming Income & Capital** income shares, and **Shires Income.** The new vulture fund **Advance UK** took its first declared stake in **British & American** and we felt there would be pressure for corporate action at **Govett Oriental,** where US arbitrageurs took their holdings up to 12.4%.

1998 – Some Volatility; Plenty of Action from Split Capital Trust Shares

In the newsletter at this point we regularly covered directors' dealings, and pointed out at the start of the year there was a good amount of buying. As a speculation we recommended the capital shares of **Finsbury Income & Growth** at 15.75p, and we also recommended **Scottish Mortgage Investment Trust,** noting it "typically trades on a discount of around 14%". Both HSBC James Capel and NatWest Securities were bullish on the investment trust sector, feeling there was value waiting to be unlocked.

In February we noted the very strong performance of capital shares in split capital investment trusts, saying we had recommended eight over the previous eleven months, with all showing double-digit percentage gains. The **Fleming Income & Growth** capital shares had jumped from 155p to 287p. We reiterated our recommendation of **Archimedes Investment Trust** capital shares at 642.5p, having first tipped them at 537p.

In March we were able again to report on strong performances from the capital shares of split capital trusts, with the **Finsbury Income & Growth** capital shares up nearly 50% already from our January recommendation. Both **Fleming Income & Growth** capital shares and **Danae Investment Trust** capital shares had doubled since recommendation. We recommended another capital share, this time in **Rights & Issues Investment Trust.**

Henderson Greenfriar announced plans to unitise, sending its shares up by 10%. We rated **Aberdeen European** a good 'each-way bet' at 136.5p to perform or restructure. Around the turn of the tax year there was a surge in directors' dealings and also in trust buybacks. Stockbrokers said that Budget changes to tax and to PEPs and ISAs should be good for the sector.

In May we produced a table of all of our recommendations to date, showing nearly five out of six in profit (of a total of 65) and an overall average gain of 25.6%. Three capital shares led the way with triple-digit gains. In June we interviewed Ian Rushbrook of **Personal Assets Trust,** Colin McLean of **Undervalued Assets Trust,** and Stephen White of **Foreign & Colonial Eurotrust.** We also wrote about the new **Dresdner RCM Income Growth** split capital trust. Advance UK took a stake of 3.65% in **Martin Currie Moorgate** that we thought might be a prelude to some corporate action. **Healthcare Reform** announced its liquidation and **Govett Oriental** a restructuring.

The new vulture fund **Advance Developing Markets** took stakes in **Murray Emerging Economies, Morgan Grenfell Latin American, Taiwan Investment Trust** and **Edinburgh Inca Trust.** There was a great deal more corporate activity too, with **Murray Ventures, Murray Split,** and **Exmoor Dual** all restructuring and **Govett American Smaller Companies** winding up. We suggested taking profits on a number of the capital shares that had performed so well. Nick Train left **GT Income Growth** following the takeover of the management group. Several Lloyd's insurance vehicles gave up their investment trust status.

In the first half of 1998, **TR European Growth** was the top performer, up by 52.3%. The trust was managed by Stephen Peak, who spoke at our Meet The Managers conference in November 1997. We would host the conference again in London this year.

In August we spoke to Max Ward, the manager of **Scottish Mortgage Investment Trust,** and in September, Peter Webb of **Eaglet Investment Trust,** where the shares were 118p. We launched a new website called trustnews, featuring a discussion group, but this was later abandoned. We looked at UK smaller companies trusts trading on wide discounts to net asset value of around 20%, and private equity trusts, which we called venture capital trusts back then.

It was a tough summer. In the three months to the start of October, the investment trust sector dropped by 23.6%, not helped by a widening of discounts as prices fell. The average discount was 15%, with many emerging markets trusts on 30% and UK smaller companies on an average discount of 22%. Even **Scottish Mortgage Investment Trust** went out to a 20% discount and **Henderson Technology Trust** to 23%. Capital shares of split capital trusts were hammered.

Sentiment recovered quite quickly in the autumn, as did activity. **Gartmore European** bid for **Aberdeen European,** the Liverpool Partnership arbitrageur increased its stake in **Foreign & Colonial US Smaller Companies** to 7%, and the £1bn-plus trust **Scottish Eastern** was targeted by Advance UK. We covered new split capital issues from Commercial Union and Jupiter, offering attractive potential returns.

1999 – Strong Performances and Discount Narrowing as the 'its' Campaign Launches; But We Warn Repeatedly on Split Capital Trusts

We started the year with a few suggestions for self-select PEPs (personal equity plans, in case you have forgotten). For beginners we suggested **Alliance Trust.** We interviewed Anthony Bolton, the manager of **Fidelity Special Values.** In February we wrote about the new **BGI Endowment Fund III,** investing in second-hand endowment policies. We liked its projected returns of 11.1% a year. Another split capital trust was also launched – **Govett Enhanced Income.** Picking out some discount and valuation anomalies, we alighted upon **Henderson Technology Trust** on a 16.1% discount, **Dresdner RCM Smaller Companies** on a 36% headline discount (27% with debt at fair value), **Aberforth Split Level Trust** package on a 14.7% discount; and **Mercury European Privatisation** on a 17.7% discount. The annual review from the stockbrokers BT Alex Brown was somewhat sombre, saying that capital outflows from the sector had accelerated in 1998. **Henderson American Capital & Income** was the latest to wind up. **3i Group** made an unsolicited approach to **Electra Investment Trust.**

Our performance review in March noted an average gain since launch of 16%, ranging from a 134% gain on **Danae Investment Trust** capital shares to a thumping 60% loss on **East German Investment Trust,** which we had at least labelled as a gamble. We did particularly well from the split capital recommendations, nearly all of which we had since advised selling. Of eight new issues we liked, six were in positive territory, the best being **Henderson Technology Trust.** We suggested investors avoid the new split capital **Edinburgh Income & Value Trust.**

In April 1999 we reported on the AITC's big 'its' initiative to launch a national advertising campaign, due to start in September. We hoped it might help to generate extra demand and reduce discounts. At the same time we noted that investment trusts were now able to buy in their shares without suffering advance corporation tax. Expecting more buybacks in the international generalist sector, we repeated our buy recommendation for **Foreign & Colonial** on a 14.5% discount to net asset value (with debt at fair market value). We also reiterated our buy recommendation for **Schroder Ventures International Trust.**

Schroder UK Growth changed its manager; **Mercury European Privatisation** decided to drop the privatisation part of its remit (and its name), and we rated it a buy. We noted several positions where arbitrageurs had built up stakes. In our review of the new split capital trust **Premier High Income** we said we had steadfastly declined to recommend the ordinary income shares of any splits, and we said "the incestuous nature of the split capital market worries us. In particular we do not like to see in any of these split capital trusts a statement that they will invest in the ordinary income shares of other split capital trusts". We also said "if the UK stock market falls ... we think that this trust, and many other of the new split capital trusts, will struggle to return 100p for every 100p you have paid for your ordinary income shares". Those words would later prove prescient.

There were changes of manager for **Fleming Geared Growth, Fleming Claverhouse, Fleming Indian,** and **Fleming Asian.** Corporate activity continued, with **Dartmoor Investment Trust** making a hostile bid for **Pictet British Investment Company.** In July we recommended the new split capital **Close FTSE 100 Trust,** basically a split capital tracker, but reiterated our warning for both **Govett European Enhanced** and **Framlington Second Dual,** which said they would invest in the shares of other split capital trusts. We interviewed Dr Mark Mobius of **Templeton Emerging Markets.**

Markets were strong during this period, helping **Eaglet Investment Trust** shares to rise to 176.25p. Manager Peter Webb was still bullish. Share buybacks gathered pace, and about 50 trusts had started the process, the most enthusiastic proponents being

Fleming Overseas, Mercury European, and **RIT Capital Partners.** The discount on **Mercury European** narrowed to 8%. Arbitrageurs increased their stake in **Foreign & Colonial US Smaller Companies** to 16.2%. **Martin Currie Japan** took over **Edinburgh Japan.**

In August the newsletter opened with the statement "we are nervous of the markets right now, and indeed as we write the FTSE 100 Index has fallen by more than 140 points to below the 6000 level. We fear for the capital entitlement of some of the highly geared ordinary income shares which we have not recommended, and suggest you avoid them". We focused on special situations, looking at **British Assets Trust** and **Acorn Income Fund.** We also sought out what we believed to be the safest and cheapest zero dividend share on the market – on **JZ Equity**. We suggested holders who might have doubled their money since launch in **Henderson Technology Trust** "could be forgiven for wanting to take some profit". We were not keen on the new split capital technology trust from Aberdeen, feeling it had high gearing and that its timing might be poor. **Martin Currie Moorgate** decided to wind up, as did **St Andrew Trust.** HSBC Securities recommended **Jupiter European Opportunities** under its new manager Alexander Darwall. Nils Taube retired as the principal investment adviser for the quoted element of **RIT Capital Partners.**

The "its" campaign to promote the industry got underway in the autumn, with high hopes that it might boost money flows into the large international generalists such as **Witan Investment Trust** and **Foreign & Colonial** in particular. Average discounts had already narrowed to 10.4%.

One of George Soros's Quantum Funds invested in **Foreign & Colonial Special Utilities** 'S' shares. **AIM Trust** and **Beacon Investment Trust,** two of our recommendations, soared in value, the former doubling in six months. **Henderson Technology Trust** moved to a 9% premium to net asset value amid much excitement in the sector. **Finsbury Technology Trust** shares leapt 39% in two months; **Technology & Income Trust** announced its NAV was up by 42% in the first three months since launch. As the year drew to a close, so the bullish activity intensified, with trusts jumping by 9% in November, **3i Group** moving to a 48.9% premium and **Henderson Technology Trust** to a 20.8% premium. **Beacon Investment Trust** converted to open-ended status. **Gartmore Fledgling Index** succeeded in its bid for **Themis FTSE Fledgling Index.** Jupiter raised £400m for the launch of its **Dividend & Growth** investment trust – the largest ever split capital trust issue. 1999 was a dramatic year in which the FTSE Investment Trusts Index rose by 47.6%.

2000 – Arbitrageur Activity and More Technology

We felt the start of the new millennium seemed a decent time to recycle some money from the big winners of 1999 to some cheaper quality vehicles, or to carefully continue with monthly savings plans to build longer-term positions. Tom Walker took over as manager of **Martin Currie Portfolio Trust.** We noted director selling at the private equity trust **Thompson Clive.** In February we reported on the new **Amerindo Internet Fund,** which was initially hoping to raise £300m, later raised to £400m. Research from Deutsche Bank Benchmarking confirmed the outstanding performance of technology trusts in 1999. It also singled out **Fidelity Japanese Values, Fleming European Fledgling, Scottish Value Trust, Abtrust Scotland, Mercury European,** and **Electra Investment Trust** for praise.

The US arbitrageur Sierra Trading increased its stake in **Bankers Investment Trust** to 5%. The AITC's "its" marketing campaign said it attracted 75,000 requests for information from consumers in its first two months, and revealed its intention to continue the campaign for a second year. The excitement over technology stocks continued to build. The **Invesco Enterprise** small cap trust announced plans to convert into a technology trust, **Invesco techMARK Enterprise; Fleming Geared Growth** planned to convert into the **Fleming Applied Science & Technology Investment Trust;** and **Hambros Smaller Asian Companies** into **The Asian Technology Trust.** Framlington launched the **Framlington NetNet.Inc** fund and 3i launched the **3i European Technology Trust.**

In March the backlash against technology stocks began, with the FTSE techMARK 100 Index falling by 29% in less than a month. There were some sharp price falls and some discount widening across the sector as well, encouraging more reconstructions and arbitrageur activity. **US Smaller Companies** decided to convert into an open-ended fund and **First Ireland** proposed a reconstruction. We wrote about the launch of another 'vulture' fund, **Value Catalyst Fund,** and on more aggressive moves from trust agitators. Shareholders requisitioned an EGM at **Govett Emerging Markets** to consider realisation options; Advance Developing Markets raised its stake in **Murray Emerging Economies** to 14.5% and also took stakes in **Morgan Grenfell Latin American** and **Dresdner RCM Emerging Markets.** Amongst the large international generalists, both **Bankers Investment Trust** and **Monks Investment Trust** found Sierra Trading on their share registers. There were calls for a reconstruction at **International Biotechnology Trust,** and the arbitrageur Millennium Offshore Partners also took a stake of 5.1% in **Montanaro UK Smaller Companies.**

An upheaval at the fund management group Jupiter, triggered by the departure of the boss, John Duffield, cast a shadow over some of its trusts, with **Jupiter Primadona** losing its premium and both **Jupiter Split** and **Jupiter Dividend & Growth** serving 'protective notice' on their management contracts. **Merrill Lynch Japan Enhanced Performance** launched, using derivatives in its structure. The managers of **Henderson Technology Trust** chalked up an impressive £43.1m performance fee for the year.

We met Robert Knapp of Millennium Offshore Partners to discuss its investment trust forays, which now included **Scudder Latin America.** Sierra Trading, meanwhile, topped up its holding in **GT Japan.** The technology sector showed it still had some life in it with the launch of **Close Finsbury Eurotech Trust.** The annual Credit Lyonnais Securities Europe yearbook argued that trusts should be more actively embracing share buyback programmes, which reduce discount volatility and can place a floor under discounts. Repurchases became viable after the abolition of Advance Corporation Tax in 1997.

In September 2000 we invited subscribers to switch to delivery by e-mail if they wished, taking delivery in the form of a PDF instead of a printed copy in the post. The colourful manager John Johnston resigned from fund managers Murray Johnstone, and as a result the discounts widened on **Murray Enterprise** and **Murray TMT,** two aggressively-positioned technology growth trusts. A vibrant new issue market saw new offerings from **Henderson European Micro Trust, Merrill Lynch New Energy Technology,** and **LeggMason American Assets.** In the autumn, global markets shuddered again, driven lower by Nasdaq in the US. Aberdeen raised £300m for a new split capital trust, **American Monthly Income Trust,** with its US equity element being managed by Katherine Garrett-Cox. **Independent Investment Trust** was also launched, while the shareholders of **Scudder Latin America** voted to wind up the trust. **Mercury European** rebranded as **Merrill Lynch European Investment Trust.**

At the end of the year we wrote about some more new issues being cued up for the start of 2001, including **Lindsell Train Investment Trust.** Research from Merrill Lynch showed that 129 trusts had bought in shares since the start of 1999, contributing to narrower discounts, averaging 10% (ex-private equity). Repurchases in 2000 were dominated by **Edinburgh Investment Trust, Scottish Mortgage Investment Trust,** and **Monks Investment Trust.** Credit Lyonnais Securities Europe advised holders to reduce exposure to battered technology trusts where they felt the premium ratings would erode.

2001 – Heavy Price Falls and The Split Capital Crisis

At the start of the year we noted that it had become harder to find discount bargains in the sector. Deutsche Bank data showed the average discount for all conventional trusts had narrowed to 5%, with some technology trusts including **Amerindo Internet**

Fund still sporting large premium ratings. We fretted a little as well about the chase for income, wondering whether fund structures and hurdle rates could be stretched to provide tasty headline yields.

In our start of year round-up we noted the strong performance of Anthony Bolton's **Fidelity Special Values** trust. We also picked out **Eaglet Investment Trust** in the smaller companies sector, the **AIM Trust,** and **Murray Enterprise,** now reunited with its manager John Johnston at LeggMason Investors. Nick Train became the investment adviser to **Finsbury Growth & Income Trust,** and **Capital Gearing Trust** manager Peter Spiller decided to leave Cazenove and set up his own boutique firm – the board signalled they intended to follow him.

The US arbitrageur ST Partners tried to force tender offers at some big international generalist trusts, **Scottish Investment Trust, Murray International,** and **Foreign & Colonial Investment Trust.** Separately, **Beta Global Emerging Markets** decided to wind up. **GT Japan's** board switched the management contract from Invesco to Sloane Robinson.

In February we reiterated our recommendation of **North Atlantic Smaller Companies Investment Trust** as a long-term buy at 662p. The furious pace of reconstructions and winding-ups continued, particularly in the emerging markets sector that had earned the unfortunate nickname of 'submerging' markets. A review of the private equity sector by UBS Warburg rated three trusts as strong buys, **Candover, F&C Private Equity,** and **Mercury Grosvenor.** The **Framlington NetNet.Inc** split capital trust paid back £40m of borrowings, leaving it with just £7.8m of assets, just a year after launching with £100m. We said it was vying with **Amerindo Internet Fund** for the title of highest-profile technology disaster.

We shared the key points of an article by Dr Andy Adams and Robin Angus in Professional Investor magazine that warned of the risks of 'barbell' investment trusts in the split capital sector. Problems had already arisen due to high gearing levels in falling markets, but this article warned of higher than realised costs, questioned whether distress calls would continue to be met, and also criticised the 'magic circle' of managers investing in each other's trusts. We spoke to some bankers who lend money to investment trusts and found they preferred traditional trusts too. None of this stopped BFS Investments from launching a barbell split capital trust called **BFS US Special Opportunities Trust.** Not all trusts were finding fund-raising easy at this time – there were stumbles for **3PC Investment Trust** and the **First Housing Investment Trust** – but the volume of new issuance remained strong.

For investors wishing to obtain data on split capital shares we highlighted a new website, www.splitsonline.co.uk, run by Aberdeen Asset Management and Fundamental Data. Research at this time indicated that 40% of Britons had access to the internet. In July we reported on the premature end for the AITC's "its" marketing campaign, which had limited success in attracting large numbers of new private investors to the sector. The following month we noticed that Credit Lyonnais Securities Europe had changed its tune about buybacks, arguing they had contributed to falling liquidity in the sector, leading to the withdrawal of Merrill Lynch from investment trust market-making.

The FSA warned fund managers to strengthen the risk warnings attached to split capital trusts as Aberdeen's **European Technology & Income Company** saw its asset value slump after sharp falls in both its technology portfolio and its high yield bond portfolio, exacerbated by high gearing. The stockbroker Cazenove warned of the possibility of a systemic collapse in the 'barbell' part of the split capital sector. Other trusts, such as **Govett High Income** and **LeggMason Investors Income & Growth** had to issue new equity to reduce the risk of breaching loan covenants, yet in the same month the new **BFS Managed Properties** split capital trust raised £200m from a new launch and Britannic Asset Management launched a new split offering high headline yields. Splits had grown from 8.8% of the investment trust sector in 1994 to 19.9% by August 2001, accounting for £14.3bn out of £71.9bn of assets.

UBS Warburg noted that technology funds had reverted to trading on discounts. **GT Japan** decided to reconstruct and **Aberdeen Emerging Economies** received a winding-up requisition. Trust prices fell heavily over the summer and then tumbled again after the September 11th terrorist attacks in the US. Split capital and technology trusts both took a pounding. The first nine months of 2001 saw investment trusts fall on average by nearly 29% before a fourth quarter rally restored some value.

Peter Webb of Unicorn Asset Management had built a strong reputation with his top-performing **Eaglet Investment Trust** and launched another trust called **Falcon Investment Trust** to invest in mid-cap stocks. More split capital trusts raised capital to improve their asset cover. Ben Rogoff took over as manager of **Murray TMT.** Aberdeen closed its Fund of Investment Trusts unit trust after its assets dropped from £90m to £8.1m. Its **European Technology & Income** split was taken over by the **Technology & Income Trust.**

2002 – A Year of Change in Tough Market Conditions

The year started with some licking of wounds after a terrible 2001, and the FSA issued a discussion paper on the failings of split capital trusts, followed by a series of visits to fund managers. We hosted our third Meet The Managers conference in London. **Henderson EuroTrust** bid for **Charter European Trust,** which rebuffed its proposals and ultimately fended it off successfully with its own reconstruction plan. The board of **Britannic Smaller Companies** introduced a symmetrical performance fee that penalised poor performance as well as rewarding good. The performance of **Eaglet Investment Trust** started to dip. Stockbrokers began to trawl through the wreckage of the split capital sector – sometimes dubbed the *spilt* capital sector – to hunt for bargains from better quality trusts. We recommended shares in **Aberforth Split Level Trust** which we felt was being unfairly punished for its structure. Collins Stewart launched a **Zero Dividend Recovery Fund.**

Michael Moule, the manager of **Bankers Investment Trust** and the industry's longest-serving manager, announced he would retire and hand over to Alex Crooke. The £1.4bn **Edinburgh Investment Trust** put its management contract out to tender, a blow for Edinburgh Fund Managers. It chose Fidelity as its new manager. Prices fell again in the summer, pushing some split capital trusts to their final sad conclusions. Some trusts such as **Aberdeen High Income** called in the receivers, the fourth Aberdeen split capital trust to do so. A House of Commons select committee quizzed the AITC head Daniel Godfrey, three executives from Aberdeen Asset Management, and John Tiner of the FSA.

By October the average discount had widened out to 15% in a sector battered by weak equity markets and the split capital crisis. Technology trusts and UK smaller companies trusts were particularly sharp fallers, including **AIM Trust, Eaglet Investment Trust,** and **Polar Capital Technology Trust.** Neil Hermon took over as manager of **Henderson Smaller Companies** and John Pennink took over from John Walton at **British Empire Securities & General Trust.** A number of trusts decided to reconstruct, including **Baring Emerging Europe, Fleming Technology Trust, Investec Extra Income,** and **Invesco Tokyo Trust.** Arbitrageurs targeted **Amerindo Internet Fund.** At the end of the year the **Standard Life Investments Property Income Trust** launched with a target yield of 6.5%, but was unable to reach its minimum funding target in depressed conditions.

2003 – More Corporate and Regulatory Activity as Markets Start to Recover

The FSA proposed new rules for investment companies in the wake of the split capital crisis, with limits on cross-holdings and stricter requirements about the independence of directors. Markets continued to fall as sentiment was hurt by the impending Iraq war, with UK smaller companies trusts suffering badly, and an AITC survey found that 51% of investors were not planning to use their ISA allowances. **Witan Investment Trust** addressed the benefits of staying invested in its marketing literature, quoting

David Brent, the fictional star of the television series 'The Office', who said "quitters never win".

Mark Barnett became manager of **Keystone Investment Trust,** which moved from Merrill Lynch to Invesco Perpetual. **Jupiter Dividend & Growth** purchased a two-year FTSE 100 put option aimed at providing downside capital protection. **LeggMason Investors Enterprise,** a popular trust at the height of the technology boom, shifted to Schroders with a new UK mid and small cap mandate. **Mercury Grosvenor Trust** renamed as **HgCapital Trust.** Markets rallied in the spring and Anthony Bolton, the manager of **Fidelity Special Values,** proclaimed the start of a new bull market, but Ian Rushbrook of **Personal Assets Trust** remained resolutely bearish. Discounts narrowed as investors started to buy again, and there was a rash of corporate activity with a whole group of tenders, reconstructions and offers. Trusts affected included **Aberdeen Latin American, AIM Trust, 3PC Investment Trust, Henderson Absolute Return Portfolio, Liontrust Winners, New Opportunities Investment Trust, Jubilee Investment Trust, Piccadilly Growth Trust, Smaller Companies Investment Trust, Special Utilities Investment Trust,** and **Schroder Emerging Countries.** Newspaper reports suggested that **Edinburgh Small Companies** was preparing for a change of management company. We recommended **Acorn Income Fund** at 77p and also took a look at geared trusts well positioned to motor in a recovery.

After **Edinburgh Small Companies** moved its management contract to Standard Life Investments and **Edinburgh Worldwide** moved to Baillie Gifford, Edinburgh Fund Managers was taken over by Aberdeen Asset Management. Govett, the manager of six trusts, sold its management contracts to Gartmore. We reiterated our recommendation of **Acorn Income Fund** at 95.5p. A clash erupted at **Caledonia Investments** between the board and activist shareholders seeking a realisation of the portfolio.

From December 2003 trusts could start to hold their own shares in 'treasury' for later re-sale. **ISIS Property Trust** was launched to great demand with an initial yield target of 7% and was later joined by **Standard Life Investments Property Income Trust**. The Times newspaper recommended **Amerindo Internet Fund** shares at 14.75p. Both **Martin Currie European** and **Henderson European Micro** received 'perform or else' ultimatums from their boards. **Witan Investment Trust** said it planned to appoint a chief executive and to allocate assets to specialist managers. **Scottish American Investment Company,** known as SAINTS, moved from First State Investment Management to Baillie Gifford. We reported on **JPMorgan Indian,** whose shares had nearly doubled in six months.

2004 – Japanese and UK Smaller Companies Trusts Sprint Ahead and New Property Income Trusts Arrive

The year began with an air of optimism after a decent 2003 and a sense that more orderly markets were giving some trusts a breathing space to reconsider their positions. A number of individual manager changes were followed by some corporate manoeuvres, with the arbitrageur Millennium Offshore Partners instigating wind-up proposals for **Amerindo Internet Fund, Merrill Lynch World Mining Trust** making a bonus issue of warrants, **Caledonia Investments** creating an exit for its disgruntled minority, and **Merrill Lynch European Investment Trust** deciding to reconstruct. Credit Lyonnais exited from the investment trust sector.

Japan performed very strongly in the first quarter, pushing some Japanese smaller companies trusts up sharply. By the time of the May newsletter, **Atlantis Japan Growth Fund, Invesco Japan Discovery,** and **Fidelity Japanese Values** had all doubled their assets over twelve months. Geared smaller companies trusts in the UK were also performing well, with **Active Capital Trust, Eaglet Investment Trust, Gartmore Fledgling** and **Invesco English & International** all growing their assets by at least 70% over twelve months. We suggested some caution might be prudent at these levels. Chris Turner and Marcus Phayre-Mudge, the managers of **TR Property,** resigned from Henderson Global Investors, triggering the board to give notice to terminate its management contract and undertake a selection process for a new manager. The FSA was close to concluding its enforcement against firms involved in the split capital crisis, but the mediation process stumbled over the £350m it was seeking in compensation payments.

Ruffer Investment Company launched, along with **Insight Foundation Property Trust.** The fund management companies ISIS and F&C announced a merger to create the fourth largest asset manager in the UK. Never ones to miss out on a topical link, the AITC conducted an 'Investment Trust Olympic Games'. In the ten year consistency decathlon, **Fidelity European Values** beat off **Aberforth Smaller Companies** and **Candover Investments** to take the gold. In the sprints, Japanese trusts swept the board, with **Invesco Japan Discovery** on top of the podium. We recommended **Law Debenture** shares. **Scottish Investment Trust** and **JPMorgan Fleming Claverhouse** decided to pay back expensive debt, and the management contract for **TR Property** was awarded to Thames River Capital, where the previous management duo had relocated.

More property income trusts arrived, promising yields of around 6%. We arranged access to the placing for **Invesco UK Property Income Trust. Henderson Electric & General** gave the international generalists sector a shock wake-up call by announcing a change of management company to Taube Hodson Stonex, dropping the 'Henderson' part of its name at the same time. A series of presentations by international generalists trusts, hosted by UBS, suggested guarded optimism for the outlook.

The whirl of reconstructions and switches in management mandates kept on spinning. 3i decided to seek an exit from its management contracts for **3i Smaller Quoted Companies Trust** and **3i European Technology Trust,** but plans to move both trusts to DWS – the investment trust management arm of Deutsche Asset Management – were abandoned when DWS announced its own strategic review. **3i Bioscience** moved to Schroders. **Aberdeen Convertible Income** became **New City High Yield Trust.** A formal performance target was imposed on the managers of **Charter Pan European,** with the threat of a wind-up if the target was not met, and the board effectively issued a similar ultimatum to **F&C Emerging Markets Investment Trust. Alliance Trust** and **Second Alliance Trust** rejoined the AITC after a three-year absence. The Treasury issued a consultation paper seeking views on whether there was a need to introduce additional regulation for investment trust companies. At the very end of the year, the FSA and 18 firms involved with split capital trusts agreed a compensation package of £194m for investors.

2005 – Rising Markets Attract More New Issues

F&C Commercial Property Trust was launched to swell the assets of an already popular sector. In contrast, the large shareholders of **3i Bioscience** wanted to exit and the trust announced reconstruction proposals. **3i Smaller Quoted Companies Trust** moved to Merrill Lynch, and **F&C Income Growth** and **F&C Capital & Income** entered into merger discussions. **Gartmore Global Opportunities** came under siege from arbitrageurs. The early part of the year saw plenty of personnel changes at a number of trusts. Dresdner Kleinwort Wasserstein's annual review noted that board initiatives had helped discounts to narrow towards the 9% 'glass ceiling' that had been in place since the mid-1990s. The broker thought markets might struggle this year after two years of good gains.

After a few periods of lacklustre performance, **Foreign & Colonial Investment Trust** made a partial shift towards a multi-manager approach. **F&C Pacific Investment Trust** replaced F&C Management with Aberdeen Asset Managers and Nomura Asset Management and planned to change the name to **Witan Pacific. Perpetual Income & Growth** bid for **Securities Trust of Scotland,** a rare hostile takeover bid in the sector, but did not ultimately succeed. **AXA Property Trust** became the latest addition to a burgeoning sector. **Finsbury Life Sciences** appointed OrbiMed Advisors as its new investment adviser. **Jupiter Global Green** just survived a liquidation vote. We met the managers of **Polar Capital Technology Trust** when the shares were 185.5p

– their message was "get ready to buy". UBS suggested caution on private equity trusts, as they saw a less buoyant outlook and some relatively expensive valuations.

The founders of Amerindo Investment Advisers were arrested in New York on alleged fraud charges, so the board of **Amerindo Internet Fund** served notice on the managers and the trust was liquidated when it became clear there was insufficient support from shareholders for it to continue. **Deutsche Equity Income** also served protective notice on its managers, DWS. F&C purchased Martin Currie's private equity fund of funds business and changed the name of **Martin Currie Capital Return Trust** to **F&C Private Equity Trust. Taverners Trust** became **Midas Income & Growth Trust.**

By mid-year the FTSE 100 Index was rising, up and away from the 5000-mark that had been something of a magnet. The rash of property funds spread to Bulgaria, although we had reservations about the **Lewis Charles Sofia Property Fund.** Over in Japan, **Atlantis Japan Growth Fund,** managed by Ed Merner, was a strong performer, trading on a premium to NAV. **City Merchants High Yield** agreed a merger with **Exeter Selective Assets Investment Trust.** At the start of October The Times newspaper reported that Fidelity was preparing to launch its first new investment trust in ten years, aiming to raise £80m-£100m for an emerging markets trust for launch in the first half of 2006. **ING UK Real Estate Income Trust** was the latest big launch in the property sector, targeting a 6.25% dividend yield. The fourth quarter saw a real flurry of new issues in specialist fields, including **Aberdeen Asian Income Fund, Merrill Lynch Commodities Income Investment Trust, The Ukraine Opportunity Trust, Morant Wright Japan Income Trust, India Capital Growth Fund,** and **AcenciA Debt Strategies.**

Presentations from several well-known UK managers, including Anthony Bolton, Mark Barnett and Job Curtis, indicated that while British shares were some way into the bull market, they could have further to go. **Lowland** won the award for best UK trust at the annual Investment Week awards in London, with **British Empire Securities** winning the award for best global trust and Baillie Gifford picking up the prize for best group. **Baillie Gifford Japan** snatched the Japan title from **Atlantis Japan Growth Fund,** which had won for the previous four years. The Nikkei 225 Index moved ahead strongly to round off a good year.

2006 – The Sector Diversifies into Alternative Assets

Rounding up some fund managers' views for the year ahead, in the January 2006 newsletter, we quoted Bruce Stout, the manager of **Murray International.** He said "unprecedented credit-fuelled consumer spending and irresponsible fiscal policies have enabled the US and UK economies to grow only by living well beyond their means. Such debt-dependency has produced unsustainable deficits that history tells us are exceedingly painful to correct. We believe the post credit-binge hangover is rapidly approaching for such 'Debtor Nations'". How prescient his words would become, though not just yet. Most fund managers expected a good year ahead.

The JPMorgan trusts started to drop the word 'Fleming' from their titles. Ben Rogoff took over from Brian Ashford-Russell as manager of **Polar Capital Technology Trust.** Investment trusts seemed to be moving into previously unchartered waters, including infrastructure with the launch of **HSBC Infrastructure Company,** targeting a 5.75% yield. WINS Investment Trusts said the largest fund facing a high probability of corporate action in 2006 was **JPMorgan Fleming Continental European,** in which the arbitrageur Carrousel Capital held a 13% stake. The broker had a long list of trusts with large arbitrageur stakes on their shareholder registers.

A number of smaller investment companies listed on the AIM, including **Eastern European Property Fund**, **Aurora Russia,** and **Puma Brandenburg.** Hedge funds were also in vogue, with new listings from companies such as **Dexion Alpha Strategies** and **PSolve Alternatives. Alliance Trust** and **Second Alliance Trust** finally decided to do the obvious thing and merge, forming the largest generalist investment company on the London Stock Exchange. Simon Gergel took over from Nigel Lanning as manager of **Allianz Dresdner Income Growth.** Noting the rise of AIM-listed and Guernsey-domiciled investment companies, the Association of Investment Trust Companies (AITC) announced plans to change its name to the Association of Investment Companies (AIC). The new issue market continued full steam ahead, including **ING Global Real Estate Securities, RCM Technology Trust, Jupiter Green Investment Trust,** the **Close AllBlue Fund, Canadian Income Trusts Investment Company, VietNam Holding,** and **Macau Property Opportunities Fund.**

In May, markets fell sharply, with UK and Japanese equities suffering badly. It felt like a correction after three years of fairly solid gains. In March The Financial Times had pointed out that "not since the 1950s has the London stock market enjoyed a longer uninterrupted bull run". **JPMorgan Fleming Continental European** announced restructuring proposals. **Acorn Income Fund** scraped through a continuation vote.

We noted in September that the sector was strong, with average discounts standing at just 2.2% (or 8% excluding private equity). New managers were coming into the sector, with new AIM listings helping the industry to grow. It was a busy time for two-way capital flows. In the year to the end of August, new inflows amounted to £6.7bn from fund launches, extra gearing, 'C' share issues and warrant exercise, with £4.1bn leaving the sector through capital distributions, winding-ups and liquidations, tender offers, redemptions, and share repurchases.

Standard Life Investments Property Income Trust was trading on a large premium of 8.4%, and we questioned its sustainability. There were warnings of slower future returns from UK property. **Edinburgh UK Smaller Companies Tracker** and **Resources Investment Trust** both decided to wind-up. **Gartmore Asia Pacific** switched its management mandate to Aberdeen. More alternative asset trusts arrived, including **Babcock & Brown Public Partnerships, Prospect Epicure J-REIT Value Fund,** and **CQS Rig Finance Fund.** At the annual end-of-year awards sponsored by Investment Week, **British Empire Securities & General** won in the global category again, making it four years out of five.

2007 – More of the Same: Arbitrageurs and Alternative Assets

In January 2007 we reported on the market debut for **Phaunos Timber Fund**, illustrating the breadth of the industry, along with the hedge funds **BH Macro** and **Gottex Market Neutral Trust**. **Henderson Strata Investments** made some changes and became **Henderson Opportunities Trust. 3i Infrastructure** announced its intention to float. Katherine Garrett-Cox joined **Alliance Trust** as chief investment officer. **Gartmore European** came under attack from the arbitrageur Carrousel Capital.

Finsbury Technology Trust moved the management of the trust's portfolio to RCM, part of Allianz Global Investors, under the guidance of Walter Price and Huachen Chen. **SR Europe** issued subscription shares, a relatively new variant of warrants. **August Equity Trust** and **Rutland Trust** announced proposals for a merger to form **New Star Private Equity Investment Trust.** The AIC released data showing that trusts managed by the same manager for at least ten years had handsomely outperformed the average, although the results might be rather flawed as poorly-performing managers are replaced. In the May newsletter we looked at two trusts with long-serving managers, **TR Property** and **Invesco English & International.**

Stock markets generally, investment trusts as a group, and emerging markets in particular, had all been performing well. Plenty of analysts saw good reasons for the bull run to continue, citing the combination of strong growth with weak inflation and low P/E ratios, similar to the economic configuration that saw such a long bull period prior to the oil shock of the 1970s. One dissenting voice though was Anthony Bolton, the outgoing manager of **Fidelity Special Values,** whose parting shot was a warning about the possibility of a drop in stock markets. He was worried about the ease with which credit markets were financing M&A and private equity deals. He said "I can't tell you when it's coming but I can tell you the precursors are there" for a stock market slump. Sanjeev Shah took over as manager of the Fidelity trust.

Nicola Horlick launched **Bramdean Alternatives** to invest in private equity, hedge funds, and speciality funds. It raised £131m from its launch, rather less than the £250m it was seeking. **RCM Technology Trust** made a bonus issue of subscription shares to shareholders. There was a spat between the board and managers of **UK Balanced Property Trust** that looked like heading towards a reconstruction of some kind.

In July the newsletter led with the news that the AIC together with **JPMorgan Claverhouse Investment Trust** had won its case against HMRC relating to the charging of VAT on management expenses. Dating back to 1990, the excess VAT wrongly collected was estimated to amount to £300m.

Brokers recommended property trusts, with Dresdner Kleinwort opting for **Invista Foundation Property Trust** and UBS for **F&C Commercial Property Trust.** In the summer the market wilted on fears of a credit crunch, and in the August newsletter we wrote the words "sub-prime mortgage market" for the first time. The gravity of the situation was not clear, so we looked at trusts for pessimists and for optimists. The assets of **Invesco Japan Discovery Trust** dropped to £25m, so it decided to throw in the towel and reconstruct. Complex capital reorganisation proposals from **Templeton Emerging Markets** were rejected by shareholders and abandoned.

Aberdeen Asset Management bought Glasgow Investment Managers; **Edinburgh Small Companies** became **Standard Life UK Smaller Companies Trust.** In November the London Stock Exchange started the Specialist Fund Market for specialist investment companies with more sophisticated investment propositions. The Chancellor, Alastair Darling, introduced a new single rate of Capital Gains Tax (CGT) of 18%.

Some European property and financial sector trusts fell heavily towards the end of the year as the US credit crisis began to bite. Dresdner Kleinwort published a chunky survey of listed hedge fund vehicles that could perhaps provide some downside protection in volatile market conditions. **BH Macro** was the best performing company in the sub-sector at this point, but **Dexion Absolute** snagged the Investment Week award for the sector at the annual awards ceremony. **Eaglet Investment Trust** came under attack from a group of arbitrageurs, and Carrousel Capital also established a stake in **Fidelity Asian Values. JPMorgan Japanese** moved the management of its portfolio from London to Tokyo, with a change of management.

2008 – A Bad Year for Markets as the Credit Crisis Deepens

Managers started the year in a reasonably optimistic mood, although some did suggest the short-term could be bumpy. WINS research indicated 2008 could be another busy year for corporate action as trusts struggled to attract new demand. New issues were not easy to get away, with **Close Agricultural Commodities** and **Jupiter Equity Income** both failing to raise the capital they were seeking at the turn of the year. In contrast, there was demand for hedge funds – **Absolute Return Trust** increased the size of its 'C' share offering from £100m to £125m in response. **Terra Catalyst Fund** launched to target distressed property situations.

In March we considered ISA selections for the year, noting that the amount you could invest was rising from £7000 to £7200 for the 2008/09 tax year. This time we plumped for **Caledonia Investments, Law Debenture,** and for more speculative investors, two JPMorgan emerging markets trusts – **JPMorgan Russian** and **JPMorgan Indian.**

After a number of board changes, **Eaglet Investment Trust** proposed a change in remit and manager. At the annual AIC conference for directors we heard about how the sector was changing, with more performance statistics online, more offshore investment companies, and more thoughtful use of the investment trust structure. Board independence was being expressed more often by changes of fund manager, and some trusts such as **Gartmore Growth Opportunities** started to experiment with a quasi open-ended structure allowing regular exit opportunities.

Mark Barnett, the manager of **Perpetual Income & Growth,** warned in a conference call that the slowdown in the UK economy was not yet priced into the equity market. He suggested focusing on large caps. The stockbroker Cenkos preferred Japan and recommended **Baillie Gifford Japan** on a discount of 16.4%. Some degree of risk aversion was evident in the IPO market, as JPMorgan launched a convertibles trust, BlackRock sought up to US$500m for a new fund of hedge funds, and the infrastructure trusts **Babcock & Brown Public Partnerships** and **HSBC Infrastructure Company** both tapped the market for extra funds through 'C' share issues.

ING UK Real Estate Income sold off some properties to reduce its borrowings. **Japan Accelerated Fund II** was in the news because it was backed by two Icelandic banks that had seen their credit ratings cut. **JPMorgan Chinese** made a bonus issue of subscription shares while **JPMorgan Fleming Mercantile** changed its name to **The Mercantile Investment Trust.** Several Merrill Lynch trusts re-branded to BlackRock.

In the May newsletter we introduced a number of 'alternative asset' trusts, **Thames River Multi-Hedge PCC, Ludgate Environmental,** and **Vietnam Property Fund.** In June we reported on the WINS Investment Companies Conference, where the price of oil was a recurring theme, as well as the difficult equity market conditions. Bob Yerbury, the CEO of Invesco Perpetual, said that it had been critical to have exposure to emerging markets and to mining stocks over the previous five years to have achieved the best returns. He said there were still problems to work through in the UK and US, where the unwinding of excess leverage had further to go. Chris Turner, the experienced manager of **TR Property,** advised that it was too early to buy into the depressed property sector. He felt the bottom for property equities would come no earlier than the end of 2008, and perhaps later. **Throgmorton Trust** received a merger proposal from **Gartmore Growth Opportunities** but decided instead to hold a 'beauty parade' of managers and plumped for BlackRock.

Discussing the bear market in the July newsletter, we examined the merits of monthly savings plans and also looked at some relatively high discounts on offer from the sector. These included **Alliance Trust** on a discount of 19.6% and **Lindsell Train Investment Trust** on a discount of 12.7% against a twelve-month average of 1.2%. The broker WINS issued a positive note on **Monks Investment Trust,** which was performing very well under the management of Gerald Smith. **Perpetual Japanese** decided to issue reconstruction proposals.

In September 2008 we made some changes to the style and design of the newsletter, adopting the paper and masthead that we still use today. We were able to report on a radical economic step in the US, where the two main mortgage organisations – Fannie Mae and Freddie Mac – were effectively nationalised. This worked well to restore some confidence in the US, so we reviewed the trusts focused on that region – just before Lehman Brothers went bankrupt and shattered that fragile confidence. Glitnir Bank also went into receivership in Iceland, damaging the capital value for **Close Enhanced Commodities,** which held some of its debt securities. We reiterated our advocacy of monthly savings plans as a way of building long-term investments.

Henderson Smaller Companies sought approval from its shareholders to allow investment in short positions, including derivatives such as CFDs, following changes to the listing rules allowing their use. **Edinburgh Investment Trust** moved its management contract from Fidelity to Invesco Perpetual, with Neil Woodford as the new manager. The financial website Citywire launched a new investment trust data service online.

In November the US elected a new President and the level of volatility in global markets abated somewhat. AIC data showed the five most consistent performers over a decade to be **JPMorgan Russian Securities, Genesis Emerging Markets, Advance Developing Markets, Aberdeen New Dawn,** and **BlackRock World Mining Trust** – not the 'boring' international generalists one might have expected.

Invesco Leveraged High Yield Fund ran into trouble as the fixed income market deteriorated, and sought additional equity capital. **Kenmore European Industrial Fund** started to de-gear by selling an industrial site in Germany. We were sad to report the death of Ian Rushbrook, the manager of **Personal Assets Trust.** At the annual Investment Week awards, **Hansa Trust** took the award for UK trusts, with **Charter European Trust, Perpetual Japanese,** and **Biotech Growth Trust** amongst the other prizewinners. We rated **3i Infrastructure** shares a buy on a discount to NAV of 19% at 88.5p. **Gartmore Smaller Companies Trust** decided to merge with **Standard Life UK Smaller Companies.** The arbitrageur Carrousel Capital served requisition notices on **Henderson Smaller Companies** and **Herald Investment Trust** to try and force cash exit facilities at values close to NAV. A string of JPMorgan trusts decided to issue bonus subscription shares to ordinary shareholders. The year closed with a loss of 36% in the FTSE 350 Equity Investment Instruments Index, not helped by some discount expansion as assets dropped.

2009 – Shares Rally as Trusts Deal with the Aftermath of the Credit Crisis

In our January round-up we highlighted the resilient performance of **Lindsell Train Investment Trust** in the downturn, along with **RIT Capital Partners. Templeton Emerging Markets** continued its yo-yo performance, this time falling to the bottom of the sector rankings. Nicola Horlick's **Bramdean Alternatives** trust had 9.5% of its assets invested in hedge funds run by Bernard Madoff in New York, who was accused of operating a 'Ponzi scheme' fraud. **New India Investment Trust** suffered as well – its largest holding was Satyam Computer Services, where the company's chairman admitted fraud. Markets kept falling at the start of the year. Jupiter bravely tried to launch a new trust – **Jupiter China Sustainable Growth** – at this difficult time, but the IPO was later abandoned.

3i Group was demoted from the FTSE 100 Index after a sharp fall as investors worried about its funding and the valuation of its holdings. **Candover Investments** also slumped after disastrous results, and **SVG Capital** raised fresh capital and launched a strategic review. Along with property, the private equity sector was generally a distressed area due to its structural borrowings.

At the start of March the stockbroker Collins Stewart issued a research note titled 'bear market rally imminent?' and asking whether this might be a time to be greedy when others were fearful. They picked out several trusts with higher beta characteristics for the brave. A lower beta trust, **Personal Assets Trust,** appointed Troy Asset Management as its new investment adviser, with Sebastian Lyon as lead manager.

Shares rallied sharply from their March lows, with private equity trusts rebounding very strongly. Graham Birch handed over the management of **BlackRock World Mining Trust** to Evy Hambro. **Foreign & Colonial Trust** returned to the FTSE 100 Index briefly, falling back out again as more volatile shares rallied later in the year. **Manchester & London** proposed a merger with **Osprey Smaller Companies Income Fund,** both managed by Midas Investment Management. A fight arose for the assets of **Principle Capital Investment Trust.**

Alastair Darling's Budget introduced a new tax framework for investment companies, enabling tax-efficient investment in interest bearing assets, notably bonds. Charlie Ricketts, head of investment funds at the broker Cenkos Securities, said at the AIC Directors' Conference that the sector had exploded out of the conventional investment trust format into a multi-asset class, multi-currency, multi-exchange investment vehicle managed from around the world. Only 4% of the money raised in the sector over the previous five years had been for onshore trusts listed on the London Stock Exchange. More was for offshore trusts or AIM listings.

We examined warrants and subscription shares in the May newsletter, picking out eight for investors with a high risk tolerance. **Bramdean Alternatives** received a takeover approach, and **Eastern European Trust** moved its management mandate from Pictet Asset Management to BlackRock.

Daniel Godfrey left the AIC after eleven years as Director General, with Ian Sayers becoming the acting head. In the late summer the FTSE 100 Index recovered the 5000 level for the first time in a year. **Impax Asian Environmental Markets** was launched, raising £104.5m. **The City of London Investment Trust** not only raised its dividend for the year, but also continued to add to its revenue reserves. **Candover Investments** shares more than trebled in four months from a low base as confidence was restored in the company's finances and the discount narrowed dramatically. **Invesco Perpetual European Absolute** decided to wind up, and **Gottex Market Neutral Trust** received a cash offer. **Advance Developing Markets** re-domiciled in Guernsey. **Alliance Trust** finally bought back some shares after a long period of reluctance to do so. **Matrix European REIT** continued to struggle with debt problems, negotiating with its bankers and trying to sell assets. **Kenmore European Industrial Fund** attracted a bid. The fund was one of the top performers over the year, after **Invista European Real Estate.** At the annual Investment Week awards, **HgCapital Trust** picked up the award for the private equity category for the fifth consecutive year.

2010 – New Arrivals, and Others at the Exit Gate

We noted in January that **Edinburgh Worldwide, Scottish Mortgage Investment Trust,** and **Monks Investment Trust** all did well in the more buoyant market conditions of 2009. The conservatively positioned **Lindsell Train Investment Trust** fared less well in relative terms. **Murray International** was another top performer, reflected in a premium of 3.7% to net asset value. **Templeton Emerging Markets** bounced back to the top of its sector after doubling its net asset value in a year.

Advance UK Trust failed its continuation vote. **Witan Investment Trust** announced that Andrew Bell would become its new chief executive. Fidelity announced plans to raise up to £630m for **Fidelity China Special Situations,** to be managed by the renowned manager Anthony Bolton. We had reservations about the trust's launch, noting issues about its size, its charges, and its level of country-specific risk. The launch actually raised £460m, mainly from retail investors. JPMorgan launched **JPMorgan Brazil** to complete its 'BRIC' line-up. **Perpetual Income & Growth** planned an issue of 'B' shares that would offer returns purely in capital, but later withdrew the proposals after they received insufficient support.

A new coalition government was formed in the UK. New investment trusts continued to arrive, including **Baker Steel Resources Trust**, **Polar Capital Global Healthcare Growth and Income, Aberdeen Latin American Income Fund, GCP Infrastructure Investments,** and **JPMorgan Global Emerging Markets Income.** Most new issues were being received well, starting at a small premium to NAV in the market. Research from the broker Winterflood though suggested that trusts with market capitalisations under £50m might face pressure to consider reconstruction. **Ceres Agriculture, F&C UK Select, Invesco English & International,** and **Melchior Japan** decided to wind up, while **Candover Investments** received a takeover approach, although these discussions eventually came to nothing. **Pacific Assets Trust** changed managers, moving the contract from F&C to First State Investments. Separately, F&C acquired Thames River Capital, the managers of **TR Property.**

Sovereign debt defaults in Europe put pressure on prices in the middle of the year, and the UK market was troubled as well by BP's Deepwater Horizon oil spill. Winterflood warned about future dividend cuts. It pointed out that only one income growth fund, **Securities Trust of Scotland,** had cut its dividend in recent times, but also said that in that peer group, nine of fifteen trusts paid uncovered dividends in their most recent financial year, using revenue reserves to bridge the gap. Management problems arose at **Quorum Oil & Gas,** a trust that we rated a sell. **F&C Commercial Property Trust** and **UK Commercial Property** proposed a merger, but this met with some opposition and was dropped. **Investors Capital Trust** cut its dividend. We reiterated our caution on **Fidelity China Special Situations** on a premium to NAV of 7.8%. **TR European Growth** dropped its formal discount control mechanism, opting for more flexibility. Oriel Securities rated **Jupiter European Opportunities** as a buy at 229p. Numis Securities recommended **VinaCapital Vietnam Opportunity Fund,** which subsequently rallied strongly. The well-known fund manager Gervais Williams resigned from Gartmore, and **Gartmore European Investment Trust** also lost its high profile manager Roger Guy, who retired.

At the end of the third quarter, Numis Securities estimated that almost £2.7bn of capital had been raised by the sector through new and secondary issuance. The demand was across a broad range of asset classes, but Numis identified four main themes: emerging markets, income, emerging markets income, and absolute return. **BlackRock Frontiers Investment Trust** introduced some new markets to the sector, seeking to raise US$150m from its IPO.

The resumption of the US quantitative easing programme in the autumn gave markets a fillip, and towards the end of the year the Nikkei 225 Index reclaimed the 10,000 level, boosting **Baillie Gifford Japan, Baillie Gifford Shin Nippon, JPMorgan Japanese, Schroder Japan Growth,** and **Fidelity Japanese Values.** The Schroder trust bagged the annual Investment Week prize for the Japan category, while **HgCapital Trust** held on to its private equity award for the sixth year running. **Artemis Alpha Trust** scooped the UK growth title. At the end of the year **John Laing Infrastructure Fund** started trading after raising £270m but **Electric & General Investment Trust** recommended a winding-up. The top performer over the year was **Princess Private Equity,** topped only by subscription shares on trusts such as **Schroder AsiaPacific** and **JPMorgan Emerging Markets.**

2011 – Sector in Reasonable Health, Although IPO Demand Weakens after Difficult Summer

At the start of the year **Fidelity China Special Situations** raised more capital through a 'C' share issue. **Gartmore Irish Growth** decided to wind up and **Henderson Global Property Companies** failed its continuation vote. **Alliance Trust** came 'under attack' from the arbitrageur Laxey Partners, although its resolutions were later defeated at the AGM. The board of **Foreign & Colonial Investment Trust** reviewed the management fees and removed the performance fee.

Strong demand for income-producing trusts saw more new issues including **Henderson International Income Trust** and **The Diverse Income Trust,** the latter marking the return of Gervais Williams as an investment trust manager. In March there was an earthquake and tsunami in Japan that knocked asset prices in the region, but managers indicated the likelihood of a quick recovery. Matrix Corporate Capital noted that John MacDougall, the manager of **Baillie Gifford Shin Nippon** was "surprisingly bullish". Stephen Peak stepped down from **TR European Growth** after 21 years as manager, handing over to Ollie Beckett.

Research from the AIC identified the cheapest trusts in terms of their annual charges, namely **Independent Investment Trust, Edinburgh US Tracker, Bankers Investment Trust,** and **Law Debenture.**

Securities Trust of Scotland changed its investment remit from the UK to global, reflecting concerns over UK dividends and also the growth of income from developing markets elsewhere. **Personal Assets Trust** started to pay dividends quarterly rather than twice a year. **Gartmore Fledgling** became **Henderson Fledgling, Gartmore Global Trust** became **Henderson Global Trust,** and **ING UK Real Estate Income** became **Picton Property Income.** Aberdeen Asset Management's website won the 'best website' award from the AIC for the seventh year in succession. We noted the irony that Alex Crooke, the manager of **Bankers Investment Trust,** was adamant that he would not invest in UK bank stocks, preferring telecoms, oil services, and insurance.

The appetite for new IPOs started to wane, with **Schroder Opus Commodity Fund, Aberdeen Emerging Markets Smaller Companies Trust,** and **Trade & General Investments** failing to garner sufficient support. Investors became even more nervous over the summer months, spooked by debt problems in the US and Europe. Several experienced trust managers said there was still good value to be had from equities. Both Numis Securities and Oriel Securities issued notes about the steadier attractions of infrastructure trusts. Julie Dent retired as the manager of **British Assets Trust. Fidelity China Special Situations** struggled with the volatile markets and its shares sunk well below their issue price, down to 80p.

Several property trusts entered a process of change. The near-bankrupt trust **Invesco Property Income** formulated a plan to sell off its portfolio in an attempt to repay its loans. **Invista Foundation Property** gave notice to its managers and announced plans to appoint Schroder Property Investment Management, whilst at the same time receiving a merger approach from the stronger trust **Picton Property Income,** which we rated a buy at 46p.

On the newsletter's 15th anniversary in November 2011 we noted that the sector seemed to be in reasonable health, with an average discount of 8%, although it was trickier at this point to raise new money from IPOs. **Gartmore European** became **Henderson European Focus Trust.** At the annual Investment Week awards,

Standard Life UK Smaller Companies Trust picked up two prizes, and **HgCapital Trust** retained its private equity crown for the seventh consecutive year. **Jupiter European Opportunities** also kept its European award. Our analysis focused on single-country trusts, finding that **Aberdeen New Thai** stood out amongst some disappointing performers. **The Biotech Growth Trust** saw its shares jump to 186p after a takeover approach for its largest portfolio holding, Pharmasset. At the end of the year the infrastructure trust **Bilfinger Berger Global Infrastructure** listed after its £212m offer was oversubscribed.

2012 – Plenty of Demand for Income, but some Growth Trusts also Flourish

Although markets began the year in very good form, attention remained on more conservative assets. Numis Securities issued a note on the booming infrastructure funds. This sub-sector was in the enviable position of attracting capital in 2011. Investors were seeking exposure to the stable, inflation-linked yields of 5%-7% on offer, coupled with low NAV volatility and low correlation with other asset classes. At the same time, infrastructure managers were seeing strong growth in their investment pipelines, with over a billion pounds invested or committed in the year. Numis regarded the outlook as positive, as **HICL Infrastructure** announced a £135m 'C' share issue. **International Public Partnerships** was the broker's core buy.

Collins Stewart suggested **The MedicX Fund** for portfolio diversification with a compelling dividend yield, and JPMorgan Cazenove compiled a portfolio of seven 'portfolio protectors', namely **3i Infrastructure, BH Macro, BlueCrest AllBlue, HICL Infrastructure, John Laing Infrastructure, Personal Assets Trust,** and **Ruffer Investment Company. British Portfolio Trust** moved its management contract from Allianz RCM to BlackRock, and the trust was renamed **BlackRock Income & Growth** – we met the new joint manager Adam Avigdori; **Henderson TR Pacific** became **Henderson Asian Growth Trust.** We highlighted some big discounts in the private equity sector, including a 29% discount on **Graphite Enterprise,** a 27% discount on **Electra Private Equity,** and a 35% discount on **F&C Private Equity.** This sector performed strongly in the first quarter.

Research from Citywire for the AIC indicated that 42% of investment advisers intended to increase their allocation to investment companies over the next three years. This was ahead of the introduction of the Retail Distribution Review (RDR) at the end of the year.

The arbitrageur Laxey Partners tried to suggest that **Alliance Trust's** management be delegated to external managers, although its resolution was defeated at the trust's AGM. **Edinburgh US Tracker** switched to an active remit. **Jupiter Green** introduced an innovative proposal for an embedded annual subscription right – we were not too keen on the idea.

As the search for income continued, we wrote about Convertible Unsecured Loan Stock (CULS), with a new issue from **Aberdeen Asian Smaller Companies.** A report by Westhouse Securities identified a strong relationship between yield and discounts, indicating that investors were prepared to pay up for income, even though growth trusts topped the performance tables over three and five years. **Foreign & Colonial Investment Trust** hiked its dividend by 20% and moved to quarterly payments. **Aberdeen Private Equity Fund** also started to pay dividends.

A new measure of 'ongoing charges' replaced the old 'Total Expense Ratio' as a way of measuring costs. **Securities Trust of Scotland** scrapped its performance fee. Scottish Widows pulled out as manager of the £30m **UK Select Trust.** Another trust of a similar size, the long-established **Albany Investment Trust,** decided to reconstruct. Susie Rippingall, the manager of **Scottish Oriental Smaller Companies,** decided to retire. June saw a flurry of activity in the surprisingly small North American sector, with two new IPOs from **F&C Barrow Hanley US Trust** (which ultimately failed to reach its fundraising target) and **BlackRock North American Income Trust,** while **Edinburgh US Tracker** changed into **The North American Income Trust.**

Data from JPMorgan Cazenove showed that the private equity sector was the top performer in the first half of the year, where trusts were also on the widest discounts, averaging 32.5%. We felt the sector offered value. The three small Blue Planet financial trusts merged into one, **Blue Planet International Financials.** At this time when so many investors were focused on income, Nick Train of **Finsbury Growth & Income Trust** was a rare dissenting voice. He viewed the outlook for equities as "hugely encouraging", driven by emerging markets and digital technology. He warned that too much focus on income could propel investors into investments less likely to protect the long-term purchasing power of their capital. **Picton Property Income** refinanced its debt successfully, removing some concern that had held the shares back, but it also flagged a likely dividend cut.

BlackRock World Mining Trust struck an innovative deal directly with an investee company to buy rights over a future income stream - a mine royalty. We felt this added complication and reduced the trust's flexibility at a time when more trusts were aiming for simplicity ahead of the new RDR regulations. Ahead of the London Olympics, the AIC could not resist the opportunity to present some performance statistics with the theme. In the sprint, **Biotech Growth Trust** took the gold medal. The broker Winterflood questioned the suitability of **Fidelity China Special Situations** for retail investors. **SVM Global Fund** fell sharply as its fund manager left suddenly and the trust revised its net asset value downwards. Its management contract was later put up for grabs and the trust became **Henderson Value Trust.**

In November we changed the format of the front page to include the biggest risers and fallers in two tables, for the first time. **India Capital Growth Fund** topped our first monthly table of risers, while **Biotech Growth Trust's** gain of 62.6% over the previous twelve months placed it in first place over a year. Many trusts with exposure to Asia and to UK smaller companies were also performing well.

BlackRock North American Income Trust didn't raise as much as it was seeking, but its initial £65m of capital was sufficient for the trust to get started. At the annual Investment Week awards **Jupiter European Opportunities** scooped the European award for the third year in a row, and **Lindsell Train Investment Trust** won in the global category.

2013 – Booming Markets Support Growth and Expansion

At the start of 2013, which saw the introduction of the Retail Distribution Review (RDR), we argued against the introduction of rigid discount control mechanisms, which we felt reduced this distinct feature of investment trusts that helps them to establish equilibrium. Average discounts started the year at only 7.4%, with yields at 2.3%.

AXA Property Trust recommended a managed wind-down of its portfolio before its scheduled continuation vote in 2015. **Greencoat UK Wind** was amongst the new launches, seeking more than £200m for its IPO. **Bankers Investment Trust** dropped its performance fee, as did **City of London Investment Trust** later in the year. Both **BlackRock Income & Growth** and **Invesco Perpetual Select** announced new zero-discount policies designed to keep the shares trading around NAV.

Advance Developing Markets faced opposition to its continuation vote from a major holder, but survived with 55% support. Richard Buxton and Errol Francis, the managers of **Schroder UK Growth,** announced they were leaving. Julie Dean took over as manager. **Impax Asian Environmental Markets** moved to wind up. Anthony Bolton announced he would retire as manager of **Fidelity China Special Situations** in March 2014.

In April we revisited **Aberdeen Private Equity Fund,** the top-performer over twelve months with a share price gain of 64%. We had recommended the shares in June 2012, since when the discount had narrowed very sharply, from 42% to 17%. Our view at this time was that the private equity sector no longer had quite the spellbinding allure it held for us a year or two previously when discounts were grossly extended. Across a number of sectors we noted many trusts on premium ratings, and we argued many were a bit rich, fuelled by the exciting bull run in equity markets in the first half of the year – we highlighted **BACIT, Edinburgh Investment Trust, Aberdeen Latin American Income Fund, Polar Capital Global Healthcare,** and **Altus Resource Capital.**

The **Polar Capital Global Financials Trust** launched, raising £153m to invest in what the manager called "the world's largest and most unloved sector". **JPMorgan Global Convertibles Income** raised £136m from its launch, and **Bluefield Solar Income Fund** raised £130m. The infrastructure sector continued to raise more cash from willing investors – **HICL Infrastructure** was one of our ISA recommendations in the March issue, and the yields in the sector were proving a big attraction. The broker Cantor Fitzgerald said that emerging markets valuations were low relative to the developed world, having lagged by 40% since 2011. **Aberdeen All Asia Investment Trust** switched to a Japanese-only mandate to become **Aberdeen Japan Investment Trust.**

At the end of August, the AIC said there were 294 investment companies (excluding VCTs), comprising 277 conventional trusts and 17 split capital trusts, with an aggregate of £103.09bn of assets. Their combined market capitalisation was £85.88bn. From this data we could easily work out that the average trust size was £351m in terms of assets and £292m in terms of market capitalisation. Trusts had been getting modestly larger as the pressures on performance and costs weeded out some of the smaller and weaker players. Back at the start of 2007 the average size was £269m in terms of assets and £226m in market capitalisation. The industry had grown since then in overall terms, up by 22% in assets, and 21% in market capitalisation.

Markets had enjoyed the generous monetary conditions, meaning investors had benefited from some very impressive growth winners such as **Baillie Gifford Japan, Biotech Growth Trust,** and **Schroder UK Mid Cap Fund.** As the year drew to a close, we thought there was a case for aiming a little lower down the leader board, taking on less risk. Tim Stevenson, the manager of **Henderson EuroTrust,** said that he was cautious about being too greedy in the near-term. **The Diverse Income Trust** bought a put option on the FTSE 100 Index to provide some portfolio protection.

Scottish Mortgage Investment Trust overtook **Alliance Trust** as the largest traditional investment trust, with a £2.5bn market capitalisation. Neil Woodford said he would be leaving Invesco to set up a new firm, so Mark Barnett added the management of **Edinburgh Investment Trust** to his already extensive responsibilities. With its half-yearly results the chairman of **Lindsell Train Investment Trust** cautioned potential new investors about the risk of buying the trust's shares on an elevated premium, 15.7% at the time of our report.

Research from JPMorgan Cazenove identified fifteen trusts that had dropped their performance fee arrangements since 2011 as boards scrambled to simplify in reaction to the RDR. For 2013, **Ukraine Opportunity Trust** was the top performer in the sector, followed by **Baillie Gifford Japan.** Ukraine was to be in the news for entirely different reasons in the year to come.

2014 – Continuing Demand for Alternative Assets

Electra Private Equity attracted a stake of 13.7% from an activist investor called Sherborne, and rose in value, but we felt a full bid was unlikely. Another activist investor, Elliott Advisors, increased its stake in **Alliance Trust** to more than 10%. **BlackRock New Energy** was wound up. Jupiter took over as managers of the **F&C US Smaller Companies** trust, and Paul Niven took over from Jeremy Tigue as the manager of **Foreign & Colonial Investment Trust.** Oriel Securities upgraded the trust from neutral to positive. **Global Resources Investment Trust** had a dreadful start, losing nearly a third of its net asset value very quickly. We classified it as a trust to avoid.

The Chancellor's Budget announced an increase in the annual ISA limit to £15,000. With the removal of the requirement to buy an annuity for pension plans as well, the prospects looked bright for the sector's future as more self-directed investors might consider trusts. All was not entirely rosy though, and we explained why the EU's new Alternative Investment Fund Management Directive (AIFMD) was causing unintended problems for some self-managed trusts that were having to decide between costly 'full scope' authorisation, or 'smaller company' registration that did not allow them to use gearing. **Witan Pacific, Independent Investment Trust,** and **Pacific Assets Trust** all chose this latter course.

Mid Wynd International moved its management contract from Baillie Gifford to Artemis following the retirement of the long-standing manager Michael MacPhee. In June we changed the data source for our performance tables from DigitalLook to Morningstar, noting a rise in some Indian trusts after a welcome general election result. The **Fundsmith Emerging Equities Trust** was launched, aiming for between £100m and £250m and actually raising £192m. We advised against investing at launch, feeling the shares would likely fall to a discount over time. **P2P Global Investments** raised £200m to buy loans on peer-to-peer lending networks, and its shares moved to a premium rating. **Martin Currie Pacific** issued proposals to drop its Japanese and

Australian investments to concentrate on Asia. The managers of **RCM Technology Trust** bagged a £6m performance fee before a revised fee plan was implemented by the board. We noticed that the comparatively new **Aberdeen Japan Investment Trust,** which hedged its currency and invested across the capitalisation spectrum, was outperforming its large cap opposition. **GCP Sovereign Debt** raised US$125m, realised during the due diligence process that it would not be able to invest it as promised, and handed the money straight back. **F&C Global Smaller Companies** issued £40m of CULS, which we felt offered a decent each-way bet. **Midas Income & Growth Trust** changed its name to **Seneca Global Income & Growth.** The **Tamar European Industrial Fund** succumbed to a takeover offer, a rarity in the sector.

At the Winterflood Edinburgh conference, Garrett Fish, the manager of **JPMorgan American,** showed that in historic terms, markets have had a fairly long period now without a correction. "We could have a mid-cycle correction", Garrett said, noting that "a 10% fall shouldn't surprise anybody – this is a frequent occurrence".

In August we introduced a new form of analysis, time-series performance data that collated rankings over longer periods of time. We applied it to the global growth sector and found that **Lindsell Train Investment Trust** was the obvious standout trust that had kept its place at or near the top over the entire period. The data also supported the gradual warming of our opinion towards **Witan Investment Trust**, which had slowly gained ground on its peers. We said that our doubts about its multi-manager approach were in the past by this time. Applying the same method to the UK All Companies sector identified **Schroder UK Mid Cap** as the most consistent winner. Julie Dean, the high-profile manager of **Schroder UK Growth,** surprised many with the news that she was leaving Schroders.

Westhouse Securities pointed out that excluding VCTs, there were currently almost 120 trusts with a capitalisation of less than £50m, which probably made them sub-scale. The broker argued this created a fertile area for future rationalisation and change. While **Alliance Trust** continued to struggle with personnel changes and **Electra Private Equity** fought off the attack from Sherborne Investors, which wanted to appoint new directors and lead a strategic review, both **Foresight Solar Fund** and **Greencoat UK Wind** sought £100m from new equity fundraisings at a premium to net assets, highlighting both the availability of assets and investor enthusiasm for bond-like returns from new energy infrastructure. **River & Mercantile UK Micro Cap** announced an IPO, aiming for £100m and with a performance fee arrangement for the managers, bucking the trends towards larger trusts and lower fees. It only raised £51m, but that was sufficient to start trading. **Perpetual Income & Growth** agreed a fee reduction with the managers. Winterflood highlighted the strong performance record of the UK smaller companies trust **Strategic Equity Capital. BlackRock World Mining Trust** ran into trouble with the failure of its large royalty investment in London Mining's Marampa mine, but the managers were not deflected from the idea. The loss of income put a question mark over future dividend payments. **British Assets Trust** moved from F&C to BlackRock, ending 116 years of history with F&C, and we turned the spotlight on some of the large amounts paid to managers for their work. Our view was that shareholders have the right to expect good results and to be able to demand changes if those are not delivered over a sustained period.

Tumbling oil prices, a snap Greek election, and talk of slowing growth in China quickly created an uncomfortable backdrop for equities at the end of the year. Some investors turned towards the group of newer investment trusts in the 'alternative assets' domain that march to the beat of a different drum, particularly when hunting for reliable yield. That demand had pushed many trusts to premium ratings. Figures from the AIC showed the average discount of 3.3% in February 2014 hit a record low since it began gathering this data in the 1970s. It moved lower again at the end of the year (3.2% in October and November). That was good news for those who had been holding trusts, but it made it a tougher task to find good discounts. The AIC calculated that industry assets were also at an all-time high of £122bn at the end of November. Falling fees were another positive trend for investors. A dozen more trusts announced they were abandoning their performance fees in 2014, and 10% of all trusts cut the fees they were paying to their managers. **New India Investment Trust** pipped **JPMorgan Indian** to the top spot in terms of performance over the year, followed by the biotechnology trusts.

2015 – A Record-Breaking IPO and Plenty of Change in Election Year

A performance table carried by The Telegraph newspaper at the turn of the year showed the top performing investment trusts since the start of 2000 – a 15-year period. What the results showed is that it had paid to take risk in emerging markets and elsewhere. The winners over that period - when the FTSE 100 Index stalled and we had both the dotcom bust and the credit crisis, let's not forget – saw the best returns come from **Scottish Oriental Smaller Companies, Aberdeen Asian Smaller Companies, Aberdeen New Thai, TR Property, Worldwide Healthcare Trust, Biotech Growth Trust, Fidelity Special Values,** and **Genesis Emerging Markets.**

Canaccord Genuity examined the personal investments of board members and managers in investment companies, in detail. Their report, titled 'Skin in the Game' found that 55 chairmen or directors had a personal investment in excess of £1m, together with 48 managers or management teams. On the flipside, 16% of directors had no personal investment. Picking out a few, the largest directors' holdings included

Lord Rothschild OM GBE/Hannah Rothschild (£155m) at **RIT Capital Partners;** Christopher Mills (£65m) at **North Atlantic Smaller Companies;** Jon Moulton (£46m) at **Better Capital;** Pierre Lapeyre Jr/ David Leuschen (£44m) at **Riverstone Energy;** and Simon Borrows (£40m) at **3i Group.**

Henderson Value Trust survived a continuation vote, although we noted the manager would have to deliver better performance before the next vote in 2017. **RIT Capital Partners** agreed to buy GVO Investment Management, the managers of **Strategic Equity Capital,** and to acquire **Hansa Trust's** holding in SEC. Ongoing debt problems in Greece raised the question again of whether it might leave the Eurozone. After listening to the views of Sarah Whitley, the manager of **Baillie Gifford Japan,** at the annual Winterflood conference in London, we thought there was a good chance of further gains in the Nikkei 225 Index from its level of 17,650 and said we would be happy to increase holdings of **Aberdeen Japan Investment Trust** or **Baillie Gifford Japan.** The index was quickly within touching distance of the 20,000 mark.

Neil Woodford announced his return to the sector through a new issue for his **Woodford Patient Capital Trust.** Initial indications suggested a target of £200m, but the scale of the demand was such that the trust became a record-breaker, raising a remarkable £800m, the largest investment trust launch of all time. We argued against buying on a premium rating. The **Gabelli Value Plus+ Trust** raised £100.1m from its launch. Winterflood said that "a market capitalisation of £100m is often quoted as being the minimum size for a fund to be considered by private client brokers and wealth managers". Some 67% of investment companies met this criterion at this point, of which 43% had market caps higher than £250m. There were 93 trusts with market caps below £100m at the end of 2014, of which 44 were below £50m. The broker suggested that some of these may not be viable, or may at least suffer wider discounts as a result of illiquidity. **Electra Private Equity** reduced its management fee and said it would start to distribute cash to shareholders. **The Cayenne Trust** looked as though it was approaching the end of its life after the investment team signalled it was time to move on.

In April we produced our first Statistical Supplement along with the newsletter. We had previously thought that most investors would search for up to date statistical information online, but we received excellent feedback from this physical document.

Extending our time-series performance data analysis to Europe and to the technology sector showed **Jupiter European Opportunities** to be consistently top of its sector, and **Allianz Technology Trust** and **Polar Capital Technology Trust** to be neck-and-neck in theirs.

The brokers Dexion Capital pointed out that the listed investment company universe had evolved considerably over the last decade. They calculated that conventional equity investment companies, which used to account for over 70% of assets, accounted at this point for only around 50%. Alternative investment companies have dominated inflows with substantial amounts of capital being raised for illiquid assets (private lending, CLOs, infrastructure, leasing, property, etc) and illiquid strategies (activism, distressed, sector-specific private equity). The **Ranger Direct Lending Fund** was the latest in line to seek US$200m to invest in loans originated by US direct lending (P2P) platforms, and we wrote a guide to alternative asset trusts that we sent with the June newsletter. **Monks Investment Trust** made a change of investment manager, with Charles Plowden taking over from Gerald Smith. In emerging markets, Chinese stocks roared ahead in the early part of the year, while Indian stocks fell back. Some writers suggested some caution though, and within a couple of months there were some sharp market falls.

A surprise UK election result proved good news for UK smaller companies trusts such as **Acorn Income Fund, Henderson Smaller Companies, BlackRock Smaller Companies Trust,** and **Strategic Equity Capital,** all of which moved up smartly. It was less favourable for environmental trusts, as the new government started to halt subsidies. **The Bluefield European Solar Fund** and **NextEnergy European Solar Utility** both abandoned their proposed IPOs. The Chancellor's summer Budget introduced a radical change to the taxation of dividends.

While resisting the temptation to create a 'one size fits all' model portfolio, we created a mini-portfolio of high-discount trusts to see how they fared. Its subsequent performance was not very good. We followed up with a long-term growth mini portfolio that has done much better. Stifel initiated coverage of the **Woodford Patient Capital Trust** with a 'sell' rating, pointing out its high premium to net asset value. There were some changes involving long-standing managers. Dr Mark Mobius handed over the reins of **Templeton Emerging Markets** to Carlos Hardenberg as lead manager, and at **British Empire Securities & General Trust** Joe Bauernfreund succeeded John Pennink to become the trust's third portfolio manager in 30 years. Rosemary Banyard announced she was to leave as manager of **Schroder UK Mid Cap Fund,** with Andy Brough becoming the lead manager.

In the summer, a yuan devaluation and disappointing macroeconomic data from China caused investors across the globe to turn bearish. This felt like more of an overdue setback than anything more fundamental. Advance Emerging Capital, the investment manager of **Advance Developing Markets Fund**, was sold to Aberdeen Asset Management. **Alliance Trust** tweaked its management approach again after a strategic review. Another new peer-to-peer lending trust arrived, **Funding Circle SME**

Income Fund, while **VPC Specialty Lending Investments** raised a further £183m through a 'C' share issue, confirming the popularity of this sector with institutional investors. A proposed takeover by AB InBev for SAB Miller – the largest ever for a UK company – was particularly beneficial for **Lindsell Train Investment Trust,** which had large holdings in the brewing sector. **JPMorgan Private Equity** said it was considering moving its contract to Fortress Investment Group. The ongoing saga at **Electra Private Equity**, where the activist investors Sherborne Investors had been agitating for board representation and for change for nearly two years, took a new twist. In the latest vote, Sherborne won the day with 53% of the vote, securing two board seats and starting a new strategic review. At the end of the year there was a brief bid battle for **Japan Residential Investment Company,** providing a good uplift to shareholders. **Juridica Investments** and **BlueCrest AllBlue** decided to wind down. **Menhaden Capital**, which raised £80m from its IPO at 100p at the end of July, had a very poor start. Our analysis on convertible unsecured loan stock (CULS) led us to recommend **Standard Life UK Smaller Companies** CULS at 136.5p.

2016 – The Brexit Vote, and More Money Flowing into Alternative Assets

The AIC introduced the new 'Flexible Investment' sector for multi-asset trusts. We considered **RIT Capital Partners** to be the leader amongst its peers.

Intermediate Capital Group was appointed as the new manager of **Graphite Enterprise Trust** following its acquisition of the private equity fund investment business of Graphite Capital Management, renaming the trust **ICG Enterprise Trust.** Similarly, **JPMorgan Private Equity** became **JPEL Private Equity** after the management team moved to Fortress Investment Group. And still in the private equity sector, **Dunedin Enterprise** sought (and received) shareholders' approval for a managed wind-down after selling its largest holding. **Henderson Global Trust** also decided to throw in the towel and offered holders the chance to switch into either **Henderson International Income Trust** or **Bankers Investment Trust.** Money kept flowing into the specialist property sector, with **Tritax Big Box REIT** raising double its £100m target for new shares.

The market had a dreadful start to the year, falling very sharply on fears of a severe economic slowdown in China and a steep drop in oil prices. We suggested investors remain calm and perhaps pick up a few trusts at lower prices, reporting on the views of several experienced managers who were more optimistic than might have been expected. None of the managers speaking at Winterflood's annual conference in London felt the sell-off was the beginning of another longer-lasting crisis. The market weakness prevented any new issues though, marking the first barren quarter since the start of 2009.

The highly successful **Lindsell Train Investment Trust** amended its management fee arrangements, which had been throwing an unintended bounty to the managers while the shares were on a large premium to net asset value. Fees were very much under the spotlight at this time, with many being cut, and performance fees being axed. **BlackRock Greater Europe** just missed out on £50m of additional funds through the exercise of subscription shares, as the ordinary shares fell a few pence short at the crucial time. **Atlantis Japan Growth Fund** narrowly survived a vote on a winding-up resolution.

In May we reported on interesting research from Numis Securities, who identified four distinct periods of IPO activity since 1990. The first was the privatisation fad of 1993-94, including the mega-launches of **Kleinwort European Privatisation** and **Mercury European Privatisation,** when retail investors were key buyers and warrants came as part of the packages. Second was the TMT Bubble of 2000-01, including **Amerindo Internet Fund,** and the third period was alternative assets and AIM from 2005-07. This was a little more varied, from the property funds such as **F&C Commercial Property Trust** and **UK Commercial Property Trust** through to **HICL Infrastructure, BH Macro, Conversus Capital,** and numerous AIM funds including single-country funds for Bulgaria, Vietnam, China and India. Finally, there was the alternative income boom from 2013-15 as investors looked for an attractive yield at a time of low interest rates. There were a lot of specialist debt funds, plus renewable energy, and secondary issues from infrastructure and UK property. The key buyers this time were multi-asset funds and private wealth investors. Separately, the academics Gordon Gemmill and Dylan Thomas studied UK-traded closed-end equity-fund IPOs from 1984–2006 and concluded "it is a puzzle why investors buy closed-end funds at IPO, given that within a year most funds move from trading at a premium over net asset value (NAV) to trading at a discount". In our view, **Woodford Patient Capital Trust** was the latest IPO disappointment. We never recommended the trust and said repeatedly that we felt uncomfortable with its premium rating, which eventually eroded.

Witan Investment Trust made an unusual agreement to buy back a large stake from Aviva, which was trying to exit some legacy positions in the sector. **RIT Capital Partners** approached **Alliance Trust** with the idea of a merger, but decided not to proceed with an offer. Alliance pressed on with another strategic review. Over at **Electra Private Equity,** the first indications from its strategic review suggested it might be taking the management in-house, with Electra Partners given notice.

HarbourVest Global Private Equity, a top-performing fund-of-funds private equity trust, was added to our list of trusts to consider in the only sector offering large discounts, as was **Apax Global Alpha**. We had been recommending **Aberdeen Private Equity Fund, HgCapital Trust,** and **Pantheon International**

Participations for some time. At the other end of the spectrum, another one of our long-time favoured trusts **3i Infrastructure** took advantage of its strong rating to rake in another £385m of capital by issuing shares at a premium. **Ecofin Water & Power Opportunities** announced reconstruction proposals.

In June we published a new Statistical Supplement for subscribers as a bonus, having received extremely positive feedback about the first edition in 2015. The column showing the date of our last comment on each trust said much about the comprehensive nature of the newsletter's coverage over time.

In July we reported on another market shock, this one following the UK's surprise referendum result in favour of leaving the EU. There was a sharp divide in performance between UK and overseas trusts as sterling took a big hit. Commercial property trusts were particularly weak as investors tried to sell out of open-ended funds that slammed their exit doors shut. Markets bounced quickly and strongly as the benefits of the sterling devaluation washed through first, but we counselled some caution about the higher level of risk inherent in markets and suggested some profit-taking in certain sectors.

The demand for infrastructure assets remained strong, with **GCP Infrastructure, International Public Partnerships, HICL Infrastructure,** and **The Renewables Infrastructure Group** all scaling up their offerings of new shares. **BlackRock World Mining Trust** slashed its dividend, as expected, after many of the mining companies reduced their payouts. The large private equity trust **SVG Capital** received a takeover offer and quickly found itself with competing bidders for its portfolio. At Winterflood's Edinburgh conference, one of the managers we met was Carlos Hardenberg, who had a very good start as the new manager of **Templeton Emerging Markets Investment Trust. International Biotechnology Trust** asked shareholders for permission to introduce an annual 4% dividend, paid out of capital. While we have seen a lot of innovations over our twenty years, we disliked this particular idea. We met Ben Rogoff, the manager of **Polar Capital Technology Trust,** for an update, bringing us full circle from when we met his predecessor Brian Ashford-Russell back in 1996.

In November we reported on face-to-face meetings with the managers of **BlackRock Smaller Companies Trust, Herald Investment Trust,** and **Witan Investment Trust.** Our longevity in the sector has given us first-rate access to managers and research that we think is hard to duplicate. We also reported on Daniel Godfrey's innovative idea for **The People's Trust,** causing us to wonder how this dynamic sector might evolve over the next ten or twenty years.

2017 - More Gains as the Long Bull Run Continues

At the start of 2017, many managers and commentators seemed wary of forecasting more gains after the devaluation-fuelled advance of 20% for investment companies in 2016. The US was widely tipped though, and we said that **North American Income Trust** was one to consider. We also discussed the artificial dividend created out of capital by **International Biotechnology Trust,** saying that it did not make sense to us and left us less comfortable with the structure. Average discounts in the private equity sector still looked enticing, from trusts such as **Aberdeen Private Equity Fund** (24.1% discount), **HarbourVest Global Private Equity** (19.9%), and **NB Private Equity Partners** (21%).

Alliance Trust decided after a strategic review to follow the lead of **Witan Investment Trust** in switching to a multi-manager set-up under the management of Willis Tower Watson. In February we noted a seasonal bump in manager contact, with a large number of meetings on which to report. Improving communications technology was contributing as well, with conference calls and webinars now supplementing our face-to-face manager meetings. Amongst other write-ups, we introduced subscribers to **India Capital Growth Fund** and we admired the lower-risk income-generating qualities of **GCP Asset Backed Income.** We had another look at the GCP trust later in the year, when the stockbroker JPMorgan Cazenove said that 'alternatives' trusts accounted for 41% of the sector's market capitalisation compared to 22% five years previously.

The strong performance of **Scottish Mortgage Investment Trust** boosted its assets and it joined the FTSE 100 Index, making it the third equity investment trust to do so, after **Alliance Trust** and **Foreign & Colonial Investment Trust,** which both subsequently dropped out again. Two giant asset managers with trust mandates announced a merger to form Aberdeen Standard Investments. We did not expect any immediate changes, but wondered about the future for **Dunedin Smaller Companies** and **Standard Life Equity Income.** Takeover activity reared its head in the investment companies sector with the takeover of the commercial property trust **Industrial Multi Property Trust** by Hansteen.

Noting that a reduction in the nil band tax rate for dividends made ISAs even more attractive as a wrapper for investment trusts, we made four seasonal ISA recommendations, **Temple Bar Investment Trust, RIT Capital Partners, Baring Emerging Europe,** and **Kennedy Wilson Europe Real Estate.** We noted some takeover talk about the latter, at odds with a wide discount and high yield. Two months later it received a bid from its manager, although not on great terms. These were later improved, and there was also an offer for **Prospect Japan Fund.**

In June we sent a third edition of our popular Statistical Supplement to subscribers, helping them navigate markets made more complicated by an indecisive British general election.

We wrote about **Tetragon Financial Group,** a little-known US$2bn fund trading on a 34.7% discount to net asset value and offering a 5.3% yield. Unfortunately many subscribers found it difficult to deal on trading platforms that did not have the shares on their systems.

Caledonia Investments joined the elite group of investment trusts to have raised their dividends for 50 consecutive years. A music royalty investor called **Hipgnosis Songs Fund** was looking for £200m from an IPO, but we noted the fees looked high – eventually the IPO was not a hit and was pulled.

At the half way stage of the year, trusts had done reasonably well, gaining 9% against the FTSE 100 Index's gain of 3%, helped by narrowing discounts, tightening to just 4.1% on average.

In August we reported on a fizzing performance from **Independent Investment Trust,** where its largest holding in Fevertree Drinks had been soaring in value. This trust would go on to become the best performer of the year. **Woodford Patient Capital Trust** also recovered its issue price, moving back over 100p, but on a 2.1% discount we said "with more than half of the assets in unquoted companies and a concentration in biotechnology we consider this a high risk trust and would normally demand a much higher discount to compensate for greater uncertainty".

Dunedin Enterprise, in 'run-off' mode, saw its shares rise as it began to return capital to investors after some successful disposals. In the same sector, **Aberdeen Private Equity Fund** agreed to sell its entire portfolio at a premium. Sarah Whitley, the long-serving manager of **Baillie Gifford Japan,** announced she would retire in April 2018. Japanese trusts enjoyed a strong autumn as Mr Abe's ruling party was re-elected and the Nikkei 225 Index hit its highest level since 1992 after a storming 16-day winning streak in October. Daniel Godfrey was forced to abandon his **People's Trust** project after it failed to raise sufficient capital to be viable. Towards the end of the year, Gervais Williams, the manager of **Diverse Income Trust,** expressed caution about equity markets, as did a number of other managers. In 2017, the FTSE 350 Equity Investment Instruments Index rose by 14.4%.

2018 - New Regulations Cause Confusion, but Flourishing IPOs Enliven a Tough Final Quarter

New MIFID II and PRIIPS financial regulations that came in at the start of the year caused confusion, as mandatory 'Key Information Documents' (KIDs) appeared misleading in some cases, or were absent, leading to disruptions in dealing. Later in the year the AIC would issue its own stinging criticism and said it would not put KIDs on its website.

In January, in our usual industry round-up, we said we felt there was some value in the global emerging markets sector, from trusts such as **JPMorgan Emerging Markets** (10.7% discount) and **Templeton Emerging Markets** (12%). We warned again that **Woodford Patient Capital Trust** was "a far riskier proposition" than its KID suggested.

A market correction shook out some complacency, and there was a surprising name amongst the worst fallers, with **HICL Infrastructure** dropping more than 10% due to its contracts with Carillion, a giant construction firm that went into liquidation. The trust estimated the impact at £50m. **River & Mercantile UK Micro Cap** also came thumping down as its successful manager was sacked for professional misconduct. Manager Carlos Hardenberg announced he was leaving **Templeton Emerging Markets.** In a completely new sector, **Gore Street Energy Storage Fund** sought capital for its IPO, and Baillie Gifford announced a new US trust, its first launch for 32 years. They would have contrasting success, with Gore Street postponing its launch and eventually struggling to raise just £30m, but Baillie Gifford capping demand for the **Baillie Gifford US Growth Trust** at £250m. Baillie Gifford also took over as managers of the UK trust that was formerly **Schroder UK Growth,** renamed **Baillie Gifford UK Growth.**

Foreign & Colonial Investment Trust celebrated its 150th anniversary and decided to adopt a more modern name, simply **F&C Investment Trust.** F&C rebranded most of its other trusts as BMO, to reflect the management name. The AIC conducted some research on the longest-held shares by trusts, and Alex Crooke of **Bankers Investment Trust** said he believed the trust had held HSBC continuously for 129 years.

CATCo Reinsurance Opportunities fell sharply as the fund was forced to raise its loss reserves for the catastrophic events of 2017, notably Hurricanes Harvey and Irma. More bad news arrived later in the year from the Californian wildfires, Hurricane Michael and Typhoon Jebi.

Invesco resigned as managers of **Invesco Perpetual Enhanced Income** over a fee disagreement, and a board shake-up was then demanded by a group of shareholders. After a public spat, Invesco were reappointed and the trust's chairman stepped down. Many trusts have been cutting the fees they are paying to managers. **Tetragon Financial Group** introduced a new sterling quote for its shares. **BlackRock Emerging Europe** decided to wind up after an enthusiastic shareholder response to its tender offer. **Picton Property Income** converted to UK REIT status from a Guernsey property company, to be more tax efficient.

Research from the Cass Business School comparing the performance of closed-end and open-ended funds from 2006 to 2016 found that investment trusts outperformed significantly, perhaps because managers do not have to contend with constant inflows and outflows.

In July – when we also sent out our Statistical Supplement again - we reported that **Dunedin Smaller Companies** was proposing a merger with the larger **Standard Life UK Smaller Companies Trust.** That was not a great surprise, but we had not expected to see the **Hipgnosis Songs Fund** finally strike the right note and raise £200m from a refreshed IPO. Usually, when an IPO fails first time around, that's the end of the project.

As the FTSE 350 Equity investment Instruments Index passed through 10,000 for the first time in August there were some dramatic price movements including a monthly rise of 175% for **Infrastructure India** as its major holding secured a critical refinancing. **Lindsell Train Investment Trust** also jumped by more than 25%, up to a premium of 49.2%, which we felt was "unlikely to be sustainable". Much as we admired the performance, we felt the risk/reward trade-off looked poor. There was also a jump of 22% in the value of **John Laing Infrastructure Fund** after a recommended cash offer at a premium to net asset value. We looked again at **Tetragon Financial Group,** by now on a 43% discount to NAV.

In the autumn, weathering some choppy market conditions, the new issue market sparked into life. **The Mobius Investment Trust,** managed by Mark Mobius and Carlos Hardenberg, raised £100m, and **Merian Chrysalis Investment Company** picked up the same amount. **AVI Japan Opportunity Trust** came to the market with a distinctive offering focused on corporate change in a highly conservative market, raising £80m. **Smithson Investment Trust,** a global smaller companies trust, also arrived with the managers bearing all the costs of the IPO, and raised a record £822.5m. We said "holders must hope the trust can break the hoodoo sadly established by previous record IPOs that have subsequently run into problems and become disappointments". **Woodford Patient Capital Trust** shares were back below their

100p April 2015 launch price and were relegated from the FTSE 250 Index in May. To some extent this mirrored the experience of many of the largest trust launches, which have raised capital on the back of mass optimism about a particular theme or strategy that has then struggled to meet high expectations. Launches such as **Fidelity China Special Situations, Amerindo Internet Fund,** and further back, **Mercury European Privatisation** and **Kleinwort European Privatisation,** have failed to match their grand designs. In the IPO market, it's easy to squash the assertion that big is beautiful with historic examples.

The November newsletter contained an article on trusts paying dividends out of capital, which we said might destroy value for many shareholders. We urged caution towards trusts with this policy, including **Aberdeen Emerging Markets Company, BB Healthcare Trust, European Assets Trust, International Biotechnology Trust, JPMorgan Global Growth & Income, Martin Currie Asia Unconstrained, Montanaro UK Smaller Companies, Princess Private Equity,** and **Securities Trust of Scotland.**

Over the year the FTSE 350 Equity Investment Instruments Index fell by 3.8%, outperforming the FTSE 100 Index (-10.9%) and the MSCI World Index, down by 10.3% over the same period.

2019 - Climbing the Wall of Worry; Woodford Loses Grip

January brought rare news of M&A activity in the sector, a merger between **Primary Health Properties** and **MedicX Fund,** effectively a takeover by the larger trust, PHP. A de-merger of a different sort was still on the cards as the UK headed uncertainly towards Brexit, and manager Mark Barnett said at the annual Winterflood conference that **Perpetual Income & Growth** and **Edinburgh Investment Trust** were both positioned to benefit from a potential re-rating of UK revenues once there was more clarity on the future of Britain's relationship with the EU.

Markets started the year well after a difficult last quarter of 2018, helped by the US Federal Reserve softening its stance on interest rates and the Chinese government injecting more fiscal stimulus. We still worried about too many investment trusts being on premium ratings, and about more trusts starting to pay dividends out of capital, which we felt was sleight-of-hand that would actually depress long-term returns.

We met a lot of investment trust managers, some for the first time, including **Regional REIT, Impact Healthcare REIT, Gresham House Energy Storage Fund, Dunedin Income Growth, Odyssean Investment Trust,** and **Ecofin Global Utilities & Infrastructure.** Some managers were clearly expanding their horizons to reach new groups of potential investors and to explain the investment case for their trusts. Others were fortunate enough to find instant popularity: **Merian Chrysalis Investment Company** quickly returned to the market to raise more capital once it had invested its IPO proceeds, and with minimal marketing Baillie Gifford raised US$477m for **The Schiehallion Fund,** investing in unlisted equities, and its shares went to an immediate premium.

Jupiter European Opportunities manager Alexander Darwall said he would be stepping down from his management commitment to his open-ended funds, but would continue to manage the investment trust in which he has a large personal stake. Later in the year, the trust would transfer the mandate to his new investment firm, Devon Equity Management. Lord Rothschild, meanwhile, stepped down as chairman of **RIT Capital Partners.** A number of very experienced managers reached retirement, but their trusts had sensible succession plans that were implemented smoothly. Another long-established trust, **British Empire Securities,** succumbed to the pressures of the age and changed its name to the far less colourful **AVI Global Trust.** Similarly, **Scottish American Investment Company,** commonly known as SAINTS, changed its ticker code from SCAM to SAIN.

In April the AIC revamped its investment company sector classifications, partly to reflect the greater amount of investment in alternative assets. The AIC said the amount of money invested by investment companies in alternative assets had grown by 92% in five years, from £39.5bn in 2014 to £75.9bn in 2019. The result was more sectors for debt and property, plus new sectors for growth capital and for royalties.

In the June newsletter we reported the serious news that the largest open-ended fund run by renowned fund manager Neil Woodford had suspended dealings while he disposed of illiquid and unquoted assets. His investment trust, **Woodford Patient Capital Trust,** continued to trade normally, although at a lower price, sending a reminder that the investment trust structure is a far better choice than open-ended funds for strategies involving illiquid assets. Terry Smith's emerging markets trust, **Fundsmith Emerging Equities Trust,** also owned up to some sub-par performance, perhaps raising a question about paying up for access to 'star' fund managers.

Research by the AIC found the three investment companies that outperformed most often over the previous ten years were **Finsbury Growth & Income Trust, Jupiter European Opportunities,** and **BlackRock Smaller Companies Trust,** each outperforming in nine out of ten years.

When we sent the Statistical Supplement in August, investment trusts were being supported by strong international market conditions and a lower sterling, as the tough rhetoric of new Prime Minister Boris Johnson proved divisive. The UK market was depressed in relative terms against other global equities, due to ongoing Brexit uncertainty, which kept overseas investors away. Simon Gergel, the manager of **Merchants Trust**, showed us a chart of the cyclically-adjusted P/E ratio that showed the UK trading below the long-term US historic average, joined only by markets like Brazil, Spain, Turkey and Russia.

In November we reported that Woodford Investment Management was closing, and that Schroder Investment Management would be taking over the management of **Woodford Patient Capital Trust** and renaming it the **Schroder UK Public Private Trust.** Changes were afoot in Parliament too, with an early General Election called for December after the impasse on Brexit proved impossible to break.

In the US, biotechnology enjoyed a late-year rally, from which **Biotech Growth Trust** was a particular beneficiary after a disappointing spell of performance, and UK smaller companies trusts rose on hopes for a clear Conservative victory to shift the political logjam. When the result confirmed that optimism, **JPMorgan Smaller Companies** would become the year's strongest share price performer with a rise of 67.5%. Mark Barnett ran out of time though as manager of **Edinburgh Investment Trust** and was replaced by James de Uphaugh of Majedie Asset Management. **Hadrian's Wall Secured Investments** became the latest debt provider to run into problems and be severely punished by the market, but there was no reduction in the enthusiasm for other alternative assets, including the IPO for **Octopus Renewables Infrastructure Trust,** which was enthusiastically received. **Hipgnosis Songs Fund** had also been growing, and moved to the Premium Segment of the London Stock Exchange.

In spite of much hand-wringing over Brexit and the state of trade relations between China and President Trump's US, markets made good progress over the year and investment trusts rose on average by around 15%, outpacing the FTSE 100 Index.

2020 – The Covid-19 Pandemic Strikes

Markets began the year in good form in spite of some worrying global events in the form of the UK's impending EU exit, impeachment proceedings against President Trump, and the spread of a coronavirus from China. After our usual seasonal round-up of the industry in January we reported on the sector news in February. **Henderson Alternative Strategies Trust** decided to seek shareholder permission to realise its assets and wind up. **SQN Asset Finance** ran into some difficulties with its loans and warned of a potential impairment, and **US Solar Fund** was the victim of fraud. **Nippon Active Value Fund** launched its IPO. At Winterflood's 16th annual conference in London we listened to presentations from some major trusts and reported on **Monks Investment Trust, BlackRock World Mining Trust, Aberdeen Smaller Companies Income,** and **Pantheon International.**

In March, all previous analysis was swept away by the rampaging coronavirus, now named Covid-19, which sent global stock markets into a spin. The market rout did not prevent us from naming our ISA tips as usual, but we did change the format for the April newsletter to focus on how to react after another tumultuous month. The pair of hedge funds, **BH Global** and **BH Macro,** managed to swim against the tide, as did **Pershing Square Holdings,** which had cashed in a remarkably successful derivatives trade.

Prices did start to bounce back, but the uneven nature of the recovery meant it was possible to identify a number of trusts that looked cheap. With open-ended property funds again in trouble, the advantages of the investment trust structure became more apparent under stress. The use of revenue reserves to support dividends was especially welcome, although some alternative asset trusts did cut or suspend dividends. **3i Infrastructure** found itself in the right place at the right time with its interest in the oil storage company Oystercatcher when oil prices turned briefly negative because storage facilities were full. Some growth-oriented trusts started to outperform strongly in the lockdown period, including **Pacific Horizon Investment Trust** and **Baillie Gifford European Growth,** but it was tougher going for some value trusts. **Perpetual Income & Growth** served notice to dismiss Mark Barnett and Invesco, and both **Temple Bar Investment Trust** and **Securities Trust of Scotland** also started to search for a new manager. The Perpetual trust would later decide to merge with **Murray Income Trust.** Ten years on from its IPO, **GCP Infrastructure** re-set its dividend at a lower level in response to lower interest rates and falling subsidies.

Manager access improved dramatically during lockdown, with numerous video calls hosted on Zoom, enabling regular updates from experienced managers in the sector. This helped to explain exactly how they saw the outlook and how they had re-shaped their portfolios to adapt. **Allianz Technology Trust** was one of the clear beneficiaries of accelerating trends towards greater use of technology. Alexander Darwall's **European Opportunities Trust** was in the news for the wrong reasons though, as a major shareholder of the German payments company Wirecard, which discovered a €1.9bn hole in its accounts. This raised questions about the concentration of large holdings in the trust.

As the pandemic news continued into the summer, interrupting the usual holiday season, a rising gold price proved good news for **Golden Prospect Precious Metals, CQS Natural Resources,** and the other commodities trusts. Buyers were digging for value through some unusual corporate actions as well, with **UK Mortgages** rejecting an approach from an M&G fund, and **HWSI Realisation Fund** recommending an offer at a massive 91% premium to its previous closing price. The broker Numis Securities issued a detailed report asking whether a new wave of consolidation might be underway to deal with trusts that are sub-scale or trading on wide discounts. We said we saw some value on this basis in **JPMorgan Mid Cap, ScotGems** and **Jupiter Green.**

Witan Pacific said it was changing its manager and mandate to become a China-specific trust with Baillie Gifford, named **Baillie Gifford China Growth Trust.** The Edinburgh-based management house was enjoying a spectacular run, and in September, accounted for four of the top ten performers over the previous twelve months, including the sector's flagship **Scottish Mortgage Investment Trust,** up nearly 90% over the period. Another much-favoured trust, **Lindsell Train Investment Trust,** dropped to a rare discount – briefly – as markets continued to struggle with the implications of Covid-19.

Japan was in favour in the autumn, following news that Warren Buffett's investment company Berkshire Hathaway had spent US$6bn building stakes in Japan's large general trading houses. The Japanese investment trusts, with less in the way of liquidity constraints, were generally invested in other stocks, but still rode the wave of capital flowing into the sector. **Baillie Gifford Shin Nippon** led the way with a one-month rise in excess of 20%. Biotechnology was also in vogue, with both **The Biotech Growth Trust** and **International Biotechnology Trust** benefiting from the US$21bn takeover of Immunomedics at a big premium.

Towards the end of the year there was a rush of new issues trying to raise capital with varying success. **Triple Point Energy Infrastructure Company** scraped £100m, and both **Home REIT** and **Round Hill Music Royalty Fund** raised reasonable amounts, but two British trusts from the boutique managers Tellworth Investments and Sandford DeLand Asset Management failed to reach their minimum requirements. **Schroder British Opportunities Trust** just managed to raise its £75m minimum. Another wave of IPOs followed in December.

The international investment wheel of fortune spun around to China, which rose very strongly around the time of the US presidential election on hopes that a Trump defeat would ease trade tensions, and also because the 'first in, first out' rule seemed to apply to Covid-19 infections. A sharp rally and re-rating took all three China specialist trusts up strongly, with **JPMorgan China Growth & Income** recording a 108% rise over the twelve months to early November.

Towards the end of the year, news of breakthroughs with Covid-19 vaccines buoyed the UK market, and in November the FTSE 100 Index recorded its best monthly performance since January 1989, although it remained 15% lower in the year to date, near the bottom of the global rankings. We looked at some UK trusts, but noted again the dominance of Baillie Gifford-managed trusts over the last year, with **Pacific Horizon Investment Trust** at the top of the tree.

Index

3

A

B

C

D

E

F

G

H

I

J

K

L

M

N

S

T

U

V

W

Y

Z